D1626826

WITHDRAWAL

*The Legal Environment
of International Business*

The Legal Environment
of International Business

A Guide for United States Firms

by
Don Alan Evans

McFarland & Company, Inc., Publishers
Jefferson, North Carolina, and London

KF
390
.B8
E94
1990

British Library Cataloguing-in-Publication data are available

Library of Congress Cataloguing-in-Publication Data

Evans, Don Alan.
   The legal environment of international business : a guide for
United States firms / by Don Alan Evans.
     p. cm.
   [Includes index.]
   Includes bibliographical references.
   ISBN 0-89950-485-X (lib. bdg. : 50# alk. paper)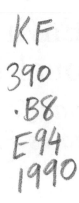
   1. Foreign trade regulation—United States. 2. International
business enterprises—Law and legislation—United States.
3. Investments, American—Law and legislation. 4. Foreign trade
regulation. 5. International business enterprises—Law and
legislation. 6. Investments, Foreign—Law and legislation.
I. Title.
KF390.B8E94   1990
343.73′087—dc20
[347.30387]   89-13729
                                              CIP

© 1990 Don Alan Evans. All rights reserved

Manufactured in the United States of America

McFarland & Company, Inc., Publishers
 Box 611, Jefferson, North Carolina 28640

To Lydia and her family,
who have made Switzerland my second country
and whetted my interest in the world,

and to Betty,
who encouraged me to put what I had learned about it
into writing and through creative scheduling
gave me the time to do it.

Contents

Introduction

When I began teaching law-related courses at Stephen F. Austin State University in 1967, the university offered no courses in international business. When I touched upon international legal problems in our basic business law course, students wondered why I bothered to confuse them with such esoterica. But today the American Assembly of Collegiate Schools of Business (AACSB), the major accrediting organization for our country's collegiate schools of business, insists that students be well acquainted with the international business environment. Here at SFASU we now offer four undergraduate and four graduate courses in various aspects of international business. We offer the student the opportunity to learn much about international management, marketing, finance, economics, and (at the graduate level) law.

As of now (June 1989) I know of no text on the law of international business that is designed for business students, either at the undergraduate or the graduate level. This work is, to my knowledge, the first of its kind. It is intended to provide students with detailed hard information on the legal systems of the world and the legal problems of doing international business.

Chapter 1 covers United States government regulation of exports.

Chapter 2 addresses the regulation of imports and Treasury Department foreign assets control regulations.

Chapter 3 inaugurates coverage of the world's legal systems with an in-depth look at the common law. Chapter 4 discusses the other major world legal system, the Romano-Germanic, found in non–English-speaking, non–Communist nations. Chapter 5 explains the operation of the Socialist legal system, while Chapter 6 examines the law of the Islamic world. Chapter 7 concludes this section with coverage of the Chinese and African systems.

The text next takes up the subject of international law. Chapter 8 deals with the United Nations, the European Community, and other international organizations of importance to the international businessperson.

Chapter 9 takes up the fundamentals of the international law system, the rights and privileges of states and governments, nationality, and human rights.

Chapters 10 and 11 cover the law of export transactions. Drafting the contract, shipping terms, and the like are the subject of Chapter 10, while Chapter 11 deals with problems of payment and finance.

Next comes consideration of doing business abroad "on the spot" in Chapter 12. Here I deal with the advantages and disadvantages of agents and distributors, licensing transactions, and joint ventures. The chapter closes with a discussion of direct investment in the host country and its associated labor problems.

In Chapter 13 I take up the problems of securities regulation, antitrust law, and product liability.

Chapter 14 addresses international accounting and taxation, tax havens, and efforts by American legislators to bring international financial crime within reach of federal prosecutors.

Chapter 15 deals with the risks of operating abroad: fluctuating currency exchange rates, inflation, exchange controls, discriminatory behavior by the host government, political risks, and the ultimate risk of all—expropriation.

Chapter 16 closes the work by dealing with the problems of law enforcement across national frontiers.

One hopes the reader will finish the work with a much clearer understanding of the nature of the legal environment of international business. May he or she who reads for intellectual stimulation be tempted to conduct further mental exploration in this fascinating area of knowledge—and may they who seek to become more knowledgeable and understanding participants in the solemn undertaking of international business reach their goal.

May the reader never cease to view the problems of business from the global viewpoint! Today's market is the entire world. What happens today in Seoul, Taipei, Kinshasa, Beirut, and Bogotá will affect markets tomorrow in Hong Kong, Singapore, Zurich, and New York. Whether we like it or not, we live and work in one world, and the technology of the latter quarter of the twentieth century shrinks it and will continue to shrink it.

Though today's most advanced technology may be obsolete tomorrow, law and the legal environment change more slowly. Successful international business managers must not only know their products, they must also have an understanding of the legal systems of the nations where they buy and sell. May this volume contribute its portion to that understanding.

Chapter 1

Federal Export Regulation

The Constitution gives to Congress the power to regulate the interstate and foreign commerce of the United States. It also gives to the president the authority to conduct the foreign relations of the country. It is therefore clear that the federal government has virtually unlimited authority to regulate both the export of goods, services, and money from the United States and the import of the same into the United States. This chapter summarizes the current law and regulation governing exports; the next chapter will cover import regulation.

Americans have been international traders since before the American Revolution; British interference with colonial foreign trade was one of the grievances that provoked the American Revolution. Since independence we have not hesitated to use diplomacy and military force to protect our international commerce. We fought an undeclared naval war with France in 1798 in part on the issue of free trade. We sent naval expeditions to the Mediterranean to punish the North African states of Algiers, Tunis, and Tripoli for their interference with United States merchantmen; and we fought our second war with England over this issue in 1812-14.

In the interest of trade the United States took the lead in forcing Japan to enter the modern world in 1853; in the interest of unrestricted trade she resisted the efforts of the colonial powers to destroy the independence of China at the turn of the century. Until very recently Americans have resented the efforts of any government — ours or someone else's — to interfere with our freedom to export whatever we will to whomever we will.

With the advent of American world power and the division of the earth into hostile camps, the environment of our export trade has changed. Any sale of American goods or technology abroad that strengthens the economy of an unfriendly nation may later give cause for regret. (Those of us with an interest in history remember the sales of petroleum products and scrap metal to Japan before 1941.) At the same time the desirability of encouragement of American exports has never been more obvious. As the volume of our country's imports increases our balance of trade becomes more and more adverse. We must sell abroad to offset the costs of what we buy abroad.

How can we increase the volume of our exports without strengthening the economies of those nations with whom we contest the mastery of Planet Earth? Do we dare help strengthen the hands of those who may some day try to destroy us? This is the dilemma facing those who make and enforce United States export policy. Understanding the problem may make the solutions attempted by present law more comprehensible.

The major piece of legislation governing United States exports is the Export Administration Act of 1985 (50 USC App. 2401–2420). The major enforcement agency is the Office of Export Administration of the Department of Commerce.

Export regulation is designed to accomplish three objectives: (1) to enhance national security; (2) to assist in the accomplishment of the objectives of United States foreign policy; and (3) to protect the national economy against short supplies of essential commodities.

Export controls apply to the following:

1. Export of commodities and technical data
2. Reexport of commodities and technical data of United States origin from one foreign destination to another (Thus if an American firm exports goods to France for reexport to Vietnam, the Franco-Vietnamese transaction would be subject to American regulation)
3. Parts and components originating in the United States used in another country to manufacture a foreign end product for export, so long as at least 25 percent of the end product comprises such (Thus if an American auto parts manufacturer ships automatic transmissions to Brazil for use in Brazilian-made automobiles exported to the Republic of South Africa, the transaction between the Brazilians and South Africans may well be subject to the American controls)
4. The foreign-produced direct product of technical data originating in the United States (Thus if an American firm licenses a Spanish firm to produce electronic components using American technical data and the Spanish firm sells the components to Libya, the Spanish-Libyan transaction would be subject to the American controls)

No license is required for reexport of most American products from a second country to a *Co-Ordinating Committee* (CoCom) country. Members of CoCom are the countries of the North Atlantic Treaty alliance (excluding Iceland) plus Japan and Australia. These nations have cooperated to create a mechanism whereby they coordinate their export policies to minimize the sale of strategic goods to unfriendly nations (primarily members of the Soviet bloc). Export of a strategic good from any CoCom nation to a controlled country must receive the assent of the committee.

Products destined for such reexport for which licenses are required include:

1. Supercomputers
2. Goods or technology for sensitive nuclear uses
3. Devices for surreptitious interception of wire or oral communications
4. Goods destined for such end-users as the secretary of commerce shall by regulation determine

A license is not required for most experts to Canada. No license or permission is required to export nonsensitive items to CoCom countries with the exception of exports to such end-users as the secretary of commerce may designate. The exporter may be required, however, to inform the Commerce Department of the export. Also, no license is required for export of items to non–CoCom countries other than controlled countries if the export of such an item to a controlled country would require no more than notification to CoCom governments. The controlled countries will be identified later in this chapter.

For virtually all other exports a license is required. The Office of Export Administration (OEA) is responsible for most of the licensing, except for the following:

1. Arms and ammunition (under jurisdiction of the Office of Munitions Control, State Department)
2. Narcotics (under jurisdiction of the Justice Department)
3. Nuclear materials (under jurisdiction of the Nuclear Regulatory Commission)
4. Watercraft (under jurisdiction of the Maritime Administration)
5. Natural gas and electricity (under jurisdiction of the Federal Energy Regulatory Commission)
6. Patent applications (under jurisdiction of the Patent Office)
7. Controlled foreign assets (under jurisdiction of the Treasury Department)

The OEA issues two types of export licenses. *General* licenses may authorize the export of commodities or technical data without the necessity of the exporter obtaining any specific license. These are essentially blanket authorizations for export of the covered goods and technology enacted in the form of administrative regulations. Most United States exports are authorized by such licenses; thus in most cases the exporter may carry out his transaction without requesting specific government approval.

If no general license exists, the exporter must apply for a *Validated* license. This is a specific license to authorize a specific export or series of exports.

To determine whether one must apply for an export license (or whether there is any point to applying for a license) the exporter must first determine to which of the Country Groupings the destination country belongs. The groupings are as follows:

     Q — Romania

     S   — Libya

     T   — All Western Hemisphere nations except Cuba and Canada

     W — Hungary, Poland

     Y   — Albania, Bulgaria, Czechoslovakia, Estonia, German Democratic Republic, Latvia, Lithuania, Mongolian People's Republic, People's Republic of China, USSR

     Z   — Cuba, Kampuchea (Cambodia), North Korea, Vietnam

     V   — All other countries except Canada (Canada belongs to no group, since no license is required for most exports to her)

The Group Z nations are under almost total embargo. General licenses authorize exports to them of publications containing data available to the general public (newspapers, news magazines, and the like) and gift parcels to relatives of the sender having a value of two hundred dollars or less. In addition, shipments to Cuba of merchandise passing through the United States in transit from another country are authorized by general license. No other general licenses cover shipments to these countries, and applications for validated licenses are almost always denied.

The Group Y nations have Communist governments to which the United States has chosen not to grant special importing privileges. Exports to them are highly restricted.

Groups Q and W are Communist nations with special privileges — W more so than Q.

Exports to Group S — Libya — are restricted because of its support of international terrorism.

Groups T and V comprise our favorite trading partners (other than Canada). Restrictions upon exports to them are relatively few.

Groups Q, S, W, Y, and Z comprise the controlled countries.

The exporter must next locate his would-be export on the Commodity Control List. This list will indicate whether the commodity is exportable at all to the country of destination, whether a general license for its export exists, or whether a validated license will be required.

Special restrictions may apply to some countries of a control group and not to others. Such countries include the Soviet Union, Nicaragua, Iran, the Yemen People's Republic (South Yemen), Syria, the Republic of South Africa, Namibia, Afghanistan, Iraq and Panama.

If export of the commodity is forbidden, the exporter can forget about making the transaction. If a general license exists, he may proceed to make his contract with his customer and prepare his shipment. If a validated license is required, he had best apply for the license before finalizing his contract. However, one must be in possession of an order for the export before applying for a validated license.

Application for a validated license is made to the OEA, unless the commodity is one of those under the jurisdiction of another government agency. Before filing a formal license application, one may informally ask the OEA if a license is likely to be issued. One must of course be able to identify the commodity, the importer, the destination country, and the commodity's ultimate destination (if it is to be reexported).

If the OEA's advisory opinion is negative, it will probably be futile to file a formal license application. If the opinion is affirmative, OEA will *probably* respond favorably to a license application. However, the agency is not bound by its advisory opinions. It could still deny a license despite a favorable earlier advisory opinion.

OEA will usually make a decision on an application within two months. If the destination is a Communist country, however, the process may take up to ten months, because obtaining CoCom approval may be necessary.

A decision will be made solely on the basis of the documents filed with the license application; no hearing will be held. A negative decision may be appealed to the assistant secretary of commerce for trade administration, who again will make a decision without holding a hearing. His decision is final; the law does not authorize judicial review of these administrative decisions.

An aspect of export administration that has long disturbed American exporters is the fact that the United States can deny a license to an American producer to export a product to, say, the Soviet Union even though the Soviets could obtain the same product from, perhaps, Sweden or Switzerland. If the Soviets may obtain the product somewhere else, runs the argument, why deprive American producers of the opportunity to make the sale?

A license to export goods or technology to a controlled country (any country other than a member of Groups T and V, or Canada) shall not be denied if the goods or technology is available to the destination country from sources outside the United States in quantity and quality sufficient to frustrate the American policy restricting the export. If, however, the president determines that national security requires the restriction of the export despite the foreign availability, a validated export license may still be required.

When a general license for an export does not exist, one may under some circumstances apply for one of four special licenses that allow the making of multiple shipments without validated licenses for each.

A *Distribution License* allows the exporter to ship goods to approved consignees for up to two years. New consignees may be added to the list during the two-year period, but the license does not authorize shipments to unapproved consignees.

A *Service Supply License* authorizes the export of goods needed to service equipment sold abroad. The license is good for one year, and may be renewed twice.

A *Project License* allows export of goods to be used in new capital expansion projects or capital facilities such as dams, power generating plants, oil refineries, and the like. These are valid for one year.

A *Comprehensive Operations License* allows export and reexport of goods and technology by a United States firm to its subsidiaries, affiliates, joint venturers, and licensees that have long-term contractual relationships with the exporter, are located in countries other than controlled countries (except for the People's Republic of China), and are approved by the secretary of commerce.

All export shipments must be accompanied by a *Shipper's Export Declaration*. This document must state the nature of the license under which the shipment is made. If it is being made under a validated license a copy of the license should be attached.

No international carrier may lawfully carry an export shipment away from American soil without Customs Service clearance. The Customs Service will require a Shipper's Export Declaration for every item of cargo on the carrier's manifest.

Shipments to Switzerland, Yugoslavia, and the People's Republic of China must also be accompanied by an *International Import Certificate* issued by the government of the destination country. Proof of delivery of the shipment to the importer must be noted on the certificate; this helps these countries enforce their own import and export control regulations.

The regulatory scheme described above comprises most American export controls; the purpose is the enhancement of national security.

In the interest of promoting the nation's foreign policy the president may restrict or entirely forbid exports to any country or countries; thus he may impose an almost total embargo upon trade with another nation. However, he should make an effort to settle our differences with the nation in question through diplomacy. In addition, if the target nation is in a position to acquire what the United States proposes to refuse to export elsewhere (so that the economy of that nation will not be significantly injured by the embargo) our nation's displeasure should be expressed by other means.

If the president finds that a product or commodity is in short supply in the United States, he may forbid or limit its exportation. Limitation is accomplished through export quotas. A quota system must be administered in such a way that firms that have not long been exporters have an opportunity to continue exporting the product or commodity in question.

Violations of Commerce Department export control regulations may subject the exporter to criminal and civil penalties. A deliberate violation of the Export Administration Act or the regulations issued thereunder is a criminal offense, for which one may be imprisoned up to five years and or fined five times the value of the export or $50,000. An unlawful export to a controlled country by a corporation is punishable by a fine of up to five times the value of the export or $1,000,000, whichever is greater. Such a violation by an individual is subject to a fine of up to $250,000 and ten years' imprisonment. He who exports goods or technology to a controlled country under a validated license and learns that the export is being used for military or intelligence-gathering purposes contrary to the conditions under which the license was issued must report this discovery to the secretary of defense; failure to do so renders one liable for the same fines as for willful violations of the act, except that the maximum imprisonment for individual violators is five years, not ten.

The secretary of commerce may revoke or restrict the export privileges of persons convicted of these offenses.

The Commerce Department may file administrative complaints against negligent or inadvertent violators. These result in trial-type hearings before administrative law judges of the Commerce Department; in such administrative proceedings there is no right to trial by jury. Violators may be fined up to $10,000; the exported commodities or technical data may be seized; or, more painfully, the exporter may have his export privileges restricted or revoked.

The outcome of these cases, too, may be appealed to the assistant secretary of commerce for export administration. Until the enactment of the Trade and Competitiveness Act of 1988 there was no judicial review of his decision. Under the new law these matters may be appealed to the United States Court of Appeals for the District of Columbia Circuit.

Since foreign business entities are subject to these regulations if controlled by Americans, they may find themselves in very painful difficulties when American export policy runs contrary to the policies of the host country. In the late 1960s the People's Republic of China belonged to Country Group Z, to which virtually all exports were forbidden. Fruehauf Corporation, the semitrailer manufacturer, owned a manufacturing subsidiary in France which had American management. The subsidiary contracted to sell a large number of trailers to Berliet SA, one of the largest truck manufacturers in France. After the Fruehauf-Berliet contract was made, Fruehauf management learned that Berliet intended to sell the trucks to which the trailers would be attached to the People's Republic of China. The U.S. government demanded that Fruehauf cancel its contract with Berliet because delivery of the trailers would violate American law. Fruehauf's American management therefore ordered the management of the French subsidiary to do just that, which it did.

Thus Berliet found itself in danger of losing its Chinese contract, and because of the magnitude of the deal employees of both Berliet and Fruehauf found their jobs in danger. All asked the French government to intervene. The government responded by making use of an extraordinary court procedure to remove the subsidiary's American management from power and place a French receiver in charge of the company, with orders to reinstate and perform the Berliet contract. Since this action was perfectly legitimate under French law, all that Fruehauf management and the U.S. government could do was make a diplomatic protest. This protest did absolutely no good because at the time French president Charles de Gaulle was anxious to prove that France could function in the world independent of the tutelage of the United States.

Ultimately the Berliet contract was performed by Fruehauf, the receivership was ended, and the Americans regained control of their property.

Dresser Industries encountered a similar problem in 1982. Its French subsidiary (Dresser France) had contracted to sell materials to the French firm Creusot-Loire for resale to the Soviet Union for use in the construction of the great pipeline to bring natural gas from Siberia to western Europe. After General Jaruzelski's coup in Poland that ended the power of the trade union Solidarity, the Reagan administration stopped export of American materials to the USSR for use in the pipeline. (It assumed that the coup was masterminded by the Soviet government.) Thus Dresser Industries was ordered to tell Dresser France to stop performing its contract with Creusot-Loire. Dresser France obeyed the orders from home. The French government then formally requisitioned Dresser France's performance of the contract, which was allowed by French law. Dresser France complied with the requisition.

The Office of Export Administration therefore issued an order temporarily revoking the export privileges of Dresser France and began administrative proceedings to make the temporary order permanent, which could have made it unlawful for Dresser France to export products containing materials or components made in the United States to any nation outside France.

The European Community and Japan refused to follow American policy on the pipeline, so the new American restrictions proved futile. The Reagan administration changed its policy and again legalized the export of pipeline materials to the USSR before the Commerce Department case against Dresser was decided. The case against Dresser was now moot, and so was dropped.

These incidents demonstrate the limited effectiveness of this sort of export restriction. Since our allies are more in favor of unrestricted exports to anyone anywhere on earth than we are at this point in time, it is very difficult to operate counter to their policy. We cannot keep goods from the Soviets when our allies are willing to sell them; should we not claim our share of the business? Present policy permits just that, within the limitations described above.

Chapter 2

Federal Import Regulation

Import regulation has been a question of political importance in the United States for at least a century and a half. In the beginning the tariff system served two vital purposes: its receipts provided much of the federal government's operating revenue; and it protected infant American industry against the deadly competition of cheap European manufactured goods. American tariff policy continued to be protectionist even after the United States had become the greatest manufacturing nation in the world. Congress reacted to the onset of depression in 1930 by enacting the Smoot-Hawley Tariff Act, which provided for some of the highest import duties in American history; it sought to preserve the shrinking American domestic market for American producers only. What the United States did in 1930, most other industrial nations also did in what they called self-defense. The gigantic tariff walls of that period choked off most of the world's international trade, adding to the almost universal distress caused by the Great Depression.

The nation began to turn away from protectionism when President Franklin Roosevelt made reciprocal trade agreements containing "most favored nation" clauses the cornerstone of our trading relationships. By encouraging other nations to export to us we could more easily encourage them to accept our exports.

The Tariff System

In the new world order after World War II the Western industrialized nations realized that the entire world would benefit if barriers to international trade were lowered. The signatories of the General Agreement on Tariffs and Trade (GATT) have striven to lower trade barriers since the late 1940s.

In those early postwar years the United States was by far the world's greatest trading nation. But as West Germany and Japan emerged from their war ruins and built up their economics, they began to compete with Americans in foreign trade everywhere on earth—even in our own backyard. American imports began to rise; as time went on foreign producers began nibbling off significant percentages of the American domestic market for their wares: automobiles, textiles, and the like.

As the world economy slowed down during the 1970s the competitive position of American firms in many markets, foreign and domestic, worsened. Inefficient American producers began to be forced out of the market at the cost of investments and jobs. Whole industries (steel, shoe manufacturing, textiles, automobiles) began to feel the pinch. The cry for protectionism, never totally silenced, increased in volume manyfold. Congress has to a degree responded to this cry.

Though our commitment to the objectives of GATT and the reality of our single world market will not permit a return to the "good old" high-tariff days, several special regulatory schemes exist for the purpose of shielding American producers from what we deem to be unfair foreign competition within our backyard. I shall first consider the tariff system and then take up nontariff regulation of imports.

The tariff regulation is accomplished under the Tariff Act of 1930 (19 USC ch. 4) as amended, which imposes import duties on goods brought into the country. Nontariff regulation is accomplished through quotas and the like.

Eugene Rossides, in his work *U.S. Import Trade Regulation,* describes the workings of the duty collection process. Import duties are assessed and collected by the United States Customs Service. When commercial shipments arrive at a United States port of entry, they are unloaded from the carrier under the supervision of Customs Service personnel and taken to a Customs warehouse. There they remain until formal *Entry* is made.

This may be accomplished by the importer, or by a customs broker hired for the purpose. Normally it must be done within five days of the arrival of the merchandise. If it is not done in a timely fashion, the goods remain in storage in the warehouse at the expense of the importer until it is done.

Entry consists of presenting to the Customs Service the documentation it needs to classify the goods and assess the duty. More often than not entry is for consumption. In such cases the documentation consists of an *Entry Manifest* or *Special Permit for Immediate Delivery,* evidence of authority to make entry, commercial invoice, and packing list. Bond must be posted at this time to ensure payment of tentative duty. The shipment is then examined, tentative duty is assessed, and the goods are released to the importer. Supplementary documentation must be filed and estimated duty paid with ten days of the release.

Shipments are examined to determine:

1. The nature and classification of goods for duty-assessment purposes

2. Whether goods are marked with their country of origin, and whether other marking and labeling requirements are met

3. Whether goods are correctly invoiced, including overages or shortages of invoiced goods

4. Whether the shipment contains prohibited articles

If articles are found in the packages that are not listed on the invoices, and if it appears that their nonlisting is deliberate, the offending package may be seized and charges may be brought against the importer.

Other types of entries are possible. The goods may be placed in a bonded warehouse for a period of up to five years, causing duty to be deferred until release for consumption. Or they may be placed in a foreign-trade zone; as long as they remain there duty is deferred. If goods in a foreign trade zone are eventually exported to another nation, no United States duty is payable.

If goods in a bonded warehouse or a foreign-trade zone are processed so that they change their form, they may later be entered for consumption and duty becomes payable on them in their altered form. Thus, for instance, fabric may be imported into the United States and made into clothing in a foreign-trade zone. Duty will then be paid on the clothing.

The duty assessed right after entry is not final. The Customs Service will *Liquidate* the entry weeks or months later, and reserves the right to charge additional duty. If it proposes to do this a *Notice of Adjustment* will be sent to the importer. He may informally contest the adjustment by submitting documentation of his case to the Customs Service, which will reconsider the matter.

After final liquidation the importer may file a *Protest* and or an *Application for Further Review* within ninety days. The review is administrative, either at the offices of appraisal specialists in New York City or at Customs Headquarters in Washington, D.C.

An administrative denial of a protest or application for further review is appealable to the Court of International Trade in New York City, and from there to the Court of Appeals for the Federal Circuit in Washington.

The classification of goods for assessment of duty and the determination of the amount of duty due are determined by consulting the Tariff Schedule of the United States. (TSUS will be replaced by the Harmonized Commodity Description and Coding System, designed to bring the American import classification system into synchronization with the system used by most of our trading partners. The changeover is mandated by the Trade and Competitiveness Act of 1988, but will require time to implement. The new system will change the method of classifying goods for assessment of duty, but will not change present tariff preference policies.) First the TSUS classification for the goods must be discovered. Then the rate of duty applicable to such goods from the source nation must be determined.

TSUS contains three schedules of duties based upon the country of export. Although it is the general objective of the General Agreement on Tariffs and Trade (GATT), of which the United States is a signatory, for all member nations to treat each other alike with respect to imports, the goal has not yet been reached. Discrimination by GATT members against nonmembers occurs, and under some circumstances domestic political considerations will excuse member discrimination against member. For the most part, however, the United States grants most-favored-nation (MFN) treatment across-the-board to GATT members.

The highest duty schedule applies to goods from Communist countries to which the United States has not granted MFN treatment. The lowest schedule applies to goods from least-developed developing countries (LDDC), to which GATT members are obligated to accord special consideration. The middle schedule applies to goods from most of our trading partners.

Romania, Hungary, and Yugoslavia have been granted MFN treatment by the United States; their exports are subject to the middle schedule. Imports from many of the poorest countries of Africa and Asia plus most lands of the Caribbean Basin pay the lowest schedule; special legislation also grants this privilege to Israel.

Most duty rates are *Ad Valorem,* a percentage of the value of the imported merchandise. Some are *Per Unit,* so much per described quantity of the merchandise regardless of value. A few are a combination of ad valorem and per unit.

Where ad valorem rates apply, the duty will be payable on the FOB (freight-on-board) value of the merchandise. That is, transportation costs will not be figured into the value of the goods.

The value will be transaction value, that is, the price the importer is paying the exporter for the goods, where this may be readily computed. When there is no evidence of transaction value or the transaction is made between closely related parties, other methods of valuation may be used. In order of preference these are:

1. Transaction value of identical merchandise (What would an exporter charge an unrelated importer for identical merchandise?)

2. Transaction value of similar merchandise (If no identical merchandise has been imported, what would an exporter charge for similar merchandise?)

3. Deductive value (Resale price in the United States less certain arithmetical adjustments too complex to explain here)

4. Computed value (Estimate of value using costs of raw material

labor, profit of manufacturer and middlemen, packing costs, and the like)

Enforcement. Customs officers may board any vessel or vehicle to inspect or search it or any person, trunk, package, or cargo on board. This may be done anywhere within the United States, or on the high seas within four leagues (twelve miles) of the United States coast.

They may also search the baggage of any person coming into the country. If the owner of the baggage refuses to open any closed container, the officer may force it open. No search warrant is necessary in these cases.

If Customs officers want to conduct searches within any building, however, they must obtain warrants. They have the authority of a peace officer for the purpose of making arrests; indeed, they may arrest persons charged with crimes having nothing to do with the customs laws.

Any vessel, vehicle, or merchandise involved in violation of customs laws may be seized. In addition, when an attempt is made to bring dutiable merchandise into the country without declaring it to Customs officers the offending merchandise may be seized and the smuggler assessed a penalty of the value of the said merchandise.

Seized property is subject to summary forfeiture if: (1) its importation is forbidden; or (2) its value does not exceed $100,000; or (3) the seized vessel, vehicle, or aircraft was used to import, export, transport, or store a controlled substance (essentially an unlawful drug). Summary forfeiture procedure involves: (1) sending notice of seizure and possible forfeiture to everyone known to have an interest in the property; (2) publication of notice of seizure and liability to forfeiture for three consecutive weeks; and (3) sale at public auction without any court action.

The owner may redeem the seized property before auction by paying the Customs Service its appraised value. He may also petition the service to mitigate the penalty and forfeiture. Such a petition is filed with the commissioner of customs; the district director of the Customs Service for the area involved decides whether to grant the petition. If the district director denies, the owner of the property may appeal to the secretary of the treasury, whose decision is final.

If the property is worth over $100,000 and otherwise is not subject to summary forfeiture, it must be turned over to the federal courts for judicial condemnation. It will remain in custody until a federal judge orders it sold, at which time it will be disposed of under court supervision.

For entering goods into the country under false statements, one is subject to criminal prosecution, but it is seldom initiated. Usually the Customs Service contents itself with assessing penalties against the violator. For a negligent violation this may consist of up to the lesser of the domestic value of the merchandise or double the duties due on it. For a grossly negligent violation the penalty is the value of the merchandise or four times the duty, whichever is less. For a fraudulent violation the penalty is the domestic value—retail value—of the merchandise.

The Customs Service begins the penalty collection procedure by issuing a claim for penalty to the importer. The importer may petition the commissioner of customs for remission or mitigation. If the commissioner denies the petition the importer may appeal to the secretary of the treasury. If his petition is denied, the importer has no more administrative appeals, but if he does not pay the penalty the Customs Service must file a petition with the Court of International Trade to enforce it. The importer may challenge the lawfulness of the penalty in that court and once more argue that he should not have to pay it. The decision here is appealable to the Court of Appeals for the Federal Circuit.

Antidumping Duties. Under 19 USC 1673 et seq, if a foreign manufacturer sells goods in the United States for less than he sells such goods in his domestic market, and if these sales cause or threaten to cause material injury to a United States industry or retard the establishment of such an industry, an antidumping duty equal to the amount by which the foreign market value exceeds the United States price shall be imposed upon that product.

The procedure for imposing antidumping duties is somewhat complex. It may be initiated either by the secretary of commerce or by an interested party on behalf of a domestic industry. An interested party may be:

1. An American manufacturer, producer, or wholesaler of a product like that being dumped

2. A certified union or group of workers engaged in the manufacture, production, or wholesaling of the product

3. A trade or business association, the majority of whose members engage in the manufacture, production, or wholesaling of the product.

If an interested party begins the proceeding (as is usually the case) it must file its petition simultaneously with the Department of Commerce and with the International Trade Commission (ITC).

Individual exporters or groups of exporters are the targets of these investigations, because dumping takes place due to business decisions of these entities. Foreign governments would not be involved unless the exporter in question is publicly owned or is located in a non-free-market (Communist) nation.

The International Trade Administration (ITA) of the Commerce Department examines the petition and must decide within twenty days whether it contains enough information to justify beginning an investigation. If the determination is affirmative, investigation; if it is negative, the petition is dismissed and the case is closed.

If the decision to investigate is affirmative, a two-pronged proceeding ensues. The ITA must determine whether dumping is occurring, and the ITC must determine whether injury is being caused to the petitioners. No antidumping duty can be levied unless it is determined that both dumping and injury have occurred.

The ITC must determine within forty-five days of the filing of a petition whether there is likelihood of injury from the alleged dumping. A negative decision ends the proceeding; an affirmative decision causes it to continue.

Both investigating bodies may gather information both inside and outside the United States. Since an essential item of information is the price at which the dumped product is sold in the manufacturer's domestic market, investigation in the country of origin may well be required.

There is no way that agencies of the United States government may compel organizations or persons outside this country to divulge information, but those being investigated have every incentive to cooperate. If they do not, the antidumping duty will be imposed and their access to the American market may be damaged or destroyed.

Either investigating agency may hold hearings in the process of investigating. Hearings *must* be held if any party so demands. Such hearings do not involve the examining and cross-examining of witnesses under oath, however.

Within ninety days of the start of an investigation the ITA normally makes a preliminary dumping determination. Liquidating of entries on potentially dumped merchandise will be suspended at this point if this determination is affirmative.

The ITA's final determination is usually made within seventy-five days after the making of the preliminary determination.

The ITC's final determination of injury is required no later than 120 days after ITA's preliminary determination of dumping, or forty-five days after its final determination.

Within seven days of receipt of the final ITC decision finding injury, the secretary of commerce must publish an antidumping duty order. The duty will be imposed on all dumped merchandise to which entries have not been finally liquidated.

These proceedings may resort in "out of court settlements" when the exporter, the investigating government agencies, and the petitioners agree to an acceptable compromise.

Any preliminary determination by either investigating agency that causes suspension of the proceeding and any final determination is subject to judicial review in the Court of International Trade. Court of International Trade determinations may be appealed to the Court of Appeals for the Federal Circuit.

Antidumping orders must be reviewed by the Commerce Department once a year to determine if circumstances exist for rescission.

Countervailing Duties. Under 19 USC 1671–1677g countervailing duties may be imposed upon imports into the United States when a government or a private party is directly or indirectly subsidizing the manufacture, production, or exportation of merchandise imported, or likely to be imported, into the United States and that importation injures, threatens with injury, or retards the establishment of a competing American industry.

The procedure for imposing countervailing duty upon subsidized imports is very similar to the antidumping procedure. The major difference is that the law treats dutiable exports from nations that are not members of GATT or that have not agreed to comply with GATT standards on import subsidies differently from others.

Countervailing duties may be imposed upon nonagreement-country dutiable exports without proof of injury to an American industry. With respect to other exports proof of injury is required before imposition of the duty.

As with antidumping investigations, the procedure may be initiated by the Commerce Department or by a private interested party. Unless a dutiable import from a nonagreement country is involved, an interested party petition must be filed with both the Commerce Department and the ITC.

So far all countervailing duty complaints have been directed against government-subsidized imports. The objective has therefore been to impose the duty upon all imports from the subsidizing country.

The major foreign respondent has therefore been the offending government.

The procedure in countervailing duty cases is essentially the same as with antidumping duty cases. There is the simultaneous investigation by ITA of the existence of the subsidy and by ITC of the existence of injury (unless it is a case involving a nonagreement country, when ITC need not get involved). The outcome of both investigations must be affirmative for the duty to be imposed. Determinations by ITA and ITC are subject to the same judicial review as in antidumping cases.

Countervailing duty proceedings may well result in a negotiated settlement. The subsidizing government may well decide to cease its subsidies in order to save itself useless expense and preserve access to the American market for its producers.

Evasion of Antidumping and Countervailing Duties. Until very recently it was possible to evade antidumping and countervailing duties either by shipping component parts of the product to which the duties applied to the United States and having them assembled here; or by shipping component parts of the product to which the duties applied to a third country, having the parts assembled there, and exporting the finished product from the third country to the United States. Section 1321 of the Trade and

Competitiveness Act of 1988 tries to solve this problem by giving the Commerce Department the authority to include the two categories of product mentioned above in countervailing and antidumping duty orders.

Third Country Dumping. It sometimes happens that a foreign manufacturer will sell his product below cost or otherwise engage in dumping his product in a third country, thereby damaging competing American firms doing business in that country. Section 1323 of the Trade and Competitiveness Act of 1988 allows such a damaged American industry to petition the United States Trade Representative (USTR) to request that the third country take action under its own laws against such dumping. Since the member nations of GATT are required to enact antidumping legislation, the third country should be in a position to take legal action against the dumping.

Unfair Trade Practices. Section 337 of the Tariff Act of 1930 (19 USC 1337a) provides a mechanism for American businesspeople to take action against unfair trade practices in the importation of articles into the United States if the unfair practice will destroy or substantially injure an "efficiently and economically operated" American industry, or prevent the establishment of such an industry, or monopolize trade and commerce in the United States. Any industry operated in the United States that feels itself victimized by such unfair trade practices may file a complaint against the violator with the International Trade Commission (ITC).

Among the unfair trade practices that may violate Section 337 are: (1) importation of articles into the United States that infringe upon rights granted and protected by American intellectual property law, such as patents, trademarks, copyrights, and trade secrets; and (2) commission of acts that are regarded as unfair competition in domestic American law, such as false advertising, palming off one's goods as someone else's, or the like.

The complainant begins a Section 337 proceeding by filing a complaint with the ITC. The agency then has thirty days to check out the complaint and decide if a full investigation is warranted. If the decision is negative the complaint is dismissed. If the decision is affirmative notice of the complaint is served upon all respondents and notice of the beginning of full investigation must be published in the *Federal Register*.

The respondent(s) must file answers with the ITC within twenty days. If respondents contest the charges in the complaint, a full administrative hearing is held before an administrative law judge of the ITC under the rules of the Federal Administrative Procedure Act; this hearing includes questioning of witnesses under oath and cross-examination by the opposing party. The proceeding may be terminated by a *Consent Order* if all parties and the administrative law judge agree. Otherwise the administrative law judge will render a decision at the end of the taking of evidence. The decision of the administrative law judge in the case is appealable to the ITC, which may affirm, reverse, modify, set aside, or remand it.

The ITC may order one of two remedies if it finds the respondent(s) guilty. The most drastic is an *Exclusion Order* banning the importation of the offending goods in the future. Less drastic is the *Cease and Desist Order,* commanding the respondent to stop doing certain things that he is now doing. This may allow the continued importation of the offending product under specific terms and conditions.

Notice of ITC determination that a violation of Section 337 has taken place must be submitted to the president of the United States. The president has sixty days after receipt of the notice to disapprove the ITC action. Such disapproval ends the case in favor of the respondent.

Anyone unhappy with the final decision of the ITC in these cases may appeal to the Court of Appeals for the Federal Circuit. However, appeals by unsuccessful respondents cannot take place until the president has had his sixty days within which to review the ITC decision.

Section 1342 of the Trade and Competitiveness Act of 1988 allows the ITC to take action against the importation of certain products regardless of whether they cause injury to a United States industry, so long as there is a United States industry producing the product. Thus the ITC can initiate action against any products infringing upon United States patents, copyrights, or trademarks, or any products produced by processes that would violate a United States patent if said processes were used in the United States. In short, if the producer of the product is violating American intellectual property protection law the ITC may take action against him *even if his activity does not injure his American competitor(s).*

Enforcement of United States Rights. The United States may take retaliatory executive action against a foreign country when it is determined that it has: (1) denied rights of the United States under a trade agreement; or (2) followed a policy or practice injurious to United States trade that is inconsistent with a trade agreement; or (3) engaged in other acts or policies that are unjustifiable, unreasonable, and burden or restrict United States commerce.

Section 301(d) of the Trade Act of 1974 as amended by the Trade and Competitiveness Act of 1988 (Section 1301) provides that the subsidization by a foreign government of the construction of vessels used in the transport of goods by water between foreign lands and the United States burdens and restricts United States commerce. It also states that the following acts, policies and practices by foreign governments are unreasonable:

1. Denying fair and equitable opportunities for establishment of enterprises

2. Denying adequate and effective protection of intellectual property rights

3. Denying market opportunities to American firms, including toleration of anticompetitive activities by private firms that restrict such opportunities.

4. Export targeting

5. Denying workers the right of association

6. Denying workers the right to organize and bargain collectively

7. Permitting forced or compulsory labor

8. Permitting child labor

9. Failing to provide minimum wages, minimum hours of work, or occupational safety and health regulation

Retaliatory action may consist of:

1. Suspension, withdrawal, or prevention of the application of benefits granted the offending country under trade agreements

2. Imposing duties or other import restrictions on goods from the offending country and fees or restrictions on the services of the offending country

3. Restricting the access of service businesses to the American economy

Anyone wanting retaliatory action taken against acts of a foreign government must file a petition with the United States Trade Representative (USTR) requesting such action. The USTR must decide within forty-five days of the filing whether to conduct an investigation. During this period the petition is referred to the "Section 301 Committee" which makes the necessary recommendation. The USTR may also initiate action by such a committee on his own motion.

Should the Section 301 Committee recommend an investigation, it will be held. The USTR has from six to twelve months to conduct the necessary investigation. He may then take any of the actions authorized by law. He is required to prefer imposition of duties to more drastic action if such imposition would suffice to solve the problem. Whatever he does is subject to direction by the president; the president may overrule the USTR in these cases at his discretion.

Import Relief. Title II of the Trade Act of 1974, 19 USC 2251–2395, provides a mechanism under which a business injured by import competition may seek relief even if the competition of the imported product is not in any way unfair.

The same entities may file a petition for import relief that may file for protection from unfair import competition (that is, the injured business, unions engaged in production of the product competed against, or trade associations involved with the product). The ITC will conduct an appropriate investigation in order to determine whether import competition is actually injuring the petitioners.

The ITC must at once notify the Labor Department and the Commerce

Department of the commencement of these investigations. The Labor Department must then begin a study to determine whether workers in the petitioning industry may be eligible for adjustment assistance. The Commerce Department must conduct a study to determine whether any domestic firms in the petitioning industry are eligible for adjustment assistance.

During the course of the investigation a public hearing must take place. Here the petitioners get their opportunity to present their evidence.

Within six months of the filing the ITC must complete its investigation and report the results to the president. If its decision is negative — there is no injury to petitioners caused by imports — the proceeding ends. Petitioners may then, if they wish, wait for one year and request a new investigation. If the ITC decision is affirmative it should suggest a remedy for the problem; the remedy could be increased import duty, import restrictions, or some other solution.

The Labor Department and Commerce Department investigation reports must be made within fifteen days of the completion of the ITC investigation. All of the investigation reports are then transmitted to the president.

The president may or may not grant import relief. If he decides that such relief is not in the economic interest of the United States he may decline to take action. If he chooses to take action, it may take one or more of the following forms:

1. An increase in import duty on the product of up to 50 percent
2. Quantitative restraints on the importation of the product, but the quantity to be imported must not be reduced below the amount normally imported in a representative period
3. Negotiation of an orderly marketing agreement with the exporting nation(s)

Such relief can last for no more than five years, unless extended. The president may also choose to have the relief expire in a period of less than five years.

Under 19 USC 2436, an industry being victimized (as it sees it) by market-disrupting imports from Communist countries may petition for import relief. The procedure in these cases is similar to that described above, except that the ITC must complete its investigation within three months of the filing and the standard for determining injury is less strict.

Import Quotas. The importation of many products into the United States is limited by quota. Most quotas are administered by the Customs Service on a first-come, first-serve basis. A partial list of such products includes tuna fish, chocolate, peanuts, sugar, syrups, and molasses, motorcycles over 700 cc., and cotton. An importer desiring to bring such products into the country must file his customs entry before the quota is filled. If he files too late, the import will not be allowed.

Textile import quotas are negotiated by the United States bilaterally with textile exporting nations. Each exporting nation negotiates its own quota, and enforces it at its end of the transaction. Thus the American would-be importer of Pakistani cotton fabric must find a Pakistani cotton exporter who is able to ship cotton textiles to the United States under the Pakistani quota. If he cannot locate such a supplier who has authorization to export under the quota he is out of luck.

Sugar, syrups, and molasses quotas are established by the Department of Agriculture. The quotas are allocated to the various sugar-, syrups-, and molasses-exporting nations.

Import quotas for butter, various cheeses, and dried milk products are administered by the Dairy, Livestock and Poultry Division of the Foreign Agriculture Service of the Department of Agriculture. Would-be importers of these products must obtain licenses from the administering agency. The import quotas for these products are set yearly. Once an importer receives an import license, it automatically continues in effect for subsequent years until suspended, revoked, or surrendered.

Voluntary restraint agreements on certain commodities are bilaterally negotiated by the United States with exporting nations. Thus, under the Steel Import Stabilization Act, agreements have been signed with eleven different steel-producing nations or groups of nations, including the European Community. There has also been agreement with Japan restricting the number of Japanese automobiles exported to the United States.

Prohibited Imports. The import of many articles into the United States is forbidden. Interdicted items include:

1. Books, articles, and photographs urging treason, insurrection, or violent resistance to any law of the United States
2. Obscene or immoral material
3. Lottery tickets or lottery advertisements
4. Articles mined, produced, or manufactured wholly or in part by convict, forced, or indentured labor
5. Fish from a country that unlawfully seizes American fishing boats
6. Feathers and skins of birds, with some exceptions
7. Ermine, fox, kolinsky, marten, mink, muskrat, and weasel fur skins that are the product of the USSR
8. Pepper shells, ground or unground
9. White phosphorus matches
10. Eggs of wild birds, with some exceptions

Import and Export of Monetary Instruments. Anyone transporting over $10,000 in monetary instruments from a place inside the United States to a place outside the United States, or to a place inside the United States from or through a place outside the United States, must file a report with the Treasury Department. Monetary instruments include U.S. coins and currency, foreign coins and currency, traveler's checks, bearer negotiable instruments, and other bearer securities.

The Buy American Act. Under the provisions of the Buy American Act, 41 USC 10a–10d, the federal government must where possible acquire articles, materials, and supplies produced in the United States for public use. In addition, in the performance of contracts for construction, subcontractors, suppliers, and materialmen must use only articles, materials, and supplies produced in the United States.

The applicability of the act has been reduced by the provisions of the Trade Agreements Act of 1979, 19 USC 2503(c). Under this act, with respect to contracts involving over $161,000, the president may waive the applicability of the Buy American Act with respect to products of nations allowing use of American products in their government contracts, or with respect to products of least developed nations.

Special rules exist with respect to Defense Department procurement contracts that are too complex to cover here.

Foreign Assets Control. Under the provisions of the *Trading with the Enemy Act,* 50 USC App. 5, the Office of Foreign Assets Control of the Treasury Department has the authority to enact regulations prohibiting or restricting imports from, exports to, or financial transactions with countries whose interests are inimical to those of the United States.

Under this legislation the United States may freeze assets belonging to the governments of or citizens of such countries. The Trading with the Enemy Act was originally enacted in 1917 to sever economic relationships between the United States and Germany during World War I and to enable Uncle Sam to take control of German assets in this country. It has since been used against potentially unfriendly nations in peacetime, as when the United States placed a trade embargo in effect against Japan and froze Japanese assets in this country in July 1941, five months before the Japanese attack on Pearl Harbor.

If government means to sever or severely limit American economic relationships with another country it is not enough simply to freeze assets belonging to that country and its nationals located within the United States. Americans must be forbidden to enter such economic relationships, or their rights must at least be restricted. Thus certain regulations issued under the act apply to U.S. citizens or residents of the United States wherever located and theoretically to foreign subsidiaries and branches of U.S. corporations, though the foreign subsidiaries and branches are subject to the law of their host countries and face the problems Fruehauf's and Dresser's French subsidiaries did.

The organization must obey host country law, but its American officers, directors, and managerial personnel must not participate in unlawful transactions. Furthermore, the American parent must do all it can to force the foreign branch or subsidiary to comply with American policy. Should the American managers not try hard enough, United States assets of the branch or subsidiary could be blocked. In extreme cases its American managers could even be criminally prosecuted.

The most stringent of these regulations virtually prohibit all business dealings by Americans with North Korea, Kampuchea, and Vietnam. No person or organization subject to the jurisdiction of the United States may engage in any transaction involving these countries without a general or special Treasury Department license. Furthermore, the supplying of any petroleum product to any vessel bound to or from these nations is forbidden.

All trade with Cuba is forbidden except that authorized by the Treasury Department's Cuban Assets Control Regulations. Exports to Cuba that are authorized by Commerce Department regulation need no special Treasury license. Imports from Cuba are unlawful without a specific Treasury license.

No nickel or nickel-bearing materials may be imported into the United States without a *Certificate of Origin* from the country of export attesting that the nickel did not originate in Cuba. This is because the Castro government expropriated without compensation American-owned nickel mines on the island.

The Treasury Department will under some circumstances allow foreign subsidiaries of American firms to do business with Cuba when local law or policy favors trade with Cuba. The trade must not involve U.S. dollars or strategic goods, however.

Stringent restrictions upon trade with Iran are now in effect due to Iranian interference with the oil trade in the Persian Gulf.

Most imports to and exports from Nicaragua were forbidden in May 1985. Anyone seeking to do any business with Sandinista Nicaragua will need a Treasury Department license.

Any American seeking to purchase goods abroad for reshipment to Communist countries is subject to Treasury Department transaction control regulations. If direct export of the goods from the United States to the destination country would be unlawful under Commerce Department regulations, the indirect export will violate the Treasury regulations.

Due to Congress-mandated sanctions against the Republic of South Africa, certain exports to and imports from that nation are prohibited. Financial dealings, too, are subject to Treasury Department regulation.

Import Standards. Importation of certain merchandise into the United States is unlawful unless federal standards are complied with. Examples of the required standards for such follows:

      1. Wildfire. If documentation is required by the exporting

nation, it is also required at the American port of entry. If the creature is injurious, belongs to an endangered species, or is a marine mammal a special permit for its import is required.

2. Fur products. Some such imports are forbidden as listed above. Others must be labeled in accordance with the Fur Product Labeling Act.

3. Wool products. These must be labeled in accordance with the Wool Products Labeling Act.

4. Alcoholic beverages. Special import taxes must be paid, and a special permit is required for importation.

5. Insecticides. These must comply with Federal Insecticide, Fungicide and Rodenticide Act manufacturing and labeling requirements.

6. Narcotics. Narcotic drugs need an importation permit from the Drug Enforcement Administration. The importer must be registered with DEA as such.

7. Meat and meat products. A foreign meat inspection certificate is required for fresh products; inspection for adulteration and misbranding is also required at point of entry.

8. Electronic products. Certification of compliance with Radiation Control for Health and Safety Act by label or tag is required.

9. Hazardous substances. These must be examined by Consumer Product Safety Commission before release to the importer at point of entry.

10. Matches. A certification by government of country of manufacture that they are not made of white phosphorus is required; otherwise the import would be unlawful.

11. Textile fiber products. These must be stamped, tagged, and labeled to show country of origin and fiber composition.

12. Tobacco products. Special taxes must be paid.

13. Motor vehicles. These must be certified to comply with EPA pollutant emission standards and National Highway Traffic Safety Administration safety standards.

14. Serums. An importation permit is required. If for human use they must come from a foreign plant licensed under Food and Drug Administration regulations. They must pass inspections whether they are for human or animal use.

Chapter 3

The Common-Law System

Though every civilized nation has a legal system, no two are identical. There are three major families of legal systems on Planet Earth, which in some places are modified by one or more minor systems. The three major systems are the *Common Law,* the *Romano-Germanic Law,* and the *Socialist Law.* The minor systems are the *Islamic,* the *Far Eastern,* and the *African.*

The common law originated in England, and has been taken by English-speaking people to the ends of the earth. The Romano-Germanic law is a combination of the law of the later Roman Empire with the law of the Germanic tribes who destroyed the Western Roman Empire. The Socialist law originated in the Soviet Union after the Bolshevik Revolution of 1917. The Islamic law is found wherever there are large numbers of Muslims (believers in the religion of Islam). The Far Eastern law influences the legal systems of nations shaped by ancient Chinese culture. The African law is found in the African nations south of the Sahara.

Where the national language is English or the nation was at one time an English colony, the common law will prevail. Thus England, Ireland, the United States, Canada, Australia, New Zealand, and India are common-law nations. Other such nations are Jamaica, Belize, Guyana, Ghana, Nigeria, Kenya, and Singapore.

Where the national language is not English but a non–Communist economic system exists, the Romano-Germanic system will prevail. All of the non–Communist nations on the European continent have Romano-Germanic legal systems. So do the non–English-speaking nations of the Western Hemisphere (with the exception of Cuba), and the non–Communist nations of Asia and Africa that were never British colonies.

In a few English-speaking nations, Romano-Germanic law prevails because it was established in the area before English rule was imposed. Examples include the Republic of South Africa, Zimbabwe, Sri Lanka, Puerto Rico, and the Philippines. In the first three cases, the areas were under Dutch rule (or the rule of Dutch-speaking colonists) long enough for the Roman-Dutch law of eighteenth-century Holland to take root. The Philippines and Puerto Rico were Spanish colonies before they fell under American influence; to a large extent the old Spanish colonial law still remains in force. Portions of three other common-law nations have Romano-Germanic basic law: our state of Louisiana, the Canadian province of Quebec, and Scotland.

If the government of a nation is Marxist-Leninist, Socialist law will prevail. The purest examples are found in the Soviet Union and its European satellites.

Islamic law is an element of the law of most nations in which a majority of the people believe in Islam. It influences legal systems from Morocco to Indonesia, though only in the Arabian Peninsula does it exist in anything approaching a pure form. It is combined with common law in Pakistan and Malaysia, Socialist law in South Yemen, and Romano-Germanic law elsewhere.

China and Japan are the major nations influenced by Far Eastern law. Others are the Koreas, Vietnam, Laos, Kampuchea, Thailand, and Taiwan. The Communist nations among these have basically Socialist legal systems; the others are basically Romano-Germanic. The Chinese influence gives the law of these lands a unique influence (or — in a sense — lack of influence).

African law for purposes of this discussion is the custom of the continent's many tribes. These customs are not suited to the governing of a modern nation, but they influence the law of many African nations south of the Sahara. In African nations with numerous Muslims, the national law may be a mixture of Romano-Germanic, Islamic, and tribal concepts. In those that claim to be Marxist-Leninist (such as the Republic of the Congo and Benin) the mixture may comprise Romano-Germanic, Socialist, and tribal concepts.

General Characteristics of the Common Law

Wherever the English flag has flown for any length of time a legal system based upon the common law will probably prevail. It is a system peculiarly English, foreign and distasteful to those not steeped in English tradition. Though the white cliffs of Dover, England, are less than thirty miles from Cap Griz Nez, France, the English have always been reluctant to call themselves Europeans. Just as English government developed in unique ways, English law did likewise.

At the time of the Norman Conquest of England in 1066, the law under which western Europeans, including Englishmen, lived was local customary law. This could vary considerably over small distances. The

Norman conquerors, in order to better secure their control, strove to create and maintain a powerful central government in England. The power to administer justice was gradually centralized in the hands of royal courts composed of judges appointed by the king. The law applied by these judges came to be law created by the judges themselves in the process of deciding lawsuits.

A major characteristic of the common law was, and to an extent still is, that it reasons from the specific to the general. Common-law judges have never devised general rules to apply to a myriad of specific problems. Rather, the judges solve a particular problem in a certain way. Then when a similar problem arises, they have to decide whether to solve it in the same way as they did the earlier one, or whether it is different enough to justify another solution. The law thus grows through an organic process, adapting itself to changing conditions as the times require.

In order to keep the common law predictable, the notion of *Stare Decisis* evolved, under which the judges were normally obligated to follow their own precedents. Thus, if a case arose that was identical in kind to a case decided in the past, the judge should rule in a manner consistent with the previous ruling.

As the powers of the English Parliament grew, it became an accepted idea that Parliament could change the judge-made law by enacting legislation — but this power was seldom used.

Another unique common-law institution was the jury. The original reason for using a panel of ordinary people to act as decision-makers in a legal proceeding was that, since the jurymen were originally neighbors of the parties to the dispute, they would know more about the dispute than anyone else and would thus be able to render the most intelligent, fair decision. Over time the jury evolved from a body of persons who knew as much as possible about the dispute being tried into the body we know today: a group of people who know as little as possible about the dispute before trial begins.

It was accepted from an early time that the decision of the jury should be final unless contrary to the evidence, and that an acquittal in a criminal proceeding should be absolutely final. But for several centuries English judges had the power to instruct a jury as to how to decide a case. The jurors did not necessarily have to follow the judge's instructions. If the judge ordered a conviction but the jury decided to acquit, the accused was acquitted. However, by not following the judge's instructions the jurors had committed contempt of court and thereby risked punishment themselves. Only in the seventeenth century was it established that jurors could not be punished for making "wrong" decisions.

Because one could learn law only through the laborious process of studying court decisions, it became next to impossible for laymen to learn or understand much about the system. Only those who had the time and the opportunity to study law could comprehend the system. Thus the Englishman who got involved with the law had to hire an expert — the lawyer — to help him cope.

As Englishmen became more and more hostile to royal judges with great power, steps were taken to reduce their power. Gradually the potential for a judge to control the process of a trial was whittled down; meanwhile the power of the lawyers increased. Thus arose the adversary system of conducting trials — the judicial duel between competing lawyers carried out under the watchful eye of a referee, the trial judge. But while the power of a hostile judge to do harm to one of the parties in litigation became much more limited, the chances of the party to win his case also came to depend very much upon the skill of his champion, his lawyer. Money began to speak with a loud voice because the lawyer with great talent could demand a high price from those who wanted to use it; the best talent would too often be available only to those who could pay a high price for it.

Because jurors were ordinary folk of limited education, complex rules arose to protect them from being misled by unreliable evidence. So arose the rules that forbid laymen from expressing opinions on the witness stand and ban most hearsay testimony and the like.

Originally, if one Englishman wanted to sue another he was required to begin his suit by obtaining a writ from the royal chancellor. The nature of the writ would depend on the nature of the plaintiff's complaint. If the argument was about ownership of land, the plaintiff might have to obtain a *Writ of Right*. If it was over damage to land a *Writ of Trespass* was necessary. If it was over a breach of a written contract upon which the defendant had stamped his personal seal a *Writ of Covenant* was needed. It it was over nonpayment of a debt a *Writ of Debt* or of *Assumpsit* would be required, depending on the nature of the debt. Gradually dozens of writs were devised to fit the myriad situations in which one person might have a legal claim against another.

However, there were situations in which a person felt that he had been wronged, but the Chancellery had devised no appropriate writ for the problem and refused to invent a new one. The wronged person would then appeal to the chancellor (who was always a clergyman), as the keeper of the king's conscience, to allow him to take action against the wrongdoer despite the nonexistence of an appropriate writ. Gradually the chancellors began to permit this action.

Thus courts of Chancery began to dispense justice alongside the royal law courts, and two coexisting but in a way competing legal systems arose. The Chancery courts did not use the writs of the law courts, and they did not use juries. Law courts could decide disputes over the ownership of property, and they could order one person to pay money to another. The main weapon of the Chancery court came to be the injunction, a court order directing a person to do or not to do something.

A third court system existed in England well into the nineteenth century, the ecclesiastical courts. It was accepted during the Middle Ages that matters of inheritance and family relations were the province of the church, not the state. Thus the Roman Catholic church (and the Anglican church after the Reformation) maintained separate courts to handle such matters. Over time the jurisdiction of the ecclesiastical courts was whittled away. Family law found its way into the Chancery courts, while matters of inheritance became matters for law courts.

The English system allowed more popular participation than any other. It also allowed more protection to those accused of crime than any other.

When the English colonists settled the original thirteen colonies which later became the United States, they brought this legal system with them, except for ecclesiastical courts. When our forefathers made the American Revolution, they changed the American political system but not the legal system. The common law remained in full force and effect here, including the distinction between law and chancery (or *Equity* as it came to be known).

Though American courts were no longer required to follow English precedent after the revolution, they often did so. Many principles of contract law invented by the common law to solve new problems arising in the wake of the Industrial Revolution were first devised in English courts. When American courts later faced similar problems they often imported the English solution into our law.

In some respects American common law has diverged rather sharply from English common law. In part this is because the United States has a written constitution while Great Britain does not; in part this is because the United States is a federal nation while Great Britain is unitary; and in part this is because the historical experiences of the two nations have differed in the past two hundred years.

I will first discuss American common law, and then briefly contrast it to the common law of our mother country and of other common-law nations.

Nature of American Law

The law of the United States consists of a mixture of federal and state law. Federal law is composed of the following: (1) constitutional provisions and interpretation; (2) treaties; (3) statutes enacted by Congress; (4) executive orders; and (5) administrative regulations.

Treaties are included because the Constitution declares them to be the supreme law of the land.

Executive Orders are similar to the presidential decrees authorized in some other countries with presidential government, but in the United States they generally may be issued only with respect to housekeeping functions of the federal government or in accordance with the exercise of legislative power delegated to the president by Congress. The most noteworthy executive order in effect at the moment is no. 11246, which, as amended, imposes affirmative action requirements on all firms doing business with the federal government.

Administrative Regulations are items of legislation enacted by administrative agencies in accordance with power delegated to them by Congress.

There is no federal common law, because all federal law is based upon constitutional or legislative enactments.

State law consists of the following: (1) state constitutional provisions; (2) state statutes; (3) state administrative regulations; and (4) common law.

A sizeable portion of the law of most states consists of common law — judge-made law. Exceptions are Louisiana and California, whose legislatures have codified most if not all of their law by enacting it as statutes. American states inherited this law ready-made through statutes adopting the English common law as of such and such a date. Much state common law has been superseded by legislation or constitutional provision, but much remains unchanged.

In many states most of the law of contracts, agency, bailments, personal property, and torts remains judge-made. It is within the power of common-law judges to change the common law by refusing to follow existing precedents. But state court judges are conservative enough not to alter the common law except under unusual circumstances. Noteworthy recent examples of such alterations are court decisions imposing strict tort liability on manufacturers and sellers of defective products in the absence of statute or earlier precedent, and decisions imposing liability on employers for wrongful discharge of employees, overruling the traditional notion of employment at will.

Nature of the American Legal Profession. Only recently have the English recognized law as an intellectual discipline that should be studied in universities. Traditionally, English legal practitioners have been trained in special institutions devised for that purpose: the Inns of Court in London.

During colonial times the demand for legal practitioners in America exceeded the supply of trained Englishmen, so other training methods became acceptable. Law did eventually become a discipline to be studied in institutions of higher learning here, but in colonial times and throughout the nineteenth century most American lawyers learned their trade by study in the offices and under the supervision of successful members of the profession. As American society became more complex and the number of American universities multiplied, educational requirements for admission to the legal profession increased. Today seven years of higher education are required of aspiring lawyers, plus success on a bar examination and possession of good moral character.

Licensing of lawyers is done at the state level under provisions of state law. All American lawyers are permitted to do all things that lawyers normally do, a state of affairs that does not prevail in much of the world.

The United States has more lawyers per capita than any other nation on earth. Americans also engage in more litigation than any other people on earth — only the Israelis approach us in that regard.

Members of the legal profession are bound by strict codes of ethics everywhere in the world, but the terms of the codes vary from system to system and from country to country.

The common-law lawyer wears two hats; he serves as the advocate of his client, and also as an officer of the court. Since one of his major duties as an officer of the court is to do his best for his client, the two duties do not often conflict. It is in the area of defense of persons accused of crime that apparent contradictions exist. In nations with democratic forms of government communications between an attorney and his client are confidential. What if the person accused of crime admits to his attorney that he is guilty? Is not the attorney obligated, as an officer of the court, to disclose that information to the proper authority? The answer is clearly NO. The prosecutor in a common-law jurisdiction must prove the guilt of the accused beyond a reasonable doubt, and it is a major part of the defense counsel's job to make him do exactly that. The defense is under no obligation to assist.

On the other hand, if the client reveals to his attorney his intent to commit a crime the privilege would not apply. The attorney should naturally try to talk the client out of his plan, but if the persuasion will not work the information should be revealed to the proper authority.

The attorney must never assist his client to violate the law or advise him to do so. He must never advise or encourage anyone to lie in court.

It is permissible to advise the client *how* to tell the truth in court. The American lawyer may question a witness at length before trial, inform him of questions the other attorney might ask on cross-examination, and in general condition him as to what to expect when he testifies.

Of course he may not contact the opposing party without the knowledge and consent of his attorney.

An attorney is permitted to represent a client in most types of cases on a contingent fee basis (that is, a no-win no-pay basis). The attorney's fee is an agreed percentage of his client's recovery. Such an arrangement is not allowed in criminal or domestic relations cases.

The lawyer must be careful to avoid conflict of interest situations. He may not represent both sides of a controversy, represent one client against another, represent a client against a business in which he owns an interest, or represent a client against the attorney's relative.

Nature of the American Judiciary. The American judiciary is much more numerous than its English counterpart. It is also more political, both in its methods of selection and in its exercise of power.

The United States is one of the few federal nations that has two full court systems existing side by side—the federal court system that enforces federal law, and the state system that enforces state law. Far more typical is the Canadian system in which there is only one powerful federal court, the Supreme Court of Canada. The provincial courts serve as lower courts, which enforce both provincial and federal law.

Since Americans generate more court business per capita than almost any other nationality on earth, we require numerous judges to process the workload. Almost all American judges are trained lawyers who have had experience in the practice of law. The only major exception is our justices of the peace, for whom, usually, no educational requirement is laid down. In the past all states had justices of the peace or the equivalent to try petty cases. However, many states (such as Ohio) have abolished JPs and delegated their duties to legally trained judges.

At the state level the majority of judges are elected. Thus the game of judicial selection is played according to the same rules used for choosing executive and legislative officials. A minority of state judges are appointed. In some states the governor has an appointment power that is the equivalent of the power of the president at the federal level. In other states gubernatorial discretion has been reduced. Judicial nominations are made by a nonpartisan commission charged with studying the qualifications of judicial candidates and submitting, for example, three names to the governor for each vacancy to be filled. Of course, even with this system the governor may still be swayed by political considerations in choosing his appointee.

At the federal level judicial appointments are made by the president with the advice and consent of the Senate. These appointments have always been a political matter, since Democratic presidents tend to appoint Democrats to the federal judiciary and Republican presidents Republicans. Presently it has become even more political, because both president and senators consider the ideology of an appointee perhaps more than his judicial qualifications.

The major reason why politics plays such a role in judicial selection in the United States is because the American judiciary exercises a political power unmatched anywhere else in the world. This power stems from two facts. First, American judges have the undisputed power of judicial review; they may declare legislative acts null and void because contrary to constitutions. Second, the United States Constitution contains a Bill of Rights that employs sweeping general terms (such as "due process of law" and "equal protection of the law") that are not defined. In essence, these terms and the provisions containing them mean what the judges say they mean.

The power of judicial review is used sparingly at the moment because supreme courts, both state and federal, tend to follow election returns. What the state legislature or the U.S. Congress enacts is seen to be the will of the voters. However, the present United States Supreme Court does not hesitate to void state legislation that it finds contrary to the United States Constitution. Here, judicial review is very much alive.

It is in interpreting the Constitution of the United States while considering the constitutionality of state legislation that federal judges exercise immense power. Over the past thirty-five years the Supreme Court has brought about revolutionary changes in American society and politics. School desegregation, legalization of abortion on demand, reapportionment of state and local legislatures on a one man, one vote basis, and reformation of criminal procedure — all these major changes and more originated in the federal courts.

American Criminal Procedure. American law leans over backward to give the person accused of crime the benefit of every doubt. The person arrested must be told of his right to legal counsel and his privilege against self-incrimination almost at once. His right to legal counsel begins immediately; if he cannot afford to hire his own lawyer, one must be provided at state expense. Moreover, the counsel provided must be competent to give the accused adequate representation. The accused need not answer police questions and has the right to have his lawyer present during questioning. He is entitled to reasonable bail pending trial unless he stands accused of murder or an offense of equal gravity.

If accused of a felony the suspect must be indicted by a grand jury, and in all cases is entitled to trial by an unbiased trial jury. We go to great lengths to ensure that jurors are unbiased. Names of potential jurors are known to the lawyers in a case before the trial begins; thus it is possible to conduct simple investigations of their backgrounds. During the jury selection process the potential jurymen are questioned exhaustively about their knowledge of the case and their prejudices; indeed, the jury selection process in a criminal prosecution may take days.

The accused has the privilege not to testify at his trial. If he avails himself of the privilege, neither prosecutor nor judge may comment on it to the jury. If the accused does choose to testify he is treated like any other witness; thus he subjects himself to cross-examination by the prosecutor.

The right of the authorities to collect evidence for use in a criminal prosecution is hedged about by restrictions derived from constitutional prohibitions against unreasonable searches and seizures and against self-incrimination. Evidence unlawfully obtained by the prosecution is not admissible in court. If the only available evidence against the accused is unlawfully obtained, the charges against him must be dropped — even if this evidence proves his guilt.

The prosecution must prove the guilt of the accused beyond a reasonable doubt. If this is not accomplished the defense lawyer may ask the judge to end the trial with a directed verdict of not guilty — acquittal without any jury deliberation. If the evidence seems to show the accused's guilt beyond doubt, however, the judge may not direct a verdict of guilty. Conviction may occur only after due deliberation by the jury.

After all of the evidence has been presented the lawyers summarize the case for the jurors. The prosecutor must be careful in his summation to stick to the evidence presented during the trial and not to appeal to the passions and prejudices of the jury; improper summation by the prosecutor may result in the declaration of a mistrial by the judge. The defense attorney is not under such a strict obligation; the judge may not declare a mistrial because of defense misconduct. The only limitation upon the defense attorney's conduct at this point is the fact that he is expected to behave ethically and to obey the commands of the trial judge.

After summation by the lawyers the judge delivers his charge to the jury; in his charge the judge explains the law the jurors must apply. In most American state courts the judge must not comment on the evidence in any way. In federal courts the judges have a limited right to make such commentary.

Jury decisions in American criminal trials must be unanimous — all jurors must agree. If unanimous agreement is impossible, resulting in a hung jury, the judge must declare a mistrial.

If the jury convicts, it must do so in accordance with the judge's summary of the law. However, a jury may totally ignore the law when it acquits, since a verdict of acquittal is final for all time. If the jury ignores the judge's charge in the process of convicting, the decision may be overturned later. If it ignores the charge and acquits, the trial is over.

In case of conviction, the accused has the right to appeal. However, he may only appeal the judgment of conviction, not the sentence.

Since a convicted defendant usually claims that rights granted him by the Constitution of the United States were denied him during the proceedings against him, criminal appeals usually involve questions of federal law. He may argue that some of the evidence against him had been obtained as a result of an unlawful search and seizure and thus should not have been admitted by the judge. He may argue that prejudiced persons were allowed to sit on the jury, thus depriving him of a fair trial. He may argue that he had not been properly informed of his constitutional right against self-incrimination before he confessed to the police. He may argue that his lawyer had defended him incompetently.

Thus, such appeals of state court convictions could ultimately be carried to the Supreme Court of the United States – a long and complicated process.

Moreover, it is possible for a convicted defendant to test the lawfulness of his confinement by applications to the courts for *Writs of Habeas Corpus.* Since both state law and federal law provide for issuance of such writs, application for them may be made in both court systems. Thus a convicted accused may continue to contest the lawfulness of the proceedings against him even after his appeal of conviction has been decided against him.

American Civil Procedure. American common law is much less considerate of civil plaintiffs and defendants than it is of those accused of crime. It assumes and expects for the most part that persons involved in civil litigation know their legal rights, and it can gravely penalize the ignorant.

In most states small claims courts exist, in which people may settle arguments involving small amounts of money without involvement with lawyers and complicated court procedures. If the amount at stake exceeds one thousand dollars, however, small claims courts may not have jurisdiction; in such a case involvement with lawyers and complex procedures is unavoidable.

Everyone involved in a civil lawsuit has the right to be represented by a lawyer, but everyone is expected to provide his own. If a person cannot afford to hire one, organizations exist that will provide one at little or no cost. But the litigant must learn about and contact these groups on his own. If the lawyer hired by a civil litigant is incompetent, the law provides no remedy. One should be sure the lawyer is fit to handle one's case before entrusting him with the job.

Under the common-law adversary system, it is the responsibility of each party to civil litigation and his lawyer to acquire the evidence to prove his case. American law provides numerous devices to assist in this process. One may learn what a witness will probably say in court by taking a deposition from him before trial begins. The witness is questioned by the lawyers just as he would be in court in the presence of a court reporter. The reporter's notes are transcribed and the resulting document made available to all parties. Documentary evidence may be obtained from the other party to the case and from third parties by use of the subpoena duces tecum and other devices. In personal injury cases, plaintiffs may be compelled to submit to physical examinations by doctors hired by the defendant.

Trials in American civil cases are almost always by jury. The only exceptions are cases in which the parties agree to have the judge decide, and equity cases (except in states like Texas that do not recognize the distinction between law and equity).

Jury selection in a civil case involving a large sum of money may take as long as in a major criminal matter. Both sides might spend large sums of money investigating the backgrounds of potential jurors before the trial ever begins.

The civil plaintiff is not required to prove his case beyond a reasonable doubt; proof by a preponderance of the evidence is all that is required. If the evidence is very one-sided in favor of either the plaintiff or the defendant, the judge may end the trial with a directed verdict for the prevailing side.

The trial of a complex civil case before a jury may consume weeks, or even months. Jurors may be asked to try to understand complicated questions of business procedures, accounting, medicine, science, and the like of which they have had little or no earlier comprehension.

Often the civil jury's decision need not be unanimous. Thus hung juries are not quite as likely to occur as in criminal trials.

Either side may appeal the decision in a civil matter. Since civil cases tried in state courts usually do not involve questions of federal law, these cases remain in the state court system. The decision of the highest court of the state will be final. If, however, there is a federal question in the case it may end up in the Supreme Court of the United States.

Each side must pay its own attorney in American civil litigation. Only when the case involves violation of consumer protection legislation or the like may the loser be compelled to pay the winner's attorney fees. Thus the winning plaintiff does not get to keep his full recovery. Usually the loser pays all of the court costs. Judges have the power to divide these costs between the parties but seldom do so.

If the plaintiff's attorney is handling his client's case on a contingent fee basis, the plaintiff owes him nothing if there is no recovery. If the plaintiff wins, however, his attorney will claim a substantial part of the recovery, perhaps 25 percent or more. Civil litigation can be an expensive sport in the United States, win or lose.

American Commercial Contract Law. Most of the American law governing the making of commercial contracts is contained in the Uniform Commercial Code, adopted by all states except Louisiana. What follows is a very brief general outline of the subject.

In order for a valid enforceable contract to exist, the following requirements must be met:

1. A valid offer
2. A valid acceptance
3. The mutual assent of the parties

4. Consideration
5. Contractual capacity of both parties
6. A lawful objective
7. Sometimes, a writing

An *offer* must be an unambiguous statement that the offeror will sell or buy a specific good or service. An advertisement that one has something for sale is not an offer. Nor is a simple price quotation. An offer need not be in writing. It is not effective until received by the offeree, and it may be revoked any time before it is accepted unless it is a *firm offer*. A *firm offer* is one made by a merchant in writing stating that it will be open for a specified length of time. The offeror cannot revoke the offer for that length of time or for three months, whichever is shorter. Thus, if the offeror promises to hold the offer open for a year he may revoke it after three months (UCC 2–205).

The *acceptance* must be unambiguous. Acceptances dispatched by mail are valid when sent; thus even if the acceptance is not received by the offeror a contract nevertheless exists. (The offeror may eliminate this possibility by stating in his offer that the acceptance must be received to be valid.) An acceptance is valid even if its terms are not identical with those of the offer. If the acceptance contains terms the offer does not mention (for instance, the offeror offers to buy goods on credit; the acceptance accepts the offer but states that the buyer must pay 1.5 percent interest per month on the unpaid balance) silence by the offeror is considered acceptance of the added term. If the offeror objects to the added term it will not be part of the contract.

If the offer and acceptance contradict each other (the offeror buyer offers to buy a specific machine and states that it is to be fully guaranteed for a year; offeree accepts the offer but states the machine is guaranteed for only ninety days), the contract is on the offeror's terms unless offeror agrees to offeree's terms (UCC 2–207).

There is no *mutual assent* unless the parties have agreed to the bargain of their own free wills. Thus, if a party was tricked into making the bargain or forced into it, he may rescind it. Mutual assent is lacking if any of the following are present:

1. Fraud (deliberate deceit)
2. Misrepresentation (innocent deceit)
3. Mutual mistake (the parties thought they had agreed on the subject matter, but they had not)
4. Duress (physical or economic coercion)
5. Undue influence (psychological coercion)
6. Unconscionability (gross unfairness)

There must be *consideration* on both sides. Consideration takes four forms:

1. An act
2. A promise
3. A forbearance (a promise *not* to do something)
4. A promise to a third party

The usual contract consists of an exchange of two promises: the buyer promises to buy and the seller promises to sell. Or, the buyer may promise to buy and the seller ships the merchandise he ordered; his act of making shipment is his consideration. The two considerations need not be of equal value; inadequate consideration is not a ground for avoiding a contract. It may be proof of fraud or unconscionability, however.

The following do not constitute a consideration: (1) past consideration (a promise to pay for a service after it has been performed); (2) a promise to do what one already must do; or (3) an illusory promise (a promise that does not bind one to do anything).

All persons have *contractual capacity* except minors and mentally abnormal persons. A person who has not reached the age of adulthood is a minor; this age is eighteen in most states (though a few adhere to the traditional twenty-one). A minor need not perform a contract if he chooses not to (unless it is a contract involving a necessity: in such case he must pay fair market value for it). Persons with guardians have no contractual capacity; mentally abnormal persons without guardians have limited capacity.

The adult who makes a contract with a minor may not rescind because of the minor's lack of capacity. He who contracts with a person with a guardian may rescind, however; the law regards such a contract as void.

A century ago corporations were limited to performance of acts authorized by their *Articles of Incorporation*. They had capacity to do only that which they were permitted by their articles to do. Contracts not authorized by the articles were *Ultra Vires* and beyond the organization's capacity. This is no longer true. The fact that a corporate contract is ultra vires is no longer a defense to liability. The other party to the contract may enforce it. Those corporate agents who made it performed a wrongful act; if performance causes a loss to the company they are liable.

Contracts involving the commission of crimes or torts have *unlawful objectives* and are illegal and unenforceable. Generally, a contract that violates a statute will also be illegal and unenforceable.

The most common sort of American commercial contract that must be in *writing* is a contract for sale of goods for more than five hundred dollars. Others are contracts for sale of securities (no matter how much or how little money is involved) and contracts for the sale of land (UCC 2-201).

A commercial contract may be modified without consideration; a noncommercial contract may not. An amendment or modification of a commerical contract must be in writing if the contract as amended must be in writing (UCC 2-209).

The parties to a contract are expected to perform it as they agreed. One must do exactly that which he promised to do on or before the time he agreed to do it. Nonperformance is sometimes excused. The most common grounds for such excuse are:

    1. Performance is absolutely impossible (the seller's one and only factory is destroyed; he therefore cannot possibly manufacture what he promised to sell the buyer)

    2. A change in the law after the making of the contract rendered performance illegal

    3. Changes in surrounding circumstances frustrated the purpose of the contract

If a party does not do that which he promised and he has no legally valid excuse for not doing it, he is guilty of *Breach*. Generally, the victim of a breach may suspend his performance of the bargain, cancel the remainder of the contract, and file suit against the breaching party (UCC 2–703, 711).

The remedies available for breach of a commercial contract include restitution, damages, and specific performance. *Restitution* is available only when the breaching party has made partial performance (partial or full payment, partial or full delivery). He is entitled to recover the value of the performance. *Damages* are the commonest remedy for breach of contract. The breaching party must pay his victim enough money to compensate him for the harm caused by the breach. *Specific performance* is the remedy of forcing the breaching party to perform the contract. This is an uncommon remedy in the United States; it will be invoked only if damages will not adequately compensate the victim of the breach. It will be invoked when the subject matter of the contract is a one-of-a-kind item, or when there is such a shortage of subject matter that the buyer will not be able to acquire his merchandise anywhere else if he cannot get it from the seller.

English Common Law

The English Legal Profession. The most striking aspect of England's legal profession to Americans is the fact that it actually consists of two professions, that of barrister and that of solicitor. The barrister is essentially the trial lawyer; the solicitor is the officer lawyer. Barristers still acquire their training at the Inns of Court. Solicitors are required to complete a course of legal training either at a university or at a polytechnic institute. The majority of newly licensed solicitors now have university training.

The Englishman with a legal problem will first consult a solicitor. If the matter can be resolved without court action, no other legal practitioner needs to be involved. However, if the matter will require litigation the assistance of a barrister is essential. It is the business of the solicitor to hire the barrister, not that of the solicitor's client.

Contingent fee arrangements between solicitors or barristers and their clients are unlawful. Otherwise English legal ethics are very similar to American.

Great Britain has far fewer legal practitioners per capita than does the United States. The British do not carry their disputes to court nearly as often as we.

The Nature of English Law. The major sources of English law are statutes enacted by Parliament, treaties, and administrative regulations. Great Britain has no written constitution and therefore has no constitutional law as we understand it. Since most English law has been reduced to legislation by acts of Parliament little common law remains.

The English Judiciary. The English judiciary is also much less numerous than ours. This is because Great Britain is a unitary nation and thus has only one court system, and also because there is much less litigation in Great Britain.

The highest court of the English realm is the Judicial Committee of the House of Lords, presided over by the lord chancellor. Originally the entire House of Lords (the upper house of the British Parliament) had the authority to participate in the decision of cases appealed to it from lower courts. Now, however, this authority has been delegated to the eleven members of the Judicial Committee, plus the lord chancellor.

The lord chancellor presides over legislative sessions of the Lords and over the Judicial Committee. He is in a sense the English equivalent of the chief justice of the United States Supreme Court. But he exercises much more judicial authority than does our chief justice. He is the administrative head of the English judicial system and thus has some authority to assign sitting judges their work. More importantly, he appoints most of England's judges on a strictly merit basis.

Aspirants to the higher levels of the English bench must have years of successful practice as barristers behind them, and must have earned the respect of sitting judges. The major question asked about potential judges is, is this person capable of doing the job?

The most striking feature of the English judiciary is that the lowest courts of the system are staffed by magistrates who are not required to have any legal education and who serve without pay (other than expense and subsistence). They are appointed by the lord chancellor on the advice of local committees, and are required to complete a training program after appointment. These magistrates are in a sense the equivalent of the American justice of the peace, but they exercise much wider authority than do our JPs.

The functioning of English courts is nonpolitical. There are two reasons for this. First, because Great Britain has no written constitution, English judges cannot alter the legal or social framework of the nation by changing the interpretation of the basic law. Second, English judges have no power of judicial review. A legislative act can hardly be ruled unconstitutional when there is no constitution to measure it against. Furthermore, no English judge has dared declare an act of Parliament null and void because contrary to justice and the common law since the seventeenth century. In short, the legislative power of Parliament is unlimited; the judiciary may not challenge it. There is no reason for the English judiciary to be politicized.

Special English Courts. Contrary to American ways, but consistent with continental European ways, Parliament has created several special courts staffed in part by laymen to decide specialized disputes. Most noteworthy are the industrial tribunals that hear cases involving interpretation of written employment contracts, disputes over employee benefits (maternity pay and such), wrongful expulsions from trade unions, safety of workplaces, on-the-job sex and racial discrimination, wrongful employment termination, and the like. These courts consist of a barrister or solicitor as chairman, one employer representative, and one employee representative. The case is decided by majority vote. Cases may be appealed to the Employment Appeal Tribunal. The appeals are heard by a panel consisting of one professional judge plus representatives of employers and employees. Cases may be appealed from the Appeal Tribunal to the regular appellate courts.

The Restrictive Practices Court hears cases under the Restrictive Trade Practices Act, the English antitrust law. It consists of five professional judges and ten educated laymen knowledgeable in practices of the business world. Each case is heard by one professional judge and two laymen and is decided by majority vote. Appeal is to the regular appeals courts.

English Criminal Procedure. The ground rules of common-law criminal procedure are roughly identical wherever the common law applies, but there are some subtle differences between English and American procedure.

English police are under no duty to inform a person arrested of a right to remain silent, or of a right to be represented by counsel.

A person accused of a crime may be denied bail if there is reason to believe that he will flee, commit other offenses, or attempt to intimidate witnesses or otherwise obstruct justice.

English standards of unreasonable search and seizure are similar to ours, but evidence seized in violation of these rules may be used against the accused in court. Those who unlawfully seized the evidence are subject to criminal prosecution.

Grand juries are no longer used in England. When a person is accused of an indictable offense (such as murder, manslaughter, or rape) he undergoes an examining trial before a magistrate and that person decides whether or not he should be brought to trial.

Most English crimes—traffic violations, theft of small amounts of money or property, and the like—are not indictable offenses. These are tried by magistrates without a jury under summary procedure.

More serious crimes against property, and crimes against the person not involving rape, homicide, or serious personal injury may be tried either in magistrates' courts without a jury or in higher courts with a jury. Which type of court hears the case depends upon the exact circumstances of the crime. The majority of such offenses are disposed of by the magistrates.

Englishmen accused of crime are quite likely to give up the benefits of trial by jury to get their cases into magistrates' court, because the maximum sentence a magistrate may impose is six months' imprisonment.

Only the more serious cases get a full-blown trial by jury. In Great Britain, pretrial investigation of jurors is frowned upon, and jury selection is disposed of very rapidly. The trial itself is conducted in almost the same way as American trials. At trial's end, however, the judge has wide powers to comment upon evidence in instructing the jury.

Unanimous jury verdicts are not required by English law; the assent of ten of the twelve jurors is sufficient to reach a decision.

Acquittals may not be appealed in England. Convictions, however, are appealable, as are sentences. Even a person who pleads guilty to the commission of an offense may appeal his sentence.

The person convicted of a crime is entitled to a free appeal, as in the United States. However, once the highest court to hear the case renders a decision the case is closed. The English convict may not forever litigate his case through applications for writs of habeas corpus and the like.

English Civil Procedure. The English welfare state provides free or subsidized legal assistance for those who need it, even in civil litigation. No one is denied lack of legal assistance due to lack of means to pay for it.

Juries are not used in English civil cases, except in cases of libel or slander or in other cases where a person's character is called into question (fraud, false imprisonment, malicious prosecution). The judge decides all issues connected with the case. Otherwise, English civil procedure is similar to ours.

The English Law of Commercial Contracts. Most of the English law of commercial contracts is contained in the Sale of Goods Act. It very closely resembles the American law, but important differences exist.

Under English law, offers may be revoked any time before acceptance; as with us the revocation must be received by the offeree to be valid. Nothing like the American firm offer exists.

Whether a communication in response to an offer is an acceptance is determined by the *Mirror-Image Rule*. Unless the terms of offer and acceptance are identical, the response to the offer is a counteroffer. If after the exchange of offer and counteroffer the parties act as if there is a contract and perform it, the English courts are very likely to say that the contract is on the offeree's terms; the offeror accepted his terms by beginning performance of the contract.

English corporations generally may not lawfully do that which their charters do not permit them to do. Ultra vires contracts of English corporations are illegal and unenforceable, unless the other party to the contract entered into it in good faith, not knowing of the limitations of authority contained in the corporate charter.

English courts are less likely to allow specific performance in case of breach of contract than are American courts.

There are no other appreciable differences between English and American law in this area.

Other Common-Law Nations

The law of other common-law nations is more akin to English than to American law. This is because these other nations were under direct English rule for longer than the United States was, and the separation from England occurred peacefully.

Until 1982 the constitution of Canada was an act of the British Parliament, the British North America Act of 1867. Thus Canadian constitutional amendments had to be enacted by the Parliament in London. Since Canada is a federation, governmental power is divided between the federal government and the provinces. Most criminal law is federal, while most civil law is provincial. All courts are provincial except the Supreme Court and courts of special jurisdiction. The Canadian Supreme Court may declare acts of the federal parliament or provincial legislatures unconstitutional. However, when the court finds legislation unconstitutional because it violates the Bill of Rights of the 1982 Constitution, the federal parliament or the provincial legislature, as the case may be, may override the court decision and declare the legislation constitutional despite the court decision. Attorneys are licensed at the provincial level. The legal profession is not divided as in England. Legal ethics, criminal procedure, and civil procedure resemble the English model more than the American.

It must be remembered that one of the provinces, French-speaking Quebec, operates under the Romano-Germanic legal system; thus the law in force in that province is a mixture. The federal law is amplified by court precedent as in all common-law jurisdictions; the provincial law is contained in codes drafted on the French model.

Australia, too, is a federation. There criminal law and most civil law are state law (except for matters of economic regulation, insurance and banking, bankruptcy, protection of trade, family law, and a few other matters). Most courts are state courts; the only really important federal court is the High Court of Australia which acts as the nation's supreme court. The High Court has the power of judicial review, but since Australia's constitution contains no bill of rights the grounds upon which legislation may be found unconstitutional are narrow. Civil and criminal procedure resemble the English model more than the American. Three states (Victoria, New South Wales, and Queensland) have adopted the divided legal profession of England; the other three (Tasmania, South Australia, and West Australia) have the unified profession of Canada and the United States.

New Zealand is a unitary state. Its law is the most closely related to England's of any common-law country.

The legal systems of the former English colonies of Africa and Asia are hybrid systems, containing elements from other families of law. These nations will be mentioned later in this work.

Law of Commercial Contracts. Most common-law nations other than the United States have enacted the English Sale of Goods Act as their commercial sales law, or they have modeled their acts upon the English act. Therefore their law in this area is very similar to that of the mother country.

Chapter 4

The Romano-Germanic System

The legal systems of the European continent have influenced each other since early medieval times. All developed essentially on parallel courses; no continental nation took off in the unique direction of Great Britain. The area of western Europe that was a part of the Roman Empire lived under the law of that empire for centuries, though the Roman law never "took" in England and never became a major influence upon the law of that country.

The foundation of Roman law was the Twelve Tables, enacted in the early days of the Roman city-state. Later it was supplemented by legislation enacted by the law-making assemblies of citizens of the Republic, and by the edicts of the praetors, the exercisers of judicial power under the Republic. It was a custom that, upon election, each praetor would proclaim to the people the law he would enforce during his term of office. It was thus possible for each praetor to make his own law; a new holder of the office could in theory totally overhaul the law of the state (except for the Twelve Tables and enacted legislation). As a practical matter this did not happen; for the most part each new praetor continued in force the laws created by his predecessors.

When the Republic was replaced by the Principate at the beginning of the Christian era, the power of legislative assemblies and praetors to make law ended. Legislative and judicial authority became concentrated in the hands of the emperors and their appointees. Since the emperors and their appointees made no effort to systematically overhaul the law inherited from the Republic, the law now consisted of the Twelve Tables plus collected enactments of republican legislative assemblies, praetors, and emperors. The most authoritative statements of the law were those derived from the learned commentaries of legal scholars of the third and fourth centuries: Ulpian, Papinian, Paul, and a few others.

It was an accepted principle that the Roman law applied only to Roman citizens; non–Romans were originally outside the law. As the extent of the territories conquered by Roman armies increased, Roman law was forced to accommodate aliens. Two systems came into existence within the Roman domains: the *Jus Civile,* which applied to Roman citizens and the dealings between them, and the *Jus Gentium,* which applied to aliens. Within Rome itself the *Praetor Urbanus* devoted himself to hearing cases involving Romans, while the *Praetor Peregrinus* dealt with cases involving aliens.

When the Emperor Caracalla bestowed Roman citizenship on all persons living within the Empire in A.D. 212, the jus gentium vanished; since all persons were now Romans, the jus civile applied to all. But the principle that the law applied only to citizens continued to exist.

Such was the state of Roman law at the time of the fall of the Western Empire, in A.D. 476. The most earthshaking transformation in Roman law took place after the Empire had lost its sovereignty in most of western Europe.

The Emperor Justinian of the Eastern Empire ordered a codification of Roman law early in the sixth century. His experts studied the writings of the scholars of the mature Empire, plus earlier materials, and produced four great works that are still the best evidence of the Roman law. The most important of these was the *Corpus Juris Civilis,* in theory still one of the bases of the law of Scotland, the Republic of South Africa, and Sri Lanka. This body of law became the law of the Eastern Roman Empire (Byzantine Empire) until its demise at the hands of the Turks in 1453, and was adopted as the law of resurrected Greece when she became independent in 1822. (It has since been replaced there by modern codes.)

The Germanic component of the Romano-Germanic legal system comes from the law of the Germanic tribes who destroyed the Western Roman Empire. The conquering Germans lived under their own tribal law, but allowed the conquered Romans to continue living under their law. As time passed the conquered forgot much of their legal heritage, adapting to the simpler law of their conquerors. The Roman law disappeared from England, the parts of Germany that had been Roman, and northern France. In southern France, however, the Roman influence upon the local law never died. The south was known as the *Pays de Droit Écrit* — the land of written law — until the time of the French Revolution. (Northern France remained the *Pays de Droit Coutumier* — the land of customary law — until Napoleon unified French law in 1804.)

West Europeans rediscovered the Roman law during the twelfth century. It became a subject for study at the University of Bologna, one of the early European universities. Intellectuals trained at Bologna proposed the injection of Roman legal concepts into the existing law of the times; since the old law as codified by Justinian was much better adapted to the regulation of the developing society of those days than the inherited customary law, Roman influence upon continental European law began to increase.

Three other sources influenced the law of the Middle Ages. First, the feudal system of organization of society generated law. Questions of the relationship of lords to vassals and the rights and duties of each were dealt with in this system. Second, the canon law of the Roman Catholic church became an important influence upon the secular law of the time. Though this body of law was originally enforced only by the church in its ecclesiastical courts, concepts of canon law soon invaded the secular law. Third, the *Lex Mercatoria* of the traveling merchants became an important influence. The legal concepts governing contracts, commercial paper, and the like developed here proved themselves useful in nonmercantile situations also.

Still, continental European law before the French Revolution remained a chaotic hodgepodge of the above-mentioned influences. Even so centralized a nation as France had no unified national law — the basis of law remained local custom that varied from province to province, and could vary even within a province.

A few European monarchs sought to impose legal unity upon their disparate subjects. King Alfonso X of Castile (which later became part of Spain) caused to be drafted a comprehensive code for his realm called the *Siete Partidas.* This code later influenced the law of united Spain, and the laws of the Spanish colonies (particularly the nations of Latin America).

King Christian V of Denmark caused to be drafted a code called the *Danske Lov* in 1683. Denmark ruled Norway at the time; a similar code called the *Norske Lov* became effective in that land in 1687. The Danske Lov also became the law of Iceland because that island was ruled by Christian V. The Swedish Riksdag enacted the *Sveriges Riks Lag* in 1734. The Sveriges Riks Lag became law in Finland, because Sweden ruled that land. These codes are still theoretically in effect, though most of their provisions have been rendered obsolete by changing times.

The Dutch Republic combined its customary law with Roman law in its *Elegant Jurisprudence.* Dutch colonists carried this Roman-Dutch law to South Africa, the Guianas, and Sri Lanka; it still remains a major part of the legal systems of the Republic of South Africa, Zimbabwe (whose original European colonists came from South Africa), and Sri Lanka.

King Frederick the Great of Prussia caused to be drafted the *Allgemeine Landrecht* (ALR), which became effective in that country in 1794. It sought to unify the law of Prussia into one collection of legislation. As Prussia expanded her territory the ALR's jurisdiction expanded; it became the law of two-thirds of Germany before 1900.

The makers of the French Revolution sought to sweep away the chaotic French legal system of the monarchy and replace it with a unified system of national law. They failed — but Napoleon Bonaparte made the dream into reality. At his direction most of the law of France was codified (reduced to legislation) in the *Code Napoléon* of 1804, which remains the basis of French law to the present day. Napoleon's conquering armies carried his code to much of continental Europe; it remains the basis of the laws of Belgium and the Netherlands today. It is also the basis of the law of the Canadian province of Quebec, and of the American state of Louisiana.

The Austrian Empire followed the French example in 1811. The *Allgemeines Bürgerliches Gesetzbuch* (ABGB) decreed by the monarch in that year is still in effect in the Austrian Federal Republic. It was never put into effect anywhere outside the Austro-Hungarian Empire. For a time after World War I it was the law of Czechoslovakia and of parts of Poland and Yugoslavia, but has now been repealed everywhere except in its country of origin.

Unified Germany created the second of the great Romano-Germanic codes. The *Bürgerliches Gesetzbuch* (BGB) became the law of the German Empire in 1900. It is still the basis of the law of the German Federal Republic; it was also the law of the German Democratic Republic before 1975. It has also influenced the law of such faraway places as Japan and the Republic of China (Taiwan).

The third major Romano-Germanic code is the *Zivilgesetzbuch* (ZGB) of Switzerland, which became effective in 1912. Mustapha Kemal Ataturk, the great Turkish reformer, decreed the ZGB to be the law of the new Turkey during the 1920s, and the ZGB has influenced the codes of other Romano-Germanic nations.

Virtually all nations with legal systems based upon Romano-Germanic law followed the French precedent and reduced their law to a comprehensive scheme of legislation. Only three of these have not — Scotland, the Republic of South Africa, and Sri Lanka.

Scotland, though a part of the United Kingdom, lives under the Romano-Germanic law developed there when she was an independent kingdom. Scotland has her own courts, but has no legislature. All legislation for Scotland is enacted by the British Parliament in London; the London legislators have no familiarity with or sympathy for the Scottish legal system. Thus the English legislation persistently gnaws away at the body of Scots inherited law.

The Republic of South Africa lives under the Roman-Dutch law brought there by the Dutch settlers of Cape Colony in the seventeenth and eighteenth centuries. Cape Colony became an English colony in 1815; the rest of South Africa passed under English rule in 1902. English rule added a leaven of common law to the formerly existing Roman-Dutch law, but did not replace it. The Boer rulers of the present republic, loyal to Afrikaner cultural traditions, have returned to the legal concepts of their ancestors.

Sri Lanka was a Dutch colony before it became an English one. The

English chose not to disturb the Roman-Dutch legal system they had found in effect there. When Sri Lanka attained independence, her rulers, too, chose not to disturb the existing system.

Before the French Revolution the Roman notion that the national law applied only to citizens still had some validity, especially where Jews were concerned. The Jewish communities lived as isolated islands within the Christian communities, subject to their own laws except when they had business dealings with their Christian neighbors. The French revolutionaries bestowed French citizenship upon French Jews and made them subject to French law in all respects. The precedent was duly followed in other continental European lands; at last the notion that national law applies only to citizens died completely.

On the European continent there was little or no popular participation in government before the French Revolution. Thus no institution at all similar to the English jury could develop. Judges, as officials of the realm, exercised immense power in their courtrooms. They presided over trials in their courts; they controlled the proceedings; and they made the decisions.

Since there was no popular participation in government in most continental nations, there was no incentive to develop institutions to protect persons accused of crime. To be sure, the notion developed during the later Middle Ages that no one should be punished for commission of a crime unless he confessed to committing it. People believed that judges and witnesses could be corrupted to conspire to convict and punish the innocent. However, this effort to promote justice did just the opposite. If the accused could not be convicted unless he confessed, he had to be forced to confess. Hence the practice arose of torturing the accused in order to obtain the confession. The use of torture to compel confession was abolished in France during the 1790s. The conquering armies of Napoleon added the prohibition to the laws of occupied lands, and by the middle of the nineteenth century the practice had been abolished almost everywhere.

The heritage of the past lives on, however, in the way Romano-Germanic courts operate today. The tradition that the judge should be the most powerful man in the courtroom is still followed. Nowhere on the European continent did lawyers acquire the prestige or power that they did in England. The Romano-Germanic lawyer plays a subordinate role to the judge, as he has always done.

Structure of Romano-Germanic Code Systems. The Napoleonic law reform in France created five major codes:

1. The *Code Napoléon* (the Civil Code)
2. The Commercial Code
3. The Penal Code
4. The Code of Criminal Procedure
5. The Code of Civil Procedure

The *Civil Code* contains the basic law of contracts, torts, agency, the family, inheritance of property, ownership of property, and the like. The *Commercial Code* contains rules of law specially applicable to commercial transactions (including the law of commercial paper and the like). The *Penal Code* contains the criminal law, while the latter two codes contain the rules of court procedure.

The German codifications followed the French pattern. In Switzerland, however, only three major codes were enacted: (1) the ZGB (the Civil Code); (2) the Code of Obligations; and (3) The Penal Code. The Swiss *Civil Code* contains the law governing the family, property, inheritance, and the like. The *Code of Obligations* contains the law of contracts, torts, agency, business organizations, and the like; for the most part Swiss contract law is the same for both commercial and noncommercial dealings, though sections of the Code of Obligations establish special rules for certain special types of contracts. The *Penal Code* is a typical Western code of criminal law. Since Switzerland has a federal form of government and since court organization is a matter of cantonal law, court procedure is also a cantonal matter.

The Italian code system resembles the French, except that Italy has no separate Commercial Code.

The Scandinavian countries have not enacted comprehensive codes in modern times. The old codes of the seventeenth and eighteenth centuries still govern as amended by the various national parliaments.

Most Latin American countries have codified their law. The majority of these nations have based their codes upon the French enactments, but the more modern codes have been influenced by the BGB and ZGB.

Importance of Court Decisions in Romano-Germanic Law. Though in theory the Romano-Germanic Codes contain most of a nation's law, gaps in the code coverage are inevitable. In virtually every country judge-made law plays an important role in filling the gaps. In France, for instance, four sections of the Civil Code contain the entire basic tort law of the nation. Because the code was enacted in 1804, social changes caused by the Industrial Revolution had hardly begun to make themselves felt. The French courts were obligated to interpret these four code sections to cover situations beyond the imaginings of their drafters. Though the French Parliament has enacted several specialized statutes to supplement the basic tort law of the Civil Code, much of the national law in this area is judge-made. Since the judges of the Court of Cassation (the highest French court) tend to follow their own precedents to keep the law stable and predictable, the role of precedent in this area is not too different from what is found in English or American law.

Because the German Code was enacted almost a century after the French Civil Code, it contains many more sections on torts and other modern problems. There are fewer statutory coverage gaps here to be filled in by judicial decision. However, the German courts have not hesitated to make new law governing serious social problems not addressed by legislators (such as the dislocations caused by the horrendous hyperinflation of 1923).

Though the Swiss codes are the most recently enacted, they resemble the French in that they do not contain the detail found in the BGB and other German codes. The Swiss codes state general principles and deliberately leave it to the judges to provide detailed rules. Thus the Swiss system contains a fair amount of judge-made law; Swiss judges tend to follow precedents set by earlier decisions.

Though Romano-Germanic judges do not make law on the scale of their common-law brethren, they are far from powerless in this area.

The Romano-Germanic Legal Profession. Law has been a respected intellectual discipline taught in continental universities for many centuries. Practitioners of the law have been mainly university graduates within this legal system. At least two types of legal practitioner exist in most Romano-Germanic countries. In the German Federal Republic these are called the *Notar* (notary) and the *Rechtsanwalt* (attorney). The notary's practice consists of the drafting and recording of legal documents such as contracts for the sale of land, wills, articles of incorporation of business associations, and the like. The attorney does all other legal work; thus the German rechtsanwalt may both advise a person on legal problems and represent him in court. In nations with legal systems based on German law this division of the profession exists.

In France there were at one time five branches of the legal profession. The *Notaire* did and still does what notaries do in all Romano-Germanic systems. The *Avoué* was the office lawyer, the equivalent of the English solicitor. The *Avocat* was the trial lawyer, the equivalent of the English barrister. The *Agréé* performed the same function as the avoué in the commercial courts; if one had a legal problem governed by the commercial code one would consult the agréé about it rather than the avoué. The *Conseil Juridique* was a person trained in law but not licensed as a member of the other branches. He could give legal advice, but had no power to draw up documents or to appear in court. Reform legislation theoretically merged the functions of avocat, avoué, and agréé, but members of the French bar still practice in these specialties.

In Italy there are *Avvocatori,* the equivalent of the French avocat, and *Procuratori,* the equivalent of the avoué. Spain has a similar division between the *Abogado* and the *Procurador.*

Everywhere in the Romano-Germanic world the notary exists. He is usually not an independent practitioner; more often than not he is a state employee.

The structure of the legal profession in nations with Romano-Germanic systems varies from country to country. Before doing legal business in these lands, one must learn what divisions of the legal profession exist and what the functions of each branch of the profession are.

Romano-Germanic legal ethics are somewhat similar to those of the common law, but there are differences. The Romano-Germanic attorney may never represent a client on a contingent fee basis. It is generally unethical for an attorney to question a witness before the witness appears in court. There must be no suggestion that the attorney is in any way advising or coaching the witness as to how to testify.

The strength of the attorney-client privilege — the confidentiality of the conversations between an attorney and his client — depends upon the form of government of the nation in question. If the government is democratic and the judiciary is independent, the privilege will be as much respected as it is in common-law lands. In lands with dictatorial governments, such as Germany under Adolf Hitler or Italy under Benito Mussolini, all attorneys may be regarded as officers of the state and of the ruling party. In such cases no communications are confidential and no privileges exist other than those state and party choose to bestow.

The Romano-Germanic Judiciary. In most nations with Romano-Germanic legal systems, judges are not appointed from the ranks of practicing lawyers. The law student who desires to serve as a judge rather than to practice law as a lawyer makes that choice while in school. After graduation he enters an apprenticeship program for judges rather than an apprenticeship program for lawyers. If he successfully completes the program he becomes eligible for appointment as a judge.

In France, Germany, and most other Romano-Germanic nations judges are members of the national civil service. Thus political considerations play no role in judicial appointments or in the promotion of sitting judges. There are exceptions to this general rule. In Switzerland, all judges are elected — lower court judges by the voters of the area they serve, appellate court judges by legislative bodies. In Latin America lower court judges are chosen in many ways, but appellate judges are usually elected by legislatures or appointed by the president as are American federal judges.

In democratic countries judges play no political role, because judicial power to declare legislation unconstitutional and to interpret the constitution is either severely limited or nonexistent. A few nations possess special constitutional courts that exist to hear questions on the constitutionality of legislation. The judges of these courts typically are elected by legislatures rather than appointed through civil service procedure.

Romano-Germanic nations generally have more judges per capita than do common-law countries. Trial courts are generally composed of more than one judge, there are more intermediate-level appellate judges, and the highest courts of a country consist of large numbers of judges by our standards. Thus, the high court of Switzerland (the *Bundesgericht*) has thirty members, while the highest court of France (the *Cour de Cassation*) has eighty-four.

Another difference between European high courts and ours is that all of the judges on the court do not participate in deciding all cases. Some judges hear nothing but criminal appeals, others hear only civil appeals. Thus, the West German *Bundesgerichtshof* is divided into ten civil "senates" and five criminal "senates" of five judges each. Each case appealed to the court is assigned to one of these senates, which renders a final decision. The French Cour de Cassation is similarly organized; the panels of French judges are called "chambers." The only time when more judges than the members of the assigned senate or chamber hear a case is when one panel wishes to disagree with the holdings of another panel in a similar case. There exist rather complex procedures for resolving such conflicts.

Some nations such as West Germany give their highest court roughly the same powers as the United States Supreme Court. These courts may do one of four things in disposing of an appeal: (1) affirm the lower court decision; (2) reverse and remand — send the case back to the trial court for a new trial; (3) reverse and render — declare the loser in the lower court to be the winner; or (4) modify the judgment of the lower court.

The French Cour de Cassation may do only the first two of the above; it can either affirm the lower court decision or send the case back to a lower court for reconsideration, generally to a different court from the one that made the original decision. This court usually follows the lead of the Cour de Cassation and decides in accordance with its opinion; if it does the case is over. However, the second court is not bound by the high court decision and may disagree with it. In such a situation the case may return to the Cour de Cassation, where it is heard by a panel of judges containing representatives from several chambers. The case will again be sent to a third lower court if the Cour disagreed with the decisions of the second; the third lower court is bound by the second Cour decision.

In many nations special commercial courts exist to hear cases arising under the national commercial codes. In France these courts are not composed of legally trained judges; they consist of businessmen elected by local Chambers of Commerce. In France knowledge of business custom is believed to be more important for solving commercial disputes than is knowledge of the law. German commercial courts are composed of one professional judge and two businesspeople. These courts combine expertise in the law with expertise in business custom. In Italy there is no separate Commercial Code, and business cases are decided in the regular court system, as with us. The same is true of most Swiss cantons.

In many Romano-Germanic countries special court systems exist to hear special types of cases other than commercial cases. The German Federal Republic has administrative courts that hear suits of citizens against the government. Labor courts hear cases involving the employer-employee relationship and union-management disputes. Social courts hear cases involving disputes over welfare state benefits. Tax courts hear cases involving disputes between taxpayers and the government over tax liabilities. The patent court hears cases involving entitlement of inventors to patents and the likes. Each of these special court systems is separate and distinct from the regular courts. Each has its own highest court, whose decisions are final within its respective sphere.

In France a separate court system exists to hear complaints of citizens against the government. The French government is essentially as liable for the wrongdoings of its employees as is any private organization. Anyone with a claim against the government may have it heard in court; but the case is heard in the administrative court system. This system has its own highest court, the *Conseil d'État* (Council of State). The decision of this body is final in administrative matters.

France has other special courts staffed entirely by laymen. *Conseils de Prud'hommes* hear employment cases. These consist of equal numbers of representatives of employers and employees—two or three each. These decide cases by majority vote; in case of a tie a professional judge is called in to resolve matters. *Commissions de Sécurité Sociale* hear cases involving employee benefits and the like; they consist of one professional judge, one employer representative, and one employee representative. *Tribuneaux Paritaires des Baux Ruraux* hear disputes between rural landlords and tenants about rent and the like. These consist of one professional judge, two representatives of landlords, and two representatives of tenants.

Nations with legal systems based upon French law may very well have high courts with the limited power of the French Cour de Cassation along with administrative courts to hear cases against the government. Nations with legal systems based upon German, Swiss, or indigenous law may have a wide variety of court systems.

In nations with federal forms of government court organization and procedure may be uniform throughout the land, as in West Germany, or it may be governed by local law as in Switzerland.

In nations with dictatorial governments all judges may well be political appointees, expected to decide all cases according to the will of state and party. There may be no judicial independence; judges may be removed from office for handing down politically incorrect decisions. In Nazi Germany special courts were established to hear cases under the special racial legislation of the regime. People's Courts were established to hear certain types of treason cases. The "justice" dispensed by these was intended to be political justice, a "justice" intended to eliminate enemies of the master race and of the Nazi regime. Extraordinary courts of this sort may exist under any dictatorial government. Where government operates under no constitutional restrictions there is generally no room for organizations or people who question its will.

The Commercial Register. All nations with Romano-Germanic legal systems require businesspeople to register themselves and their enterprises in the local Commercial Register. It is unlawful to be in business without being so registered.

In nations with commercial codes, the special commercial law is applied only in cases involving commercial transactions. The definition of "commercial transaction" will vary from legal system to legal system. German law uses an objective system for identifying commercial transactions; if a participant in the transaction is registered in the Commercial Register as a businessman, the bargain is commercial (though transactions involving commercial paper are by definition commercial even if no involved party is a business person). French law uses a subjective system. If the transaction is one that the law defines as commercial the bargain is commercial, whether the parties are registered in the Commercial Register or not.

In nations with separate commercial courts, only cases defined as commercial may be heard there. Whether legal disputes between a businessperson and a consumer will be heard in regular courts or commercial courts depends upon the law of the nation involved.

The Land Register. Title to land is transferred by deed in most common-law countries. The buyer gets good title when the seller delivers to him a deed to the property, but the buyer should record his deed to protect himself against the seller deeding the property to a third party.

In Romano-Germanic countries title to land is not transferred until a contract of transfer is recorded in the local land register. Any unrecorded transfer is of no effect. Mortgages must also be so recorded. Thus the Land Register will always disclose the identity of the owner of any tract of land and the nature of all encumbrances against it.

Population Control. An important element of personal freedom under the common law is the right to live and travel as one pleases within his own country without government interference. Citizens of common-law countries need no official government identity cards. They need not register their residences with the police.

Romano-Germanic law does not accept this kind of freedom. In Spain, Belgium, and some other nations everyone lawfully present in the country—citizen and alien—must carry at all times the government-mandated ID card, and be prepared to produce it for law enforcers upon demand. Whenever one changes his residence, marital status, or nationality one must obtain a new card. In the German Federal Republic, Switzerland,

Japan, and many other nations one must register one's residence at the nearest police station. The local police are entitled to know who lives within their jurisdiction. Government frowns upon people who try to drop out of society by concealing their place of abode. To live in an area without registering with the local police is a crime.

Differences Between Civil and Commercial Law. The differences between civil and commercial law are not identical in all Romano-Germanic systems. In general, however, the civil law is more paternalistic and formalistic than the commercial. Since the businessman is always making contracts and performing them, he is considered to be wise in the ways of the world and able to protect himself from his suppliers, customers, and competitors. The man on the street, however, needs to be protected from his own ignorance and stupidity—hence the paternalism of civil law.

Differences between the two types of law are significant. Maximum interest rates, for example, are higher in commercial dealings than in civil dealings. Virtually all commercial contracts need not be in writing. Some types of civil contracts, however, must be written: the man on the street should not normally be bound to oral bargains involving large sums of money. The businessman buyer must inspect what he buys for defects on delivery; any defect he does not spot he usually cannot claim as a breach of contract by the seller. A consumer buyer may complain about defects he discovers later. Consumers are considered to need such protection more than businesspeople.

Commercial Contract Law. There are numerous differences between Romano-Germanic commercial contract law and the common law.

With respect to offers, Romano-Germanic law generally provides for the following: (1) if the offeror promises to keep his offer open for a certain time, he must do so—all such offers are deemed to be firm offers and irrevocable, even if oral; and (2) all other offers must be kept open for a reasonable time—the offeree must be allowed a fair chance to accept.

With respect to acceptances, when an acceptance is effective varies from nation to nation. In West Germany it is effective only when received. In Switzerland it is effective when sent. When it is effective in France depends on the circumstances of the case; French law provides no general rule. An acceptance may be effective even if its terms are not identical to those in the offer; thus the English *Mirror Image Rule* does not apply. However, offer and acceptance must agree on the fundamental terms of the contract (subject matter and price); if they do not the "acceptance" is deemed a counteroffer. The rules for determining the terms of the resulting contract vary from country to country.

Romano-Germanic law requires that there be mutual assent to the making of the contract; the three conditions under which lack of assent exist are deceit, mistake, and duress.

German law uses the concept of *Bonos Mores* (good morals) to determine the presence or absence of deceitful conduct on the part of the parties; generally any sort of dishonest or immoral conduct by one of the parties is *Contra Bonos Mores* and gives ground for rescission. French law allows rescission for deceit only when the deceived party would not have made the contract had he known of the deceit; if he would have made it but on different terms the contract is enforceable but the victim is entitled to damages.

With respect to rescission for mistake the law varies considerably from country to country. Generally, if the mistake is one of motive (in the head of the mistaken party) there is no ground for rescission; if it is a mistake of transaction (having to do with subject matter or the like) there is ground for rescission.

Duress in Romano-Germanic law lumps together the common-law concepts of duress and undue influence. If a party is not free to exercise his own will due to either physical or psychological pressure, he may rescind.

The concept of *Consideration* does not exist in Romano-Germanic law. A promise is binding in this system if there is *Causa,* a logical reason for making it.

Romano-Germanic law divides contracts into two types: *Onerous* and *Gratuitous.* An onerous contract is one where both parties are bound to do something. It is onerous to me because I have to do something in exchange for what I am going to get from you. It is onerous to you because you must do something in exchange for what you are going to get from me.

A gratuitous contract is one under which a party gets something for nothing — a contract to make a gift or the like. Suppose that Black promises to give White one thousand dollars with which to pay university tuition in Texas. White promises nothing in return. When Black does not come up with the money, White has no legal recourse, because Black got no consideration for his promise. Had Schwarz promised to pay Weiss two thousand Swiss francs for university tuition in Switzerland, and Weiss promised nothing in return, and Schwarz did not pay, Weiss would have recourse. There was causa for the promise (Weiss getting his tuition paid), which would make the promise enforceable. This would be a gratuitous contract for Weiss's benefit.

Austrian and French law contain concepts allowing rescission of a contract because of what common-law lawyers would call inadequate consideration. In Austria one may rescind a contract when the value of his performance would be worth more than double the value of the other party's performance. In France one may rescind due to *Lésion Énorme,* a gross disparity in value between the two performances.

With respect to capacity, the age of adulthood is eighteen in most Romano-Germanic countries. However, in Switzerland and Japan the age of adulthood is twenty and in some other lands it is twenty-one. Romano-Germanic law generally considers the contract of a minor unenforceable if the minor's parents or legal guardian do not ratify it. West Germany allows an adult to rescind a contract with a minor; other nations do not permit this.

With respect to ultra-vires acts by corporations, the corporation is bound in the nations of the European Community if the other party did not know of the limitation upon the corporation's power; in some other nations corporations may not have the capacity to make such contracts.

The notions of legality of contracts in the Romano-Germanic system are very similar to common-law notions. The concept of bonos mores is used here by the West Germans; any contract that is contra bonos mores is illegal and unenforceable. In French law the contract is illegal if the motive behind it or the object of it is illicit. Since good morals and "licitness" are to be defined by judges in the process of deciding cases, each case will be decided on its own merits.

There are virtually no requirements that commercial contracts be in writing in the Romano-Germanic system, regardless of the amount of money involved. Thus, bargains involving large sums of money entered into over the telephone may be enforceable if witnesses can convince a judge that a bargain was actually made. However, certain special types of bargains may need to be in writing, depending on the country where made:

1. Contracts for the sale of land or an interest therein
2. Suretyship agreements
3. Agreements to make gifts
4. Agreements obligating a party to transfer all or a part of his personal property
5. Leases to run more than a year
6. Mortgages and the like on land
7. Compromise agreements
8. Promises of annuities

Some or all of the above types of bargains may need to be *Protocolized,* authenticated by a notary and recorded in his office. Requirements for protocolization will vary from country to country.

Continental Europeans learned long ago that the most carefully considered contractual arrangements can be upset by war, coup, revolution, inflation, devaluation, depression, unexpected government regulations, and other unforeseen events. For that reason the *Clausula Rebus Sic Stantibus* is an implied provision of many contracts in Romano-Germanic lands. Liberally translated, it means this contract is binding as long as, and only as long as, conditions remain as they are now. If things change to the point where one of the parties would be gravely injured by performance of the bargain, the contract is discharged.

If the person who makes a contract does not perform properly and has no excuse for nonperformance he is guilty of breach in all Romano-Germanic countries. Whether breach results in cancellation varies from country to country. For instance, in Italy the victim may generally rescind. In France the victim may not himself rescind; generally the only way a contract may be rescinded is through the act of a judge. In West Germany there can be no rescission unless the breach is "fundamental"; that is, unless the breach has destroyed the value of the contract to the victim. Delay in delivery or payment is generally not a fundamental breach; the victim may suspend his performance and demand that the late party perform within a specified reasonable time. If the breaching party does not perform within this time, the victim may then rescind.

The primary Romano-Germanic remedy for breach is specific performance: the victim has the right to force the breaching party to perform if this is possible. The victim also has the option to claim damages; in the majority of cases he takes this option. If relations between the parties have deteriorated to the point where court action is necessary, the victim prefers damages to specific performance just to get the argument settled.

Abuse of Rights (French **Abus des Droits,** *German* **Rechtsmissbrauch***)*. Any person who deliberately uses rights given him by law to injure someone else is guilty of Abuse of Rights and is liable in damages to the one abused. This happens in contract situations where a party with great bargaining power imposes an unfair contract upon the weaker party. It can also happen where a party uses contract provisions to take unfair advantage of the other party. It can also be a tort when a landowner builds a spite fence to cut off his neighbor's light and air, or where the landowner digs a well intending to dry up his neighbor's well (and succeeds) or the like.

Romano-Germanic Tort Law. The common law has been very reluctant to impose liability to another upon a blameless person. The ancient principle of the common law of torts has been "No liability without fault." If the harmful act was not done deliberately or through carelessness the one who committed it should not be held legally responsible for it. The common law has departed from this principle in only two areas: workers' compensation and product liability. The employer owes compensation to his employee injured in an on-the-job accident even if the employer was not in any way at fault. The merchant seller of a defective product is liable for any harm it causes, whether or not he is responsible for the presence of the defect.

In Romano-Germanic lands social insurance covers on-the-job injuries, and the principle of no liability without fault generally prevails with respect to defective products. (A directive of the Council of the European Community has changed EC law on that point—the effect of the directive is discussed in Chapter 13.) However, most Romano-Germanic legislatures have adopted statutes making the owners of motor vehicles liable for any harm caused by vehicle or driver unless the harm is caused by an act of God or is unavoidable. The owner is liable for the act of the driver even if the driver is not negligent and the owner is not negligent to be letting the driver drive.

Liability insurance is mandatory for motor vehicle owners almost everywhere. No one may obtain license plates for a vehicle without proof of insurance. Driving without insurance is cause for revocation of vehicle registration and driver's license, and is a crime.

Romano-Germanic Criminal Procedure. The powers of the police vary greatly from nation to nation in the Romano-Germanic system. In the democratic nations of northern Europe their powers to arrest without a warrant and to conduct searches are less than in the United States; generally they cannot arrest without a warrant unless they saw the offense committed for which arrest is being made. In other nations — especially those without democratic political systems — the power to arrest without warrant is broad indeed.

When a crime is reported to police in a common-law nation, they are expected to act upon the report. When a law violation is reported to a prosecutor, he is expected to investigate. However, the authorities may exercise a measure of discretion and choose not to take action. In theory, no such discretion exists in the Romano-Germanic system. Authorities *must* act upon well-founded citizen complaints.

The person arrested theoretically need not answer police questions, and theoretically is entitled to representation by counsel. The police may not be (and usually are not) required to inform the suspect of these rights, and anything he says while in custody may be used against him in court.

The arrested person is generally entitled to bail unless he is accused of a major crime, he might flee the jurisdiction of the court if released on bail, he might commit other crimes, or he might obstruct justice by intimidating witnesses or the like. But Romano-Germanic criminal law allows investigative detention, under which a person accused of committing a crime is held in jail while the authorities investigate the charges against him. If commission of a serious crime is alleged, the investigation may take from six months to a year. The accused may well spend this entire period in prison.

Since the grand jury is unknown in Romano-Germanic law, another institution is used to perform its function. This institution is the investigating magistrate. The investigating magistrate is a judge, who qualifies for his job by meeting civil service requirements. He it is who investigates the charges of serious crime brought against an accused, to help determine whether or not he should be brought to trial. He has the duty to dig out all possible evidence in the case — that favorable to the state and that favorable to the accused. He has the power to summon and question witnesses. He also has the power to search and seize. In some countries he may search and seize without any sort of warrant; in others he may issue his own warrant; in still others (such as the Netherlands) he may not search and seize without a warrant issued by another magistrate. In all countries he works closely with prosecuting attorneys and the police. Once he has all of the evidence available in the case he makes a decision. In some countries he has the authority to bring formal charges against the accused; in others he must report his findings to an indicting authority which makes the decision whether or not to charge the accused.

If the accused has been in investigative detention during the investigation and the decision is made not to prosecute, he is entitled to compensation for the time he spent in prison. If formal charges are brought against the accused, he is tried under the inquisitorial procedure.

He and his lawyer are entitled to examine all documents in the dossier (the file accumulated by the investigating magistrate during the investigation). Thus the defense knows the evidence against the accused before the trial begins.

In common-law nations the accused may not be tried unless he is present in the courtroom. If he escapes from custody or jumps bail, no trial may take place until he is recaptured. Under Romano-Germanic procedure the accused must be present in the courtroom if possible. If for any reason he is beyond the jurisdiction of the court the trial may take place without him, and he may be convicted in absentia. If he returns to the nation where he was convicted his sentence may then be carried out.

A jury in the manner of common-law nations exists in very few Romano-Germanic nations. It is found in Denmark and some of the cantons of Switzerland, but hardly anywhere else. Japan and some other nations never use juries. More typical is the system in France, where criminal cases are heard before three judges and nine jurors. Judges and jurors deliberate together to make a decision, with the votes of eight being sufficient to decide. Another variation of the Romano-Germanic jury system is used in Sweden, where one judge and three to nine "lay assessors," in essence long-term jurors elected by local councils, decide cases. The judge makes the decision unless an extraordinary majority of the assessors overrule him.

The presiding judge is the most powerful person in the Romano-Germanic courtroom. He determines which witnesses shall be heard, and the order in which they are heard. He does most of the questioning. His colleagues on the bench and the lawyers may ask questions only after he finishes (and in some systems he is the only person who may question a witness—the lawyers may question only through the presiding judge).

The main function of the lawyer is to summarize the case to the court after the evidence is presented.

The accused is not allowed to testify under oath. Romano-Germanic logic holds that a party to a case has so much stake in the outcome that he probably will not tell the truth even if he swears to do so; therefore his testimony should not be taken at face value. He is, however, permitted (and in some systems obligated) to make an unsworn statement to the court. He is not subject to anything like the rigorous cross-examination undergone by testifying criminal defendants under the common law.

Both sides have the right to appeal criminal decisions. Thus the convicted defendant may appeal his conviction, his sentence, or both. The prosecution may appeal an acquittal, and may also appeal a sentence the prosecutor deems too light. Under some systems appellate courts may increase criminal sentences even though only the defense appealed.

When a criminal act causes the accused to incur civil liability, the Romano-Germanic system provides machinery for determining the civil liability at the criminal trial. The victim of the crime may intervene in the criminal proceeding to make his claim. Generally the jurors will play no role in determining the civil damages, only the judges participate in civil decision-making.

Romano-Germanic Civil Procedure. The concept of jurisdiction in the common-law sense does not exist in the Romano-Germanic system. In France a plaintiff may file suit against virtually any person or organization anywhere in the world, whether or not the person is physically present in France or has assets there. Theoretically the defendant is entitled to notice that he is being sued, but whether he responds to the notice, and whether he receives it, French courts will try the case in absentia. Most nations with legal systems based upon French law permit the same sort of thing.

The nations with systems based upon German or Swiss law, on the other hand, have notions of jurisdiction similar to, but not identical to, ours.

No juries are used in civil litigation in most Romano-Germanic nations. One exception is Sweden, where one judge and several lay assessors may hear such cases. Elsewhere a panel of three judges usually hears civil cases.

The plaintiff and defendant have the burden of procuring the evidence to be presented to the court. It is unethical for the Romano-Germanic lawyer to question witnesses before trial. It is also unethical for him to conduct investigations to help his client prepare his cases.

It is difficult for civil litigants to get evidence from third parties. Pretrial depositions are not used, and only the presiding judge may issue subpoenas.

The presiding judge summons the witnesses and does most of the questioning.

In some nations the attorneys must inform the presiding judge early in the procedure of the names of witnesses they want to testify. The witnesses are then required to sign documents agreeing to testify. Any witness who has not signed such a document and who has not been scheduled to testify may not do so. Thus, it is most difficult for an attorney or a party to call a new witness at the last minute.

Civil cases are not disposed of in one continual trial. The court may hear witness A on Monday, witness B on Thursday, and witness C on Friday. Additional witnesses may be called later if the judges feel their testimony would be useful — though this happens only if a considerable amount of money is involved. The process may go on for months in complicated cases. The judges continue to accumulate evidence until they are satisfied that all relevant information has been heard. Only then do they make their decision.

In Sweden — as with us — civil cases are disposed of in one continuous hearing. The Swedish witness begins his testimony by telling his story in his own words, without interruption. Only after he finishes making his statement may he be questioned. Under the Swedish procedure, either the lawyers or the judge may then ask questions.

As in criminal matters, either side may appeal the trial court's decision in the Romano-Germanic world.

The Ministère Publique. In France and most other Romano-Germanic countries, an attorney representing the government participates in the appeal of civil cases. It is his duty to argue the public interest in the case before the court. Sometimes the government supports the plaintiff, and other times the defendant. The appellate judges are not obligated to make the decision the government wishes, but they may well be influenced by what the state lawyer considers the public interest to be.

Corporations. Romano-Germanic law recognizes two dissimilar types of corporations. In Spanish-speaking countries the two types are the *Sociedad Anónima* (SA) and the *Sociedad de Responsibilidad Limitada* (SRL). In French-speaking countries they are the *Société Anonyme* (SA) and the *Société à Responsabilité Limitée* (SARL). In German-speaking countries they are the *Aktiengesellschaft* (AG) and the *Gesellschaft mit Beschraenkter Haftung* (GmbH).

The SARL or GmbH is a limited liability company. It may be organized by fewer persons than the SA or AG. The articles of incorporation are recorded in the Commercial Register of the area where the company does business. Though ownership rights are divided into shares, the organizations issue no share certificates. The ownership interest of each shareholder is recorded in the Commercial Register. All transfers of shares are accomplished by recording there.

There is flexibility in organizing the management, and corporate affairs may be conducted with a minimum of formality. The form can be very useful for a foreign subsidiary.

The SA has a management structure similar to that of the common-law corporation. The shareholders elect directors who appoint a managing director (as common-law directors appoint officers).

The AG has a more unfamiliar management structure. The shareholders elect the supervisory board (*Aufsichtsrat*) which consists of from three to twenty-one members, depending on the number of shareholders. This board elects the managing board (*Vorstand*), which may consist of one or more persons. If the vorstand has more than one member, it may choose a managing director to run the company.

In West Germany, the employees may be entitled to elect a third or more of the supervisory board. If the company has more than two thousand employees, the employees elect half. In the German coal and steel industries three interests must be represented; the shareholders elect four directors, the employees elect four, and three are chosen to represent the public interest.

In common-law countries the board of directors has the authority to manage the corporation as authorized by the Articles of Incorporation and governing law without shareholder interference (providing that the board does not abuse its powers). It must act collectively (in meetings, generally); individual directors have no power to bind the corporation in any way. As long as the board obeys the law and does not violate its fiduciary duties, its acts bind the corporation and its members are not liable to anyone for what is done.

Under Romano-Germanic law, directorial acts do not bind the corporation until ratified by the shareholders. One of the important items of business conducted at all shareholder meetings is the ratification of directorial acts performed during the preceding year. Directors are personally liable for their acts until relieved of this responsibility by shareholder ratification. Individual directors may bind the corporation without board action; the necessity for board action is not so important under this system because of the shareholder power to refuse to ratify directorial acts.

In common-law countries, all share certificates of large corporations are *Registered*. That is, they are issued in the name of the shareholder, and the shareholder's name appears in the corporate records as a shareholder. Shares are transferred by the transfer of the share certificate, but the transfer is not complete until the buyer of a certificate sends it in for reregistration, and the buyer's name is entered on the company records as the new shareholder. Thus a registered share may have two owners: the *Legal* owner who owns the share certificate and has the right to transfer it, and the *Registered* owner whose name appears in the corporate records.

The registered owner has the right to receive dividends and the right to vote the shares.

Romano-Germanic corporations may have either Registered shares or *Bearer* shares. Registered shares are similar to common-law corporate shares. Bearer shares are quite different.

The owner of the shares for all purposes is the possessor of the share certificate, as long as the certificate was acquired in an honest transaction. The majority of corporations in most Romano-Germanic nations issue bearer shares rather than registered shares. They are like bearer bonds in common-law jurisdictions in that they have attached coupons that entitle the shareholder to collect dividends. When a dividend is declared the shareholder clips the designated coupon and takes it to a bank for redemption. The bank then sends the coupon to the company for reimbursement. The owner demonstrates his right to vote at shareholder meetings by showing up in possession of his certificates.

Bearer shares have three advantages from the management point of view. First, the company does not need to maintain a register of shareholders. Second, the company does not get involved in the mechanics of the transfer of ownership of shares. Third, the company does not have to mail dividend checks to individual shareholders. The big disadvantage of bearer shares from the management point of view is that there is no way for management to monitor changes in share ownership.

The big advantage of bearer shares from the shareholder point of view is that ownership of shares is not a matter of public record. One may keep ownership of such investments secret from tax collectors, spouses, and the like. But the lack of records of ownership is also a disadvantage to shareholders, because it is difficult to replace lost or stolen shares.

Because of the danger of loss or theft of bearer shares, many shareholders turn their certificates over to their banks for safekeeping. The banks, as bearers of the shares, may vote them as they please at shareholder meetings unless the true owner instructs the bank how to vote, or unless he reclaims the shares in order to attend the meeting himself.

Bearer corporate shares are tempting targets for criminals, both private and public. The private thief may sell stolen shares without much difficulty if he knows the market. The government desiring to plunder the wealth of unpopular citizens finds these an easy target. Thus the Nazi government of Germany demanded that many German Jews turn over to it their share certificates in the corporations of Europe. The victims complied, hoping to save themselves and their loved ones from the concentration camps. In the early days of the Nazi regime some of the victims so bought life and the opportunity to leave Germany. Later there was no salvation.

Those Jews who saved their lives by turning over their share certificates to the Nazi gangsters were generally unable to regain their property. A German Jew who owned stock in a Swiss corporation was forced to turn his shares over to the Nazi government. This saved his life; later he was able to escape from Germany to Switzerland. He then demanded that the corporation issue him new share certificates and recognize him as a shareholder because he had been deprived of his certificates under duress. The corporation refused. He sued to force them to do as he asked. The Swiss Bundesgericht decided that, since the ultimate fate of the man's shares was unknown and the transfer of the shares by the shareholder to the government had been lawful under German law, it could not justifiably force the corporation to issue new shares because the old shares might still be in the hands of "legitimate" owners.

Government vaults in Berlin were filled with thousands of share certificates plundered from innocent Europeans by the Nazis. When the victorious Russians entered the city in April 1945, German and other European corporate managements shuddered to think of what might happen if they chose to claim the rights of corporate ownership represented by these confiscated shares. In order to avoid this situation, there was a wholesale cancellation and reissue of share certificates by European corporations. Shareholders had to be able to prove ownership of their old certificates to qualify for new ones. The victims of Nazi plundering were unable to recover their property, but the Russians were unable to profit from those particular spoils of war.

The existence of bearer shares, combined with Swiss banking secrecy laws, has made it relatively easy for persons who wish to conceal assets to be able to do so. Nazi war criminals, big men in organized crime, and fugitive exdictators have supposedly stashed large amounts of money in Swiss bank vaults in bearer-share form. Some Swiss corporate managements have decided to switch from bearer to registered shares in order to polish their corporate images. Disreputable shareholders in companies with registered shares may be quickly identified.

In France the decision has been made to abolish share certificates altogether. Ownership of shares in French corporations will soon be determined by the contents of the corporate share register. This will increase bookkeeping requirements for corporations, but will eliminate problems of lost or stolen certificates and will make it easy for the government to determine the identity of corporate shareholders.

Bankruptcy. The concept of bankruptcy entered European law via the Roman law, and came to England and America via western Europe. Originally the debtor's body was liable for debts. If he did not pay he could be sold into slavery and his purchase price divided among his creditors, or he could be imprisoned until he paid, or he could be killed and (at least in theory) his body divided among his creditors.

By about 200 B.C. this practice had ended; but a creditor of a debtor who did not pay his debt as it came due could have all of the debtor's assets seized and sold at auction under court supervision. The proceeds would be divided among the debtor's creditors. If anything remained afterward it was returned to the debtor; if the sum was insufficient to pay all creditors the debtor was liable for the balance. This procedure continued to exist until the fall of the Western Empire.

In the Italian merchant cities of the Middle Ages bankruptcy was revived. Only merchants were subject to the law. The insolvent merchant could be made to turn over all of his assets to a court, whereupon they would be sold and the proceeds divided among the creditors. If the debtor was reluctant to disclose the nature and whereabouts of his assets he could be tortured until he talked. He could be outlawed after the proceeding and his businessplace smashed (*Banca Rotta* in Italian, hence "bankrupt").

The bankruptcy law that later developed all over Europe was patterned to an extent on this Italian law. What all bankruptcy law has in common is the fact that the debtor is deprived of his assets by a court and said assets are liquidated. The proceeds are then divided ratably among the debtor's creditors.

There is one major difference between the nations. Is the law only applicable to merchants, or may nonmerchants go through bankruptcy? In Belgium, Italy, and Brazil it is available only to merchants, and in France only to merchants or practitioners of professions. In most other lands, it is available to nonmerchants also.

The debtor is not discharged from his debts after the bankruptcy. If his assets were insufficient to pay off his creditors, he is still liable for unpaid balances.

If debtor negligence contributes to his financial difficulties or if he has committed fraud against his creditors he is subject to criminal prosecution in Austria, France, and some other countries.

Most countries have developed rehabilitation procedures as part of their law under which the debtor may pay off his debts as he goes along under court supervision, thus sparing him some of the stigma that is attached to bankruptcy.

The major differences between the Romano-Germanic bankruptcy just described and its common-law variant in Great Britain and the United States are two: (1) any debtor, not just merchants and professionals may go through bankruptcy; and (2) if the debtor has not committed fraud, he is discharged from his unpaid debts at the end of the proceeding. The American Chapter 11 proceedings for business debtors and the Chapter 13 proceeding for consumer debtors are our versions of rehabilitation procedures.

Chapter 5

Socialist Law

The legal systems of most nations with Communist governments are based upon Socialist law. The purest form of the system exists in the Soviet Union itself, the first nation to establish Communist government. Since the legal system of prerevolutionary Russia was a Romano-Germanic system, Socialist law in many ways is akin to that system. But even before the Bolshevik Revolution of 1917 Russian attitudes toward law were different from those held in western Europe.

Russia was converted to Christianity by missionaries from Constantinople, not from Rome; therefore Russian Christianity is Eastern Orthodox. The Mongol conquest of Russia in the early thirteenth century cut her off from European culture. By the time she threw off the Mongol yoke two centuries later it could already be said that the Russians were the most Western of Asiatics, not the most Eastern of Europeans.

The Russian people soon realized the basic truth that those who governed the Russian State – the czar and the nobility – were all-powerful. The people were governed by their own local customs except in those areas where the czar chose to legislate. The notion gained ground that law, the will of the absolute monarch, was oppressive. Liberal Russians believed that the best state was one governed by custom, without any intervention by government.

The first code of law for the Russian realm was promulgated by Czar Alexis II in 1649. A more comprehensive codification, the *Svod Zakonov,* was promulgated by Czar Nicholas I in 1832. It was a combination of Russian custom and principles of French and German law.

The Russians never shared the basic notion of all West Europeans – Englishmen as well as continental Europeans – that law is essential in order to preserve order within society. To the Russian, adherence to custom was sufficient to preserve order. Law emanated from outside oppressors and tended to disrupt, not to preserve, the order of society.

The moderate revolutionaries who overthrew the government of the czar in March 1917 intended to bring about a political revolution by ending the absolute rule of monarch and nobility, but they had no intention of carrying out radical economic or social reforms. Lenin and the Bolsheviks, who overthrew the moderate revolutionaries in November 1917, were believers in the ideology of Karl Marx. To them the government of the March revolutionaries was government by the bourgeoisie. Marx had argued that the domination of the bourgeoisie would inevitably be overthrown. In its place would be erected the dictatorship of the proletariat, or the working class. The dictatorship of the proletariat would dismantle the mechanisms by which the bourgeoisie controlled the state by nationalizing all private property and depriving the middle class of political power.

The dictatorship of the proletariat would continue until all vestiges of capitalist mentality vanished from the people of the nation. Only then could the leaders of the revolution end the dictatorship and begin the task of erecting the Communist society. Once this task was accomplished, there would be no more need for government. The state would wither away, and liberated mankind would forever prosper under the economic principle "from each according to his ability, to each according to his need."

For Lenin and his Bolshevik revolutionaries, law was a mechanism of the bourgeoisie to help it to rivet its yoke upon the necks of the world's toilers. Soon after the revolution the new government abolished the legal system of the czars and the czarist court system, without replacing it with anything similar. "Comrades' courts" dispensed rough-and-ready justice according to Bolshevik ideology; no more was needed. This experiment in governing without law lasted about four years, and did not work. New codes of law very similar to existing European codes were enacted in 1922, and an organized court system was recreated.

Josef Stalin insisted upon a full restoration of legality in the Soviet Union, bestowing upon the nation a constitution and more powerful courts. In many respects his devotion to legality was a sham: Stalin recognized no legal limits upon his own power. Not only were the Russian people subjected to the rigors of a stringent criminal code, they were also subjected to the whims of a tyrant and of his obedient tool, the NKVD or secret police. Thousands were executed without trial; hundreds of thousands were deported to Siberian labor camps without ever seeing the inside of a courtroom. This arbitrary regime existed until Stalin's death in 1953.

Nikita Khrushchev denounced Stalin in 1956 for his arbitrary government and disregard of legal principles. Since then the Soviet rulers have insisted that "Socialist legality" should prevail in the USSR; that the government and all of the Soviet people should be subject to the rule of law; and that arbitrary exercise of governmental power should be a thing of the past.

The nature of the "Socialist legality" of the early 1960s is illustrated by a tale told by the emigre Russian lawyer Constantine Simis in his book

USSR: The Corrupt Society. After Stalin's death the Soviet criminal law was revised and the death penalty abolished for many offenses, including foreign currency speculation. In the early 1960s rings of such speculators "earned" profits of millions of rubles through their illegal activity. The efficient Soviet police went into action and apprehended many violators, who were duly convicted and sentenced to long prison terms. Premier Nikita Khrushchev wanted to know why these people had not been sentenced to death. It was explained that the law did not authorize the death sentence for this crime. "Change the law!" the premier commanded. The criminal code was duly amended to restore the death penalty for conviction for such speculation. Then the convicted were retried for their crimes under the revised law, sentenced to death, and executed.

This procedure is contrary to two basic principles of law in most legal systems: the accused were tried twice for the same offense (*Double Jeopardy*), and they were sentenced under a law that was not in effect when their crime was committed (an *Ex Post Facto* law).

This was Socialist legality in the early 1960s, but it would not pass muster in the common-law world or in most of the Romano-Germanic world. The extent to which "Socialist legality" prevails in the Soviet Union today is a matter of some debate, but it must be admitted that there is more government of law and less government of men in the present-day Soviet Union than there was under Stalin, or even in the early 1960s when the above-described incident occurred.

The Nature of Socialist Law. In theory the Revolution of 1917 has not accomplished its objective. This will not occur until perfect communism is achieved; until the people are prepared to live under the principle of "from each according to his ability, to each according to his need"; and until government is no longer necessary. For now people must settle for life under socialism and the principle of "from each according to his ability, to each according to his work." Thus the law, a necessary evil under present conditions, must be structured to further the objectives of the revolution and the ultimate attainment of communism.

The major objective of law in the West is to maintain order and to secure property rights. To the Russians the securing of property rights is oppression, and the maintenance of order to secure these rights is the sort of law from which the revolution liberated the people. Socialist law has three major objectives. It is designed to preserve the security of the Soviet revolutionary state; to develop production according to socialist principles to create the abundance that will allow the state to furnish everyone his needs; and to educate man in order to eradicate his selfish and antisocial tendencies.

In order to carry out the first objective the Soviet criminal code broadly defines offenses against the state. Treason is punishable by death. One sort of conduct defined as treason is "flight abroad, or refusal to return from abroad to the USSR." "Anti-Soviet agitation and propaganda" is another serious offense. One may commit this crime by "circulating . . . slanderous fabrications which defame the Soviet state and social system." Of course preservation of public order is essential to the preservation of the system, order is a *public* good in the Soviet Union, not mainly a *private* good as it is in our society.

To carry out the second objective the system encourages (and in a sense compels) productive activity without expectation of profit as Westerners understand it.

Accomplishment of the third objective is assisted by taking into account a person's attitude toward the regime and the system when he runs afoul of the law.

Our law regulates mostly private economic relationships: contractual, personal, and property. Since the private sector of the Soviet economy is so insignificant, no need exists for large bodies of law of this sort.

Since there is no private ownership of land, no complex law of land ownership and land transfer is needed. A Soviet citizen can own a house, but the land upon which the house stands remains the property of the state.

Since there are no privately owned business corporations, Soviet society has no corporate securities, no stock exchanges, and no conflicts between owners and managers.

No private individual is permitted to employ another. No private organizations that could employ persons existed before 1987. Thus no law governing private employment relationships was needed. However, cooperative business enterprises now exist that are authorized to hire employees of state enterprises on a part-time basis. They may also hire housewives, students, retired persons, and the like on such a basis.

Cooperatives may be organized to provide personal services, manufacture consumer goods, and so forth. At least three persons sixteen years of age or older must be the organizers. The co-owners must be the main source of labor within the enterprise. Part-time employees are entitled to the same rights as full-time employees of state enterprises.

Artisans may be self-employed. They must meet state educational requirements and obtain state patents from regulatory bodies to obtain this privilege. Such enterprises are one-person enterprises, since no individual may employ other individuals.

The law of the Soviet Union recognizes four sorts of property. First, there is private property, which individuals may own for use and consumption. Private property includes cash, bank accounts, clothing, household furniture, books, television sets, automobiles, a house, etc.

Second, there is state property. This consists of land, minerals, waters, buildings, factories, and almost everything else of great value. State property is the property of all of the people.

Third, there is collective property. A collective is an enterprise owned and operated by those registered with the proper state agency as owners. It is a legal entity; what it owns, it owns for the benefit of its members. Until very recently the only recognized collectives were farms. Since 1987 it has been lawful to organize and operate nonagricultural cooperatives.

Fourth, there is public enterprise property. Every productive enterprise is a legal entity. Most of such an enterprise's assets are state property, lent to it by the state. The state thus has the right to take such property away from one enterprise and give it to another. The state has most control over buildings, machinery, and the like; less control over raw materials and inventory in process of manufacture; still less control over finished inventory and currency. Yet all of these assets must be used and disposed of in accordance with the state economic plan; enterprise management may not use much discretion in dealing with them.

Obsolete machinery and the like must be disposed of under strict regulations. The central plan may allow management a choice with respect to raw material suppliers, or it may not. It may allow a choice of customers, or it may not. Even profits may not freely be disposed of by management.

It is unlawful to use private property for the purpose of gaining unearned income. To buy such property at a low price with intent to sell it for a higher price is *speculation,* a criminal offense. To use private property for purposes of earning income without a license or to practice a trade or profession with it is *parasitism,* an even more serious offense. No citizen may own more than one house, and it is difficult to rent space in a privately owned house to a tenant.

Soviet law guarantees everyone a job. In fact, it goes much farther. The Soviet constitution of 1936 contains a provision that everyone who is physically able to work must work, according to the principle "he who does not work, neither shall he eat." This rule is not included in the Constitution of 1977, but Article 60 of this constitution imposes the duty upon the citizen not to evade socially useful work. He who lives without gainful employment is most certainly guilty of parasitism and will probably be punished.

The Soviet Legal Profession. Soviet lawyers must have university degrees in law. They work either for the state or in close association with the state. There are four sorts of profession open to a Russian trained in law.

The *Jurisconsult* is the equivalent of the American corporate or civil service lawyer. He advises governmental organizations or public enterprises.

The *Procurator* is a prosecuting attorney with additional powers. His role will be discussed shortly.

The Soviet *Notary* is very similar to the Romano-Germanic notary, working in state notariat offices. The notariat serves three purposes. First, it drafts and records contracts. In the Soviet Union, these are mainly contracts for the sale of property from one citizen to another. Law enforcers monitor these records closely for evidence that citizens are engaging in unlawful speculation. Second, it drafts wills and settles estates where no dispute over the inheritance exists. Third, it makes certified copies of documents. When a Soviet citizen needs to attach a copy of his university diploma to an employment application, for example, the copy must be certified by a notary.

The Soviet *Advocate* is in a sense a self-employed independent professional. He is a member of his local College of Advocates, and generally works out of the Legal Aid Bureau operated by the college. The citizen who needs legal assistance comes to the bureau and is assigned a lawyer. He may request a certain lawyer, but the bureau is not obligated to honor his request.

The person accused of committing a crime will have an advocate as his defense counsel. In a nonpolitical case the advocate may be as diligent in defending his client as the Romano-Germanic lawyer. In cases with political overtones the advocate must be more careful because he is expected to serve the state as well as his client. By definition the interests of the state and the people are identical. The advocate who criticizes state policy is not only failing to do his job, but also making himself an enemy of the people.

The advocate's fee is set by the Legal Aid Bureau. The client pays the bureau, and the money is divided between bureau and advocate. Thus lawyer and client have no direct financial dealings.

The Soviet Court System. The Soviet constitution establishes a federal state. All courts in the Soviet Union are courts of the individual republics except the highest court, the Supreme Court of the Soviet Union.

The court systems of the individual republics are identical. The trial courts are the People's Courts. These consist of one elected judge and two people's assessors. The judge is elected in the manner of other Communist officials. The party nominates one candidate for each judgeship to be filled, and only that candidate's name appears on the ballot. To drop the ballot into the ballot box unmarked is to vote for the nominee; one must cross out the nominee's name to vote against him. Thus the official nominee is virtually always elected. (Since contested parliamentary elections were held for the first time in the Soviet Union in the spring of 1989, it may well be that contested judicial elections will occur in the future.)

The judge, like the English magistrate, need have no legal education. After his election he is required to take courses in law, but he never becomes as knowledgeable in the law as the lawyers who appear in his court.

The people's assessors are elected from among the citizenry and serve for perhaps two weeks out of the year. They are like common-law jurors in that they know nothing about law except what they learn as assessors.

Judges of higher courts are required to have legal education. They are elected by legislative bodies for specified terms. Here again the party organization nominates the candidates, who are always duly elected.

The Republic Supreme Courts and the Supreme Court of the USSR have the powers of American or German high courts; they may reverse and render lower court decisions if they wish. They are not limited to remanding decisions they disagree with to lower courts as is the French Cour de Cassation (though they may do that if they wish).

Court decisions do not produce law. Soviet courts are not bound by precedent. There is absolutely no judicial review in the Soviet Union. Legislative supremacy is absolutely essential to the carrying out of the purposes of the revolution. Thus the courts are limited to deciding cases.

Special labor tribunals exist to hear cases involving rights of employees (who of course are always state employees).

The Procuracy. The procurator-general of the USSR is responsible for assuring that the courts, the state, and society itself operate according to Socialist legality. He appoints the procurators-general of the republics; these in turn appoint the procurators that function on lower levels of government. Procurators serve as prosecuting attorneys in cases involving serious crime. They may also intervene in civil litigation to present the state's point of view, or to aid a party who is not getting proper legal counsel. They supervise the operation of the government and the state economic enterprises. Any citizen who feels that these are not operating on principles of Socialist legality may complain to the local procuracy, which is obligated to investigate the charge. Wrongdoing may be brought to the attention of higher authority, and criminal charges may be brought where warranted.

Soviet Criminal Procedure. Soviet criminal procedure is so similar to Romano-Germanic procedure that only peculiarities of the Soviet procedure will be noted here.

The preliminary investigation is not conducted by a judge in the Soviet Union, but rather by a person in the Procuracy. Once the investigation is complete the investigator decides whether or not the accused should be tried. A negative decision may be appealed to the local procurator.

Trial is held in the People's Court according to the usual Romano-Germanic inquisitorial procedure. Only the judge may question witnesses. If a lawyer wants certain questions asked, he must request that the judge ask them. If the judge refuses, the lawyer has no recourse except on appeal. The main function of the lawyers is to summarize the case after the evidence is presented.

The judge and assessors deliberate together on the decision, which is determined by majority vote. Thus the two assessors may outvote the judge.

As in the Romano-Germanic world, either side may appeal the outcome; the power of appellate courts is essentially the same as in France, Germany, or Mexico.

Theoretically the police—both ordinary and secret (the MVD and KGB)—are bound to deal with suspects on terms of Socialist legality. The Procuracy is bound to take action against abuses of justice by either type of police. Whether the Procuracy in actual practice ever interferes with the work of the KGB or MVD is another question.

The Internal Passport System. Americans who travel abroad know how important the passport is as a means of identification at national frontiers and elsewhere. The American who never travels abroad has no need for such a document, however.

But every Soviet citizen sixteen years of age or older is required to possess an internal passport and to carry it with him at all times. It contains the information you find in all passports (recent photograph, name, nationality, address, etc.) plus, in capsule form, the citizen's employment history, police history, marital history, and the like. It is *the* required document for personal identification, and must be produced upon the demand of the police or other authorized authority.

This passport must contain a *Propiska,* which is the government's authorization for the citizen to live where he lives. One may not change his residence in the Soviet Union without the permission of the MVD, the police agency for internal affairs. One may not apply for a new *Propiska* without first cancelling his old one. That is, one must give notice to authority at the old address that one is moving from before one may apply for permission to live at the new address he is moving to. It is a severe crime to live in a place for which one has no propiska.

The internal passport is invalid for travel outside the Soviet Union. For that an external passport is required, which is extremely difficult to obtain.

Soviet Contracts. Contracts between ordinary Soviet citizens are rarer than contracts between Westerners. Soviet contracts generally accomplish the sale of personal property. The most valuable property involved is usually either a used motor vehicle or a house; however, sales of both items are severely restricted.

Private loans are very rare, because the lender may not lawfully charge his borrower any interest.

Among the types of contracts between ordinary Soviet citizens that must be in writing and are void if not in writing are contracts of pledge (a borrower borrows money and gives the lender an asset to hold as collateral) and contracts of suretyship. Loans of over fifty rubles and other bargains involving over one hundred rubles should be in writing, but lack of writing will not invalidate them. They are simply difficult to prove in court because testimony of witnesses with respect to such is not authorized.

Some sorts of contracts should be both written and protocolized; among these are contracts for the sale of a dwelling, contracts to make gifts worth over five hundred rubles, and contracts to make gifts of amounts of cash amounting to over fifty rubles. However, courts may not invalidate even these contracts if there has been substantial performance by one party and no illegality (other than lack of a protocolized contract) involved in the transaction.

Offers containing a time limit for acceptance are open for the duration of the time limit. Oral offers without time limit must be accepted at once; written offers must be accepted essentially by return mail. The acceptance is valid only when received. An acceptance that varies the terms of the offer is deemed a counteroffer.

More common are contracts between citizens and retail stores for the purchase of merchandise of one sort or another. Should the merchandise be defective, the buyer may claim the following remedies:

1. Replacement of the defective goods at no cost
2. Removal of the defect
3. Reimbursement for the cost of fixing the defect, if buyer paid to have it fixed or fixed it himself
4. Rescission plus damages caused by the defect
5. Reduction of the purchase price

The buyer may choose his remedy.

State enterprises often make contracts with each other. These are not freely negotiated in the sense that the enterprise has a wide choice of contracting partner. What an enterprise produces is determined by the central economic planners. Where it gets its raw materials and to whom it sells its output may also be so determined.

When the Brezhnev Steel Mill is ordered to acquire its pig iron from Kuznetzov Iron Works, Brezhnev and Kuznetzov must perforce make a contract. What the terms of the agreement will be the parties can determine for themselves, within the parameters of the economic plan. It may be that the Red October Shoe Factory is told to sell its shoe output to retail outlets in the Kiev area. Red October's management may have some choice in such a case as to which outlets to deal with. Up to a point it may even choose its own contracting partners. Generally price is not negotiable in these bargains; price is determined by the planners. Bargaining will be over delivery schedules and the like.

If the efforts of Mikhail Gorbachev to decentralize economic decision-making in the Soviet Union continue, more authority to negotiate contracts and to choose contract partners may well be delegated to enterprise managers.

Soviet enterprises engaged in foreign trade have some discretion in the negotiation of bargains with their foreign customers. Here, of course, all terms of the contract are subject to negotiation; foreign organizations are not bound to the goals of the Soviet economic plan. However, the Soviet planners limit the freedom to negotiate of these enterprises by not permitting them to enter into contracts contrary to the state plan. Generally such contracts must be in writing and authenticated as required by Soviet law; they must be signed for the Soviet party only by persons authorized to sign. They are in essence government documents.

Soviet Bankruptcy Law. All state enterprises must have close relationships with banks. The Foreign Trade Bank, as its name implies, finances all foreign trade. The All-Union Capital Investment Bank makes long-term loans to enterprises. Day-to-day banking business is done with the State Bank of the USSR.

Enterprises are not permitted to keep large quantities of cash on their premises. All funds not necessary for day-to-day operations must be kept in State Bank accounts.

Enterprises may not grant each other credit. All business is done on a cash basis. Only the State Bank may grant short-term credit.

Though state enterprises are not required to operate at a profit, they are required to handle their financial obligations responsibly. They are required to file financial statements with the State Bank monthly. Bank agents may inspect enterprise premises when they wish to verify the accuracy of these statements.

Should an enterprise have difficulty meeting its obligations, the State Bank may take corrective action. It may refuse to make any more loans to the enterprise until current obligations are repaid. It may require that all future loans be guaranteed by the parent organization of the enterprise. This is bound to cause difficulties for the miscreant's managers with their superiors. More seriously, it may put the miscreant on a "special credit regime." The bank will not lend the miscreant anything unless its superior organization takes over its management and tries to "shape it up." Most seriously, the bank may declare the enterprise insolvent. When this happens a special commission is appointed to investigate the situation and to make recommendations. Either the enterprise will be liquidated, or an effort will be made to rehabilitate it. Usually the latter is tried — the enterprise will not be liquidated unless everything else has failed.

The result of liquidation is not the same as it is in a free market economy. The assets of the failed enterprise generally are turned over to another enterprise, which has a go at operating it.

Torts. After Lenin's revolution an effort was made to set up a system of liability without fault for torts in the USSR. The experiment was acknowledged to be a failure. Soviet tort law is now very similar to that in other legal systems. There is no liability without fault except for persons and enterprises whose operations cause "increased hazard" for bystanders and the like.

Because automobiles cause "increased hazard," auto owners incur the same liability they do in most Romano-Germanic countries. The state railways and the like also operate under "increased hazard" rules.

Soviet Civil Procedure. Soviet courts hear civil litigation on many of the same problems that bedevil ordinary people in all countries. Heirs squabble about inheritances. Married people seek divorces and argue about child custody and child support. Drivers of automobiles are negligent and cause damage to persons and property. People breach their private contracts. These cases are heard in the People's Courts, and are decided in the same way as are criminal cases. They are also appealable in the same manner as are criminal cases.

A suit by a citizen against a state enterprise will also be heard in the People's Courts unless it involves the employment relationship, in which case it is decided by a labor tribunal.

A contract dispute between two public enterprises is not resolved by the civil courts. If the two disputants are governed by the same government ministry their dispute will be decided by the arbitration mechanism of the ministry. If they are not governed by the same ministry (as where a manufacturing enterprise makes a claim against the state railways for goods damaged in transit, for instance) the case will be heard by special arbitration tribunals established for this purpose.

Foreign businesses having contractual relationships with Soviet state enterprises virtually always agree to have disputes arising under their contracts settled by arbitration. The People's Courts are obviously not suitable tribunals for deciding such cases.

Socialist Law Outside the Soviet Union. To all Marxist-Leninist governments law serves the three purposes mentioned earlier. Virtually all have almost eliminated the private sector of their economies. Virtually all have reorganized their courts on the Soviet pattern. Even so, no two Communist lands have identical legal systems.

All Communist nations of Europe, and nearly all such nations in the rest of the world, possessed well-developed Romano-Germanic legal systems before their revolutions. In these nations there was no wholesale abolition of old law and old court systems as in the Soviet Union; the transition to the Socialist system was more gradual and, in some nations, incomplete.

Originally judicial review of government actions was anathema, for the same reasons as in the Soviet Union. However, in 1963 Yugoslavia established a Federal Constitutional Court and gave it an authority similar to that of such courts in Austria, West Germany, and Italy.

In 1982 Poland amended her constitution to create a Constitutional Tribunal and gave it authority to declare legislative acts unconstitutional. It is the first such to be created in the East European satellites of the Soviet Union. It has been in operation since 1985, though its workload has been very light.

Legal systems of Communist lands differ just as their economic systems differ. Poland and Yugoslavia have not forbidden the private ownership of land. In fact, most land in these nations is still under private ownership.

Poland, Yugoslavia, and Hungary allow the private employment of labor by small enterprises; in the German Democratic Republic, too, skilled craftsmen may operate their own enterprises. Thus private business of sizes unthinkable in the Soviet Union exist in these nations.

In Hungary government price controls have been eliminated except for absolute essentials (such as public transportation fares, electricity, housing, and the like). Thus the market system determines prices and most enterprises are expected to operate at a profit. A new progressive income tax forces successful entrepreneurs to share their wealth with the state.

Yugoslav enterprises — most of them — are in essence cooperatives. The workers are treated as co-owners and exercise ultimate management authority; if the enterprise operates profitably the workers may reinvest the profits in the business or distribute them to themselves as dividends.

Cuba and Nicaragua are not as favorable to individual enterprise as are Poland and Hungary. The Asian communist states such as Vietnam and North Korea are even more hostile to individual enterprise; their legal systems are still influenced by Chinese concepts. The law of China herself will be considered in Chapter 7.

Chapter 6

Islamic Law

Islamic law is the one major legal system that is based upon the teachings of a religion. Islam is not the only religion to have developed a system of law; Judaism and Hinduism have done likewise. All three faiths have devised comprehensive rules to guide believers in all phases of their lives. But neither Jewish nor Hindu law has acquired much influence outside one country.

Though Jews are found in many of the world's nations, they have never been a majority in any nation except modern Israel. Since the leaders of that country are secularists who believe in separation of organized religion from the state, Jewish law plays no great role in the Israeli legal system. Israeli law today is a mixture of Romano-Germanic concepts inherited from the Turkish occupation of Palestine and British common-law concepts dating from the British mandate over the area (1917–48).

The majority of the world's Hindus live in India. In modern times Hindu religious law has had no influence outside that country. During the period of British rule the law of India was a mixture of religious law and common law; Hindu law leavened by common law, applied to Hindus, and the "Anglo-Mohammedan law"—a mixture of Islamic and common-law concepts—applied to Muslims. The secular rulers of independent India, too, have separated the state from organized religion. Hindu law still governs matters of family law and inheritance in India, but otherwise India is a common-law nation.

Nature of Islamic Law. The body of Islamic law is found in the *Shari'a,* the precepts of which should be obeyed by all believing Muslims. It deals with the relationship of God to man, of rulers to ruled, and of man to man. God's revelation to man is a theoretically comprehensive set of rules of conduct. The pious Muslim must obey these rules; his fate on the Day of Judgment will depend on how well he has performed these obligations.

This body of law has four "roots." The first of these is the Qu'ran, the holy scripture of the faith. Since this was revealed to the prophet Mohammed by God himself, it is the primary relation of divine law. Though it lays down some basic rules of human conduct, it is too short and its coverage is insufficient for it to be used as a comprehensive law code. The second root is the *Sunna*. This explains the way of life and the beliefs of the prophet Mohammed, the only person competent to reveal the will of God to true believers. Its main source is the *Hadith*, the collected sayings and acts of the Prophet as reported by the collators of the early days of the faith. The third root is *Ijma*, the supposedly unanimous opinions of Islamic scholars as to the interpretations of the Qu'ran and the Sunna. Actually less than unanimous opinions of these scholars have become recognized as law in parts of the Islamic world, as will be described shortly. The fourth and last root is *Qiyas*, reasoning by analogy. When a new sort of problem arose which had never been considered before by judge or legal scholar, a solution would be found by applying principles used in similar cases.

Islamic law developed with Islam and the culture it spawned. Beginning as the law of the handful of Mohammed's original followers it grew and bloomed into the law of one of the world's mightiest empires. Ijma and Qiyas permitted it to develop and adapt to new circumstances.

The great Islamic empire that at one time extended from Spain to the borders of India began to crumble during the ninth century. As the number of independent Muslim states began to multiply, the attitude of Islamic scholars toward the law began to change. The notion became accepted that the law had developed as far as was desirable. So the *Bab al-Ijtihad*, "the gate of personal reasoning" by judges, was declared to be closed. All had been revealed that was to be revealed. The law as it had developed to this point was all that was needed. The legal problems of the present and future were to be solved through the legal writings of the past.

By this time the unity of Islamic law had broken. When the faith split into Sunni orthodoxy on the one hand and Shia and Kharijite deviance on the other, the Shia and Kharijites developed their own schools of law. Meanwhile the Sunni developed four of their own schools, all of which are recognized as orthodox somewhere in the Islamic world. The *Maliki* school sought to preserve the fusion of Islamic concepts with Arab tribal custom that was the original law of Islam. The *Hanafi* school preached an Islamic law modified by a few of the civilized customs of the Tigris-Euphrates valley, conquered from the Persians in the early years of Islamic expansion. The *Shafii* school preached that the purity of Islamic law should not be diluted by local custom; that the law should be uniform throughout Islam, determined by Qu'ran, Hadith, and true *Ijma*. The Maliki and Hanafi refused, and still refuse, to accept this notion. The *Hanbali* school preached that the only sources of the law are the Qu'ran and Hadith; human reason is not an acceptable vehicle for modifying the law. Later they became willing to accept Qiyas, but they have kept an identity separate from that of the other schools.

These four schools still exist within the Islamic world. The Maliki prevails in north and west Africa and also in Kuwait. The Hanafi prevails in Turkey, Syria, Lebanon, Iraq, and Pakistan. The Shafii dominates in Malaysia, Indonesia, and east Africa. The Hanbali prevails only in Saudi Arabia and Qatar.

Shia law prevails in Iran. *Ibadi* law, the remnant of the Kharijite system, prevails in Oman.

Despite this diversity of law throughout the Islamic world, all of the schools accepted the notion of the closing of the gate of reason in the tenth century. Islamic law stopped changing to meet new conditions at that time.

As time passed the high culture of Islam decayed, while Europe underwent the Renaissance and the Reformation and prepared to conquer the world. Since the earliest European expansion was directed toward the New World and the Far East, the world of Islam was spared the trauma of violent collision with Western military prowess until the nineteenth century. Then, within the short span of a century, most of the Islamic nations of the world became European colonies or protectorates. Western law was forced upon the Muslims while they were the subjects of European colonial powers. Only those Muslims who retained political independence—the Turks, the Afghans, and most of the people of the Arabian Peninsula—avoided this fate.

In a sense, the Islamic world was dragged into modern times against its will. Muslims learned that if they were to retain their religious and cultural identity in the modern world order, they would have to adapt to the new conditions.

With the partition of the Ottoman (Turkish) empire after World War I several new Islamic nations came into existence. With the disintegration of the European colonial empires after World War II the rest of the Islamic peoples regained their political independence. All of these nations—the newly independent and the always-free—have had to create legal systems suitable for late twentieth-century conditions. How they have sought to accomplish this task depends upon whether their leaders have been traditionalist, reformist, secularist, or fundamentalist.

Traditionalists strive to minimize modern influence upon their nations and laws, and to maintain as much as possible a pure Islamic legal system. This has been possible only in the Arabian Peninsula. The laws of Oman, Qatar, and the United Arab Emirates are still basically Islamic, as is the law of Saudi Arabia. Oil wealth, however, has brought economic development and huge numbers of foreigners to these lands. The Shari'a law does not provide a mechanism for solving some of the problems of modernization; even these somewhat isolated, conservative lands have had to graft some Western notions onto their law.

Reformists have tried to marry Islamic tradition to Western culture, incorporating the best of both into their governments and legal systems. Islamic monarchies outside the Arabian Peninsula have followed this path, but have almost inevitably fallen between the stools of republican secularism and Islamic fundamentalism. The only noteworthy reformist survivors are the monarchies of Morocco, Jordan, and Malaysia.

Secularism — the divorce of Islam from the state and public law — is the rule in the majority of Islamic nations. In Albania, Afghanistan, and the Central Asian Islamic republics of the USSR, the secularism is atheistic communism. Elsewhere it is most likely to be militant nationalism.

Fundamentalism — the restoration of a purified Islam to power in the state — is the system that prevails in a few highly publicized nations. Examples are Iran, Libya, and (to an extent) Pakistan and Sudan.

Fundamental Principles. God is the one and only lawmaker of the universe. The law propounded in the Qu'ran, Sunna, and writings of the legal scholars is divinely inspired. There can be no other valid law. Thus men are incapable of making law. The legislative enactments of human rulers do not express the will of God; therefore they cannot be law. However, human political rulers hold power by the will of God and must have the authority to govern their people. They have the power to legislate, but their legislation must be in conformity with Shari'a. Thus man-made legislation is termed administrative regulation, not law.

Unique Features of Islamic Law. The Qu'ran permits a man to have up to four wives, provided that he can afford them and that he treats them equally and fairly. The groom must pay his bride a dowry, which will remain her property if the marriage fails. The Shari'a makes it easy for a husband to divorce his wife, but difficult for a wife to divorce her husband. Under traditional law, divorce is accomplished without going through courts.

Shia law permits temporary marriages, providing mechanisms for the support of exspouse and offspring after the relationship ends.

The modern codes of most Islamic countries still permit polygamy, subject to restrictions — such as proof of financial ability to support more than one wife. Turkey and Tunisia, among others, have abolished polygamy altogether. All but the most conservative Muslim nations (such as Saudi Arabia) have made it easier for wives to divorce husbands. Even Iran has taken steps toward making men and women equal in this area.

Shari'a does not permit adoption of children in the Western sense. An adoptive child can have none of the rights of a natural child. Every true believer is required to make an annual contribution of 2.5 percent of his net worth to charity. The proceeds of this contribution, called *Zakat,* are to be used to help the needy and unfortunate. Orphans are provided for from this source. Zakat is levied as a tax by Saudi Arabia and a few other conservative nations; elsewhere payment of it is voluntary.

Eight serious crimes are defined by Shari'a and punishments (Hudud, singular *Hadd*) mandated. These are:

1. Homicide—death or payment of blood money (one hundred camels or one thousand pieces of gold if the victim is male, half this amount if the victim is female)
2. Theft—amputation of the right hand
3. Adultery—death by stoning
4. Fornication—one hundred lashes
5. Slander (questioning a man's paternity or wrongfully accusing him of adultery)—eighty lashes
6. Drunkenness—eighty lashes
7. Apostasy (accepting another religion in place of Islam)—death
8. Highway robbery—death, amputation of a hand and a foot, or exile, depending on whether anyone was killed and the value of what was stolen

Other crimes are defined and punished by administrative regulations of the political authority or by the judge.

Though the criminal law described above seems incredibly barbaric and harsh to modern Westerners, it has been looked upon as too mild in most of the Islamic world. The list of crimes is short and the standard for proof of guilt is very high. In order to maintain law and order additional crimes were everywhere created through administrative regulation and their punishment spelled out.

In Saudi Arabia this traditional criminal law is still in effect. Amputation of the right hand for theft is theoretically also the law in Iran, Libya, and Pakistan. This punishment is sometimes inflicted in Iran, seldom if ever in the other two countries. Elsewhere in Islam these Shari'a provisions are not part of the national criminal law; Western-style criminal codes have replaced the traditional law.

Compensation for personal injury is based upon the blood money tariff. Loss of both hands, both legs, both eyes, or the nose, loss of hearing, and some other injuries are to be compensated as for death. Loss of one eye, arm, or leg is compensable with half the amount due for causing death.

In Saudi Arabia personal injury damages are still fixed according to the blood money tariffs. The life of a Muslim male is valued at 120,000 Saudi riyals ($32,000 as of mid-1988) unless the death occurs during the first month or the last two months of the Islamic calendar, in which case it is 240,000 riyals.

A person who directly causes damage to the goods or property of another is liable for the harm done whether or not the harm was intended. A person who indirectly causes harm to the goods or property of another is not liable unless the harm was caused by his fault. (One who smashes a vase, whether by deliberately slamming it to the ground or by accidentally knocking it off its table while walking by, causes direct damage. One who breaks the vase because the rock he threw at a bird missed its intended target and struck the vase causes indirect damage.)

A Muslim may dispose of only one-third of his property as he wishes upon his death; the rest is to be divided among his nearest relatives as provided by the Shari'a. The Sunni schools agree upon an elaborate and rigid scheme of division in which children are given preference, but a daughter may inherit only half as much as a son, and other female heirs are entitled to half as much as males equally related. Distant relatives related to the deceased through males are preferred to closer relatives related to the deceased through females. The Shia prefer close relatives to more distant ones regardless of whether the relationship is through males or females.

The Sunnis generally forbid a testator to will property to someone entitled to inherit a part of his estate by law unless the other heirs consent; this is intended to prohibit a person preferring some close relatives to others. The Shia do not restrict the making of wills in this manner.

In many areas of the Islamic world customs relating to family and inheritance that had been long in place at the time of the conversion to Islam remain in effect. Thus the Berbers of North Africa denied women all inheritance rights (and still do in Morocco, where Berber customary law still remains in effect in Berber-inhabited areas), while groups like the Minangkabou of Sumatra allowed (and still allow) woman a much higher status than Shari'a mandated in matters of inheritance and otherwise.

Today Iran and Iraq use the Shia rules for inheritance. Turkey has abolished the Shari'a rules of inheritance altogether, while a few Sunni lands have modified the Sunni system to make it more rational by modern standards.

In the *Waqf* Islamic law recognizes an institution similar to the common-law trust. The corpus of a waqf is usually real estate, though it can be anything tangible. Buildings and orchards are considered to be tangible; money and investment securities are not. Thus, one may not create a waqf in cash or corporate stock.

Awqaf (the Arabic plural of waqf) may be charitable or family. The object of a charitable waqf may be the support of a mosque or hospital, help for the poor, or the like. The object of a family waqf is usually the support of the descendants of the settlor. The duration of the charitable waqf is perpetual. The duration of the family waqf is fulfilled when the line of descendants of the settlor dies out; it must become charitable. Awqaf are managed by persons having powers similar to common-law trustees. The corpus and its income must be used for the prescribed purpose; managers must not use them for their own personal benefit. The settlor may establish the waqf during his lifetime or by will.

The existence of awqaf has been a bone in the throat of Islamic governments throughout history. No government looks with favor upon property that may never be bought or sold and is perpetually exempt from taxation. Throughout history theoretically impious rulers have ignored the privileges granted to these charitable institutions and expropriated them.

Today awqaf are strictly regulated in most Islamic countries; many have abolished the family waqf altogether.

Unique Features of Islamic Court Procedure. Traditionally the Islamic court consisted of one person: the *Qadi.* Appointed by the caliph (the political and religious head of state) in early times, he exercised both executive and judicial functions of government. With Islam's loss of political unity the method of his appointment varied from country to country. In the nations of the Arabian Peninsula the political head of state appoints him today.

The only appropriate forms of evidence in Shari'a courts are confession, testimony, and the swearing of oaths. Documentary evidence is traditionally of no value.

The following procedures are used in traditional courts:

If the person accused of committing an offense confesses his guilt before the qadi he may be punished. Generally he must confess twice, and in the case of a person accused of adultery, four times.

In the absence of confession the plaintiff must prove his case through the testimony of two reliable eyewitnesses (four in the case of prosecutions for adultery). The best witness is a free adult male Muslim of sound mind, wholly reliable, who has never falsely accused anyone of committing an immoral offense.

The defendant may challenge the reliability of a witness by producing evidence of bad character. If the qadi determines that the witness is unreliable his testimony is not to be considered. Once a person is accepted in one case as a reliable witness, he acquires the status of permanent witness. He may testify in any proceeding before the qadi who gives him this status without having to undergo more challenges to his reliability.

Women may not testify except in cases involving property. When allowed at all a woman's testimony is only worth one-half a man's, and no amount of female testimony can be worth more than one man's. The plaintiff may not prevail on the basis of only female testimony. Thus, if the plaintiff is to prevail in a case involving property he will need two reliable male witnesses, or one reliable male and two reliable female witnesses.

The testimony of a non–Muslim is of no value whatsoever.

There is no cross-examination of witnesses. The witnesses make their statements and that is all. If the witness is by definition reliable, the qadi must believe his testimony; it is assumed that reliable witnesses always tell the truth.

The defendant is not permitted to call witnesses. If the plaintiff is able to produce the two required witnesses, the defendant's only recourse is to attack their character. If he cannot convince the qadi that one of them is unreliable, he loses.

If the plaintiff cannot produce two reliable witnesses the defendant may assure himself victory by swearing an appropriate solemn oath. (If his oath is false he beats the earthly system, but he will receive the appropriate punishment at the Last Judgment.)

If the plaintiff cannot produce two reliable witnesses and the defendant refuses to swear the appropriate oath, the plaintiff may then secure victory by swearing the proper oath.

Traditionally there was no judicial appeal from the qadi's decision. The unsatisfied litigant had two recourses: he could ask the qadi to reconsider his decision, or he could appeal to the political head of state.

Since Shari'a opposes the termination of legal rights by the passage of time, there are no statutes of limitation in traditional Islamic courts. Theoretically cases may be heard many years after an incident occurs.

Saudi Arabia's Modern Islamic Courts. Though the law of Saudi Arabia is pure Islamic (with the exception of that governing modern commercial matters) the royal government has created a somewhat unique court system to apply it. Nancy Turck describes it in her article "Dispute Resolution in Saudi Arabia" (22 The International Lawyer 415).

There exist general Shari'a courts that hear ordinary cases and special judicial committees to hear more complex cases. The general Shari'a trial courts consist of one judge in civil matters, or three judges in criminal cases. These judges must be Saudi nationals with degrees from Saudi law colleges. Appeals are usually made to three-judge courts of appeal with essentially the power of the French Cour de Cassation (they may either affirm the trial court or remand the case for further proceedings). In criminal matters where the sentence is death or amputation of a hand, appeal is to a five-judge tribunal whose decision is final when approved by the minister of justice.

Shari'a court judges are trained only in Shari'a law. They apply only Shari'a law. Thus they are unequipped to decide complex cases.

The Board of Grievances is the special judicial committee that hears contract disputes between Saudi government agencies and private contractors. The Commercial Paper Committee is the special committee hearing cases involving checks, drafts, and promissory notes. The Committee for Settlement of Commercial Disputes had jurisdiction over nonbanking commercial disputes not involving the government. It is now being phased out; the Board of Grievances is in the process of assuming its jurisdiction. Commissions for Settlement of Labor Disputes exercise the jurisdiction suggested by the name.

The special committees rely mainly upon written documents in rendering decisions. Only documents written in Arabic are acceptable.

Saudi courts and special committees do not recognize stare decisis; they are not bound by their own precedents. They decide each case upon its own merits.

Riba. The Qu'ran forbids in several passages the practice of riba. The literal translation of riba is "usury," the charging of excessive interest on loans. However, many Muslim jurists hold that the charging of any interest whatsoever on a loan is riba and therefore forbidden. Fundamentalists and traditionalists take this position.

If the charging of interest is forbidden, banking as we of the West practice it should also be forbidden. In theory this is the case in some Islamic lands — notably Iran and Pakistan. In practice, however, it is very difficult to dispense with the charging of interest on loans in a modern economy.

Gharar. The Qu'ran also forbids the practice of *Gharar,* the entering into a contract the outcome of which will depend on factors unforeseen at the time the contract is made. The sort of immorality this prohibition is aimed at is of course gambling. A literal interpretation of it would make insurance in the Western manner unlawful, because only unforeseen catastrophe causes most insureds to have claims against their insurers. Any sort of speculative investment would also be gharar, because the speculator gambles that market prices will move in the proper direction to permit a large profit on the speculation.

Haram. The doing of that which is forbidden by the Qu'ran is *Haram.* Islamic law forbids the sale of that which is haram. The pious Muslim must not eat pork, drink alcohol, commit adultery, possess musical instruments, or gamble. He also must not eat the flesh of animals that have died natural deaths. The rearing of pigs is almost nonexistent in Islamic lands. Many countries forbid the consumption of alcoholic beverages. However, bars and nightclubs where alcohol is consumed are found in other Islamic lands. Generally, secularist governments do not concern themselves with the sale of haram goods. To traditionalists and fundamentalists enforcement of these prohibitions is an affair of great importance.

Islamic Contract Law. Traditional Islamic law recognizes four major types of contracts: (1) *Bay,* or sale; (2) *Hiba,* or gift; (3) *Ijara,* or hire; and (4) *Arriya,* or loan.

Three elements must be present to have a valid contract of sale. First, title to whatever is being sold must pass at once if it presently exists. A contract to sell a presently existing thing in the future (such as a contract under which I agree to sell you my car next week) involves too much of an element of gharar; who knows what might happen to the car between now and next week?

Purists have argued that no contract for the sale of something that does not yet exist (like a future crop — *Salam* — or something to be manufactured in the future — *Istisna*) should be allowed because of gharar. However, such contracts are legitimate. For a salam contract to be valid, the price must be paid when the contract is made and a definite date for the delivery of the crop must be agreed to. The istisna contract is revocable by either the buyer or seller at any time prior to the completion of the manufacture according to the specifications of the contract.

Second, whatever is being sold must have legal value. If it is haram (such as alcohol, pigs, or musical instruments) it has no legal value.

Third, a fixed price must be named, and a fixed time provided for paying the price. Making the price the future market price of what is to be sold, or making the payment date an uncertain future date, involves unacceptable speculation — another form of gharar.

A promise to make a gift generally is not binding (except under Maliki law). The donor must actually deliver the gift to the donee. (The Maliki say that if the donor promises a gift but does not deliver, a court will force him to deliver if the demand is made before the donor dies or becomes mentally incompetent.)

Hire may involve the rental of property or the employment of a person. For a contract of hire to be valid, three things must be spelled out. First, the nature of the property to be rented and its use, or the nature of the work to be done by the employee, must be designated. Second, the rent for the property or the wages of the employee must be definitely stated. Third, the term of the rental or employment must be definitely stated. Any uncertainty here would be unacceptable gharar.

When a loan of property is made the lender may restrict the borrower's use of it. Whether or not the borrower may relend depends on the governing school of law — Maliki and Hanafi say he can, Hanbali and Shafii say he cannot.

A buyer is not obligated to pay for what he does not get. Even if the buyer signs a promissory note or the like promising to pay for what the seller has sold him, but the seller does not deliver, the buyer need not pay. This is true even if the seller negotiates the buyer's note to a third party who would qualify as a holder in due course in Western law.

Islamic law does not recognize the holder in due course of commercial paper as a party entitled to special privilege.

When an offer is sent to an offeree by mail, the offeree must decide almost immediately whether or not to accept it. He has essentially the amount of time he would have if the offer was delivered by a messenger; traditionally if the messenger left the offeree's establishment without an acceptance the offer was terminated. If the offeror and offeree are negotiating face to face, any contract they make is not binding unless the parties have agreed to it when they part. As long as the negotiating session (*Majlis*) is in session, there is no binding contract.

Thus, Abdul and Rashid negotiate in Abdul's tent over the sale of Abdul's camel to Rashid. Abdul offers to sell it to Rashid for 10,000 dirhams, and Rashid accepts. Then they celebrate their agreement over cups of coffee brought in by Abdul's servant. The parties are still face to face in Abdul's tent, so the majlis is not over yet. As Rashid sips his coffee, he has second thoughts about the deal he just made. Finally he tells Abdul he will not pay more than 9000 dirhams for the camel. Abdul says he cannot sell the beast for 9000 dirhams — Rashid had better pay 10,000 because he has already agreed to do so. An angry argument ensues. Rashid gets so angry that he leaves Abdul's tent and goes home. The majlis is now over. Since there is no agreement between the parties when it ends, there is no contract under traditional Islamic law. Rashid could in essence revoke his acceptance of Abdul's offer any time before he and Abdul parted company.

Any kind of an ongoing long-term contract may be rescinded by either party at will, even if it was agreed that the contract would endure for a fixed period. Thus, if Suleiman leases his house to Hamid for a period of three years, Hamid may move out and terminate the lease at any time or Suleiman may terminate the lease and evict Hamid at any time. It may be that Suleiman has decided to move into the house himself, or he just does not like Hamid any more. It may be that Hamid has inherited a house from his father, or he just wants to move to another neighborhood. Essentially, if changed circumstances make either party unhappy with the bargain he may repudiate it.

Generally there is no requirement under Islamic law that any contract be in writing, because of the value the system places upon oral testimony.

These traditional concepts of contract law are generally found only in the legal systems of the countries of the Arabian Peninsula. Elsewhere contract law in Islamic countries is Romano-Germanic, common law, or Socialist, depending on the country.

Islamic Banking. As mentioned earlier, Western-style banks could not exist where traditional Islamic law applied. The payment of interest to depositors and the collection of interest from borrowers would be riba. The taking of a security interest in collateral put up by borrowers would be gharar because of the uncertainty as to whether or not the borrower would default on the loan and the bank would foreclose on the collateral.

In parts of the Islamic world — and even in the West — banks owned and operated by Muslims exist which seek to avoid the pitfalls of riba and gharar. These banks pay their depositors no interest.

With respect to checking account customers, this is nothing unusual; in the United States it was unlawful for banks to pay interest on checking account balances for over forty years. Islamic banks levy service charges on their checking account depositors just as Western banks do; service charges are not interest.

Islamic banks also pay no interest to savings account owners. Where then is the economic incentive to deposit savings in an Islamic bank? Savings account owners are treated as co-owners of the bank, in a sense. Their compensation for depositing their savings with the bank is a share of the bank's profits. Thus these account owners are not creditors of the bank, as Western savings account owners are. Their deposits are in essence investments in the banking enterprise. They are not entitled to any return on their investment unless the bank operates profitably. If the bank fails, their investment is lost.

If the bank is forbidden to lend money to borrowers for interest, how can it make loans and earn profits from them? The answer is found in a traditional Arab arrangement which existed before the time of Mohammed: the *Mudaraba*. The lender asks for partial ownership of the enterprise to which he lends. Instead of paying the lender interest, the borrower pays the lender a share of his profits. Lender and borrower become partners. The lending bank now enters into a mudaraba arrangement with the business borrower. Thus, the bank is not a creditor of its borrower; it is a co-owner of the borrower's enterprise. Not only does the bank earn no return on a loan to an unsuccessful enterprise, it also stands to lose the lent funds. If the borrower's enterprise prospers, the bank earns a larger return on its investment than it would by simply collecting interest.

When the bank wants to finance the purchase of something by a consumer, it enters into a murabaha or *Ijara Wa Iqtina* transaction, both of which have long been accepted in Islam. Habib wants to buy a new car but does not have the cash to pay for it now. He may make the following bargain with Islamic Bank: Habib tells the bank which car he wants to buy and who the present owner is. The bank buys the car from the owner and resells it to Habib for a higher price, which he agrees to pay at some time in the future. If Habib does not pay when he agreed, the bank may rescind the sale and reclaim the car, because of the principle that a contract may be rescinded any time before it is fully performed. This is a murabaha transaction.

Or, the bargain may be made in this fashion. The bank delivers the car to Habib. In exchange he agrees to make a stated monthly (or weekly or bimonthly or whatever) payment to the bank which is credited to an account in his name. He must continue to make these payments until an agreed amount is in the account if he ever wants to become the vehicle's owner. If at any time he decides he does not want to become the vehicle's owner, he returns it to the bank and the bank takes over ownership of the account as payment of rent. Once the required amount is on deposit the bank takes it and Habib has bought the car. This is an ijara wa iqtina transaction.

In neither transaction is the bank charging Habib interest. In neither transaction is there any appreciable element of uncertainty or speculation.

Islamic Investment Companies. Investment companies are springing up all over the Islamic world which invite the public to contribute to their capital and invest said capital in mudaraba transactions with business enterprises.

If Ibrahim wants to invest in such an enterprise he pays to it 10,000 dirhams (or another agreed sum) and gets in return a *Sakk* certificate which is a cross between a debenture and a stock certificate. The sakk provides that the company will have the use of the 10,000 dirhams for a fixed period of time and will have the right to invest them in mudaraba. In exchange Ibrahim will receive his ratable share of 90 percent of the profit earned by the company on these mudaraba.

It is accepted that the profit on these mudaraba will be divided 10 percent to the investment company itself and 90 percent to the owners of the outstanding *sukuk* (the Arabic plural of sakk is sukuk).

When the sakk matures, then, Ibrahim gets back his 10,000 dirhams plus his ratable share of profits earned during his membership.

Takaful. Insurance is abhorrent to the Islamic purist because of the large element of gharar involved. Yet insurance is necessary to the operation of a modern economy. Takaful is a gharar-less form of insurance and therefore perfectly acceptable to traditionalists and fundamentalists.

If Ahmad wants to insure his house against fire damage he may join a *Takaful Mudaraba.* He is then obligated to make a periodic contribution (monthly, quarterly, semiannually or whatever) to the organization which goes into an account in his name. The organization invests these funds in mudaraba.

The invested funds belong to Ahmad, though they are frozen for a short period after he joins. Later he may withdraw them at any time and give up his insurance protection. If he suffers a fire loss during his membership he makes a claim with the takaful. His claim is paid out of his deposit account if it is sufficient to pay it. If the loss is larger than his account, the organization pays him the balance out of its other funds.

Thus Ahmad is in essence getting self-insurance for small losses but is getting protection from the organization and its other members against large losses. Theoretically it is done without gambling and without anyone charging or collecting interest.

Islamic Law and Capitalism. From the foregoing discussion it should be clear that Islamic law assumes the right of individuals to own property, including large enterprises. In many respects its economic concepts are much closer to capitalism than they are to socialism. But this legal system does not look with favor upon some types of unearned income. By its prohibition of riba it tries to reduce the power of large concentrations of capital, and by the prohibition of gharar it seeks to restrict the investment of scarce capital resources in unproductive speculation. Thus one might say that Islam favors a guided, nonpredatory sort of capitalism.

Summary: Islamic Law in the 1980s. Two modern Islamic nations, Albania and Turkey, have totally divorced their legal systems from Shari'a. Albania's Marxist-Leninist government is officially atheist and strives to stamp out all religious influence in the country. Turkey's great reformer Mustapha Kemal Ataturk abolished Shari'a influence upon Turkish law and courts in the 1920s in the interest of modernization.

Western-style court systems have been established almost everywhere. Turkey and Egypt among other lands have totally abolished separate Shari'a courts; most other Islamic countries have reduced their jurisdiction to family and inheritance matters. But virtually all courts in present-day Iran are religious.

Virtually all Islamic nations have enacted civil and commercial codes, reducing most of their law to writing. The law governing commercial relationships has become primarily Western from Indonesia to Morocco. However, recently enacted codes in nations such as Egypt, Iraq, Kuwait, and the United Arab Emirates provide that judges should use Shari'a principles to solve cases in which the codes do not mandate the decision. Islamic commercial principles, such as the prohibitions against riba and gharar, may still influence court decisions in these lands.

Iran and Pakistan are making efforts to eliminate Western-style banking from their economies. The charging of interest on loans is also theoretically unlawful in Saudi Arabia. There banks charge interest on loans, but if the borrower defaults the courts will not enforce the obligation.

In Pakistan, Iran, and Sudan all legislation must be consistent with Shari'a principles; special tribunals exist that have the power to avoid nonconforming statutes. This notion is rigidly enforced in Iran, but not so much so in the other two nations mentioned.

Within the last thirty years fundamentalism has become a force in the Islamic world, seeking to purify culture and law by driving out Western influence. It will doubtless increase in influence in the Islamic world as Muslims strive to adapt their ancient culture and values to modern conditions.

Westerners who transact business in the Islamic world will be required to make allowances for what they consider to be the quirky way Muslims observe the world and carry out commercial obligations.

Chapter 7

Far Eastern and African Law

Far Eastern Law

The nations of the Far East that have been influenced by Chinese culture have a unique outlook upon law. Two contradicting philosophies have influenced this outlook. The first and most important is Confucianism. K'ung-Fu-tzu (Confucius) lived in the sixth century B.C. and put into writing the set of ideas that have most shaped Chinese culture. Man cannot prosper on earth, he wrote, unless two harmonies are maintained: the harmony between heaven and earth, and the harmony between man and man. The activities of men may upset the harmony between heaven and earth. When this happens natural catastrophes—floods, earthquakes, famines—make the life of man miserable and uncertain. Only harmony between man and man will maintain the harmony between heaven and earth.

The best way to maintain harmony between men is to educate them to behave harmoniously. There are five basic relationships between human beings: (1) father and son; (2) elder brother and younger brother; (3) husband and wife; (4) emperor and subject; and (5) friend and friend. Men must realize that they have no rights on this earth; they have only duties. These duties are reciprocal; the subject may owe duties to the emperor, but the emperor also owes duties to the subject. The wife may owe duties to her husband, but her husband also owes duties to her. The son owes duties to his father; his father likewise owes duties to him. If all people diligently perform their duties to each other there will no discord in society. Then heaven and earth will be in harmony and all will prosper.

If matters deteriorate to the point that people must be forced to perform their duties an unworthy society exists. Since the purpose of law is to force people to perform their duties, law is only needed in unworthy societies.

In conflict with Confucianism, with its emphasis on reciprocal responsibilities and maintaining harmony, is legalism, a close kin to Western positivism. Its essence is that law is necessary to preserve the existence of the state, and that the ruler has the power to make this law. In short, the will of the emperor shall be law.

Confucius lived three centuries before the various Chinese states were joined into a united nation. Legalist philosophy was adopted by the princes of Ch'in, the state that conquered the other Chinese states and created the Chinese empire. The judicious wielding of the power conferred by this philosophy allowed Shih Huang-ti, the first emperor of united China, to ruthlessly consolidate his rule.

Later the Ch'in dynasty of emperors was overthrown by the Han, and the legalist philosophy was eclipsed. Confucianism became the official philosophy of state and remained so for two thousand years. Still, a significant remnant of legalism lived on, because it was accepted that the emperor was the supreme legislator. What he decreed was law.

The law that began to accumulate over the centuries was a code of criminal law. Some of its provisions were called *Lu;* these provisions name acts that are forbidden and describe the punishments for performing these forbidden activities. Other provisions were called *Ling;* these provisions state actions that must be performed and describe the punishments for failing to properly perform mandated acts. There was no legislation on what we would call civil matters. The only way one could obtain justice from Chinese courts was by accusing someone of violating a lu or a ling. Accusation could be dangerous because falsely accusing someone of committing an offense was in itself a serious offense.

Furthermore Emperor K'ang-hsi decreed in the eighteenth century that any person appearing before a court in any capacity should be treated without pity, so that he would forever be disgusted with law and fearful of the magistrates. This was necessary because, said the emperor, if people thought that they could get justice from courts they would be deluded about their rights and would institute so many lawsuits that the work of society would never get done. Moreover, magistrates under the empire prided themselves on their lack of knowledge of the lu and ling. A caste of professional law clerks existed to advise the magistrates, but these were low-ranking civil servants held in near contempt by their superiors and the rest of society.

After the overthrow of the empire in 1912 China was in theory transformed into a country of Romano-Germanic law. Comprehensive law codes were enacted based upon German and French law, modern courts were established in a few places, and educational facilities were set up to train lawyers. However, Chinese government and politics were so unstable during this period that the new law never obtained a foothold in much of the country.

The Communist victory in the Chinese civil war of the late 1940s ended the reign of this system on the mainland. The old rulers retired to Taiwan, where today their sons remain in power. The law of Taiwan remains the pre–Communist Romano-Germanic law of the mainland.

Mao Tse-tung's victorious revolutionaries transformed Chinese society into something very new according to very old principles. The old China was to be destroyed, never to rise again. The Romano-Germanic codes were abolished, the study of Confucianism was forbidden, and legalism once again became the dominant philosophy in law. Mao and the Communist party, in the manner of the Ch'in emperors, decreed what was law. By government order most private ownership of property was eliminated. At the same time Mao proclaimed the abolition of law and secured obedience through exhorting the Chinese to do their duty. Because of the isolation of China from the world during Mao's rule, the system for the most part worked. The Chinese people did their duty toward the new government as they had done their duty toward the old, with minimal legal compulsion.

Since Mao's death and the reopening of China to the world, law as we understand it has returned. Since 1976 the new rulers have enacted new comprehensive law codes. Since private economic activity is again allowed and since the Chinese people are becoming more affluent, more law is required to regulate their relationships. Furthermore, with the government's present policy of encouraging foreign trade and investment a legal framework is needed within which the outlanders feel secure.

Before 1976 there was virtually no legal profession in China. Now law schools exist to train people in this suddenly needed skill; the number of lawyers grows rapidly.

The court system is organized on the Russian model; the most common court, a people's court, consists of one trained judge and two people's assessors.

Chinese Private Enterprise. Since 1983 individual enterprise has been permitted in the People's Republic of China. It is allowed in the areas of personal service and small-scale handicraft manufacturing.

One may not engage in a private individual enterprise without a business license. These are issued only to persons not employed by state enterprises. A person employed in a state enterprise cannot quit in order to set up an individual enterprise. These are authorized to combat unemployment and only secondarily to promote economic growth.

Licenses are issued for only one activity. The holder may only engage in that particular activity.

The licensee may be either a single individual or his household. If it is a household, all members of it may participate in the enterprise and share the profit.

The price the individual enterprise charges for its product is generally set by the state. Only when the enterprise buys raw material at market prices may it sell its product at an unregulated price. The enterprise may not have more than two employees and five apprentices. Their wages or salaries must be approved by a government agency.

In agriculture private enterprise has appeared in the form of the rural contract business household, which may contract with the rural collective to produce quantities of specified produce. Any rural household may assume this status; it is not limited to otherwise unemployed persons.

Perhaps the most remarkable development in modern China is the advent of the collective enterprise. Unlike the collectives of the Soviet Union and Yugoslavia, these enterprises very much resemble the corporations of the West. These organizations have some remarkable attributes. First, their operating capital is not furnished by the state, but comes from private sources. Second, they may sell securities to the public. Third, the securities holders may choose the enterprise officers, or the securities holders may choose directors who choose officers. Fourth, the securities are a cross betweeen bonds and stock. Investors are entitled to receive interest on the par value of their shares; they may also receive dividends at the option of the directors or officers. There appear to be no legal limits upon the size of these enterprises, or upon the number of employees they may hire. Such enterprises are not found, to the author's knowledge, in any other Communist country on earth. Thus China, which at one time was more collectivist than the Soviet Union, now allows more private enterprise than its big Marxist-Leninist brother to the north.

Japanese Law. Chinese culture has been a major influence on the Japanese since the seventh century; therefore Japanese society has followed the Confucian ethic.

Japan had no strong central government until the sixteenth century. Before that the organization of society was feudal in nature. Law was the will of the feudal overlord in his domain. Under the Tokugawa shoguns in the seventeenth century Japanese law became more unified. Now it was class-based; a person's legal obligations depended on his trade or profession, who his ancestors were, and where he lived. The unifying factor in this system was the shogun (the ruler of the nation, though theoretically subject to the emperor), who had the final word in settling legal disputes.

After Japan was forced to open her doors to the West in the 1850s, the shogunate was overthrown and modern government established. Japan became a country of Romano-Germanic law, with comprehensive codes based on French and German models. Elements of common law, such as the power of the Supreme Court to declare parliamentary acts unconstitutional, were grafted onto the system during the American occupation in the late 1940s. Today most of the law of Japan is contained in the usual five Romano-Germanic codes:

1. The Civil Code
2. The Commercial Code
3. The Penal Code
4. The Code of Civil Procedure
5. The Code of Criminal Procedure

Though courts have the power to interpret sections of the codes, and though court decisions are in theory an important guide to this interpretation, so few court decisions are rendered in Japan that precedent is not a very useful tool for determining the law. In the absence of precedent Japanese lawyers and judges look to the writings of legal scholars. The accepted interpretation of a code section is that adhered to by the majority of these experts.

Judges are civil servants, as on the European continent. Court procedure is essentially Romano-Germanic. No juries are used in either criminal or civil cases.

Legal theory is one thing and everyday practice another in Japan. The Confucian feeling still prevails that respectable people do not get involved with the law.

When crimes are committed, the police risk losing face (being humiliated) if they do not find a criminal; thus shortcuts in police procedures are tolerated. Judges do not always thoroughly explain the reasons for their decisions; this reticence is tolerated because most people believe that it really is not anyone else's business why judges decide as they do.

The Japanese use the law to settle civil matters only as a last resort. In good Confucian fashion they try to resolve their differences without getting outsiders involved. When the police are summoned, police officers themselves will sometimes act as mediators to try to get things settled. The Japanese judge in civil litigation is required to make a continuous effort to get the parties to compromise before he makes a decision.

Japanese businessmen, too, do their best to avoid dealings with the law. They are very likely to be concerned more with the spirit of an agreement than with its letter, and to do everything possible to compromise their disagreements.

Law in Other Far-Eastern Lands. Hong Kong's legal system is based on the English common law.

Before World War II, when Korea was a Japanese colony, Korean law was based on Japanese law. Now North Korea has a variation of Socialist law in force, while South Korea is Romano-Germanic.

Vietnam, Laos, and Kampuchea had French law while they were part of French Indochina; all three are now in the Socialist legal orbit.

Thailand, which never lost its independence during the colonial period, has adopted Romano-Germanic law. The peoples of all these lands share to an extent the Confucian ethic and the aversion to law as a method for settling disputes. It is this attitude that makes Far Eastern culture different from most others.

South Asian Law. As I have mentioned earlier, in the legal systems of the nations of the Indian subcontinent (India, Pakistan, Bangladesh) the common law is an influential element. In India this is to an extent modified by Hindu elements; in Pakistan and Bangladesh the modification is Islamic. Sri Lanka retains much of the Roman-Dutch law established by the Dutch colonists of the island in the seventeenth century.

Burma has sought to construct her own system of socialism; her law is a mixture of common law and indigenous elements. Malaysian law is a mixture of common law, Islamic law, and idigenous Malay elements. The law of Singapore is common law with an admixture of Chinese custom.

The legal system of Indonesia contains some remnants of the Dutch law that applied there before World War II. In addition there are Islamic elements, plus elements of the old *Adat* law, Indonesian custom that predates the conversion of the people to Islam in the fifteenth century.

The law of the Philippines is a mixture of the Spanish law in force there before 1898 and elements of American common law implanted in the system between 1898 and 1946.

African Law

Most of Africa south of the Sahara and inland from the Atlantic and Indian oceans had very little contact with the modern world before the middle of the nineteenth century. To be sure, Europeans established trading posts and slaving stations along the coasts beginning in the fifteenth century, but the interior of the Dark Continent was marked "Terra Incognita" on world maps for centuries thereafter.

Arab traders and Islamic missionaries began to bring Islamic religion and law to sub–Saharan Africa in the ninth century. The Portuguese found rich Islamic trading cities on the coasts of what are now Kenya and Tanzania in the sixteenth century. Though most were destroyed by the Europeans, Zanzibar has survived as a center of commerce to the present day.

The British found flourishing Islamic city-states in northern Nigeria. These lost their independence during the days of British colonialism, but became political powers to be reckoned with in the new free Nigeria of the 1960s.

Large non–Islamic kingdoms developed in Africa also. The Portuguese found the kingdoms of Congo and Monomatapa in the region later to become Angola. Dahomey flourished until conquered by troops of the French Foreign Legion in the nineteenth century.

Where there were large numbers of Muslims, the law of the Shari'a modified by local custom prevailed. Because the people of the non–Islamic empires had no written language we have no idea of the laws that governed them.

At the beginning of the colonial era most sub–Saharan Africans lived in political units no larger than tribes, and were governed by the customs they had lived by for centuries.

By 1880 European explorations of the interior of the continent and competition to establish colonies created the danger of war. The African colonial powers assembled in Berlin in 1884 to settle their differences. There they drew lines on the map to establish their spheres of influence and the boundaries of the present-day independent African nations took form. The British and French appropriated the lion's share of the continent, but Germany, Spain, Portugal, Italy, and Belgium also got shares. Germany lost her colonies in 1919 to the winners of World War I, while the other powers preserved theirs until the 1950s, 1960s, or 1970s.

The colonial powers imposed European law on the city-dwellers and inhabitants of developed areas of their colonies — common law in the British colonies, Romano-Germanic law in the others. They left the tribes of the bush to be governed by the ancient customary law.

As civilization penetrated the interior, the colonial powers began to compel changes in tribal law, especially to eliminate cruelty in the customary criminal law. The power to decide disputes between tribesmen was taken away from those who had decided such things under the ancient law and given to educated civil servants trained in European law and court procedure. The tribal law came to be enforced by judges who had not grown up subject to it and who did not know the parties to the dispute personally.

As economic development proceeded, the whole basis of the tribesman's life began to change. In the old days, he did not work for money; he simply worked to help himself and his tribe survive. The work he did and the reward he received for it were determined by his status in society. The tribesman owed duties to the tribe; the tribe owed duties to the tribesman; and everyone did his duty because he was expected to.

With the coming of economic development choice entered the tribesman's life. He could choose the work he did, and he could choose for whom he would do it. His reward came in an unaccustomed form: as money. He could choose his reward for his work in the way he spent the money.

However, his economic relationships in the new order were no longer determined by his status in the tribe; they were now determined by contract. His new employers owed him nothing more than pay for the work he did — as long as there was work for him to do. Now there was prosperity when there was work, and destitution when there was none, and little if any economic security.

The concept of contract as we understand it was totally foreign to most of the tribesmen, and remains so for many Africans up to the present time.

The colonial governments made no effort to force European law on everyone in the colony. Those who moved to developed areas were governed by it; those who remained in the bush were not. With the coming of national independence the native elites inherited this state of affairs. They assumed the governance of, in many cases, millions of people who had no sense of nationhood. In order to hold their new countries together and build a sense of nationality they decided to do all they could to unify the national law.

Efforts have been made in several African nations to comprehensively study the various tribal customs and to distill from them legal rules that would be applicable nationwide. This will make native tradition a part of the national law, certainly; but it will also destroy the nature of tribal custom. The great virtue of custom is its flexibility; the tribal headman can take the personality and background of disputants into account in deciding cases and render personalized justice. He may also emphasize compromise over confrontation. Modern law usually takes the opposite approach; personalized justice is bad because it does not treat everyone alike, and confrontation is better than compromise because one is entitled to one's rights without compromise.

Court Systems and Lawyers. Most African nations have had trouble training sufficient manpower to man their courts and serve their people. In highly developed countries like Ghana, Nigeria, and the Ivory Coast there are numerous educated judges and trained native lawyers. In countries like Tanzania and Kenya this sort of manpower is much scarcer.

Trials by judges are the rule in both civil and criminal matters. No country south of the Sahara uses the jury in civil cases; only Ghana, Senegal, and the Ivory Coast use it in criminal matters. (Interestingly, Ghana is the only one of this trio to have a common-law legal system.)

University-trained appellate judges and poorly educated trial judges are the norm. In both common-law and Romano-Germanic countries appointment of judges by the president is the rule and, since one-party government prevails in most of these nations, political considerations influence these appointments.

About half of the nations south of the Sahara are under military rule. In these nations judicial independence is rare; the rulers do not tolerate opposition from within the government apparatus. In many of these countries lawyers are mistrusted by the military rulers because they usually play a major role in civilian governments, and because they may not respect the generals merely because they wear uniforms and control the guns.

Chapter 8

International Organizations

When the average person thinks of international law, he probably thinks of law enacted by some international body that is enforceable throughout the world. No such law exists. There is no lawmaking authority in the world other than the nation-state, with a few exceptions. The most important of these is the European Community. The lawmaking authority of that body has the power to enact legislation binding upon the twelve members of the EC because the members have delegated to the organization such authority.

No international agency capable of enforcing or applying international law exists.

The United Nations

When one thinks of world-wide organizations, one inevitably thinks of the United Nations. In a sense the UN serves as a Parliament of Man, for it is the one forum where representatives of most of the nations of the world gather to debate the world's problems. Most of the world's nations (159 as of 1986) are represented in the UN. Though the UN has the potential to become a sort of world government with the authority to enact binding international law, it has not yet reached that position.

The General Assembly. In the General Assembly all member nations are represented, on the basis of one nation, one vote (except for the Soviet Union, which has three votes). The General Assembly may pass resolutions by majority vote (except for those involving admission of new members and those dealing with "important questions," which require a two-thirds vote for approval). Such resolutions are binding upon the organization itself, but not upon its members. No UN member need obey a General Assembly resolution if it does not choose to do so.

The General Assembly has adopted numerous resolutions and declarations that at least some UN members choose to treat as law. These deal with many of the great political and social problems of the world. Examples include:

1. Universal Declaration on Human Rights (1948)
2. Declaration of the Rights of the Child (1959)
3. Resolution on Ownership of Natural Resources (1962)
4. Declaration on the Elimination of Discrimination against Women (1967)
5. Declaration on Territorial Asylum (1967)
6. Declaration of Principles Regarding the Sea-Bed and the Ocean Floor (1970)
7. International Convention on the Suppression and Punishment of the Crime of Apartheid (1973)
8. Charter of Economic Rights of States (1974)
9. Resolution on the Declaration on the Elimination of All Forms of Intolerance Based on Religion or Belief (1982)

The Security Council. The executive branch of the UN, if one could call it that, is the Security Council. It consists of representatives of fifteen member nations: five permanent members (the United States, the USSR, Great Britain, France, and China) and ten nations elected by the General Assembly for two-year terms.

It has the authority to enact resolutions solving disputes, and to enforce its decisions (supposedly). For the Security Council to be able to act nine members must vote in favor, and no permanent member must vote against. Any one permanent member may veto Security Council action by voting against it; an abstention (a refusal to vote) is not a veto. On procedural questions there is no veto — any nine affirmative votes will approve procedural decisions. Originally the Soviet Union was the great wielder of the veto in the Security Council, but in recent times every great power has used the veto to protect itself or its client states against UN intervention. Though a Security Council decision is theoretically binding upon all UN members, the Security Council cannot force a member nation to contribute military forces to an enforcement venture.

The Economic and Social Council. The Economic and Social Council consists of fifty-four members, elected by the General Assembly. It has the power to study the world's economic and social problems, and to recommend solutions by majority vote. It also coordinates the activities of the specialized UN agencies.

The Secretariat. The Secretariat is the administrative branch of the organization. It is headed by the secretary-general, who is elected by the General Assembly on the unanimous recommendation of the Security Council. The secretary-general brings to the attention of the General Assembly and Security Council matters requiring their attention. He also supervises the operation of the United Nations civil service.

The Court of International Justice. The judicial branch of the UN is the Court of International Justice (CIJ), sitting at The Hague in the Netherlands. It consists of fifteen judges elected by the General Assembly and the Security Council. Each permanent member of the Security Council must be represented by one judge, and no nation may have more than one.

The court hears disputes between nations. It cannot consider a case involving the right of an individual unless some nation agrees to adopt the individual's case as its own.

The only possible enforcement agencies for the court's rulings are the nations themselves or the Security Council. The Security Council has never stirred itself to enforce a CIJ decision, and the nations reserve to themselves the decision as to whether or not to obey these rulings. Thus the power of the CIJ is essentially moral.

The only effective enforcement mechanism for international law is, then, the court of the nation-state. Even its enforcement ability will depend upon the nature of the defendant.

Specialized Agencies. The United Nations has many specialized agencies. The International Labor Organization (ILO) monitors working conditions and the like throughout the world. The World Health Organization (WHO) studies world health problems and coordinates national efforts in this area. The United Nations Educational, Scientific and Cultural Organization (UNESCO) studies world problems within the area of its expertise. The Food and Agricultural Organization (FAO) studies problems of food supply and nutrition.

Other United Nations organizations which are of interest to international businesspeople are the World Bank, the International Monetary Fund, the United Nations Conference on Trade and Development (UNCTAD), and the United Nations Commission on International Trade Law (UNCITRAL). UNCITRAL, UNCTAD, UNESCO, and ILO are all very active in the development of international law. The activities of all four may effect the international business environment.

The European Community

The most noteworthy international organization with lawmaking authority in today's world is the European Community. This organization began with the establishment of the European Coal and Steel Community in 1952. In 1958 the Treaty of Rome created the European Economic Community from six original members: the German Federal Republic, France, Italy, the Netherlands, Belgium, and Luxembourg. This treaty is still the foundation of the community.

Since 1958 the organization has increased in both powers and members. Great Britain, Ireland, and Denmark joined in 1973. Greece became the tenth member in 1979. Portugal and Spain became the eleventh and twelfth members in 1986. The original community expanded into a customs union in 1968, and now is well on the way to becoming a virtual federation of states.

Organization. The governing bodies of the community are four in number: the Parliament (or Assembly), the Council, the Commission, and the Court of Justice.

The Assembly is elected by the voters of the twelve member nations by direct popular vote. All of the nations except Great Britain elect their members from multimember districts by proportional representation; the British elect theirs from single-member districts by the first-past-the-post system.

The Assembly has 518 members, elected for five-year terms. Each of the four nations with the largest populations — Great Britain, France, Italy, and the German Federal Republic — elect eighty-one members. Spain elects sixty, the Netherlands twenty-five, Belgium, Greece, and Portugal twenty-four each, Denmark sixteen, Ireland fifteen, and Luxembourg six.

The Council consists of one member per state, who must be a member of his nation's government. The Council meets for a few days once a month. Usually each nation sends its foreign minister to Council meetings, though other ministers may attend instead when specialized subjects are being debated. Thus, when agriculture is under discussion each nation's representative may be its minister of agriculture; when problems of transport are under debate the respective ministers of transport may attend. It is possible for several Council meetings to be in session at the same time, each dealing with a specialized topic.

On most questions the votes of Council members are not equal. The German, English, French, and Italian representatives cast ten votes each, the Spanish representatives eight, the Dutch, Belgian, Danish, and Portuguese five, the Irish three, and the Luxemburger two. Fifty-four votes are required to pass a proposal under most conditions. However, a custom has become established that when a member declares that a Council action affects its vital interests, the action must be approved unanimously.

There also exists a sort of supercouncil, the European Council. This consists of heads of state of all of the members. It meets three times a year.

The Commission has seventeen members: two each from Great Brtain, France, Italy, the German Federal Republic, and Spain, and one from each of the other member nations. Commissioners are appointed by their national government for four-year terms. They are expected to act for the community, not for the nations whom they represent. Each Commissioner has one vote. The body acts by majority vote.

The Court of Justice consists of thirteen judges, chosen by unanimous agreement of the member nations for six-year terms. Each member nation is entitled to a member of the court. The judges are assisted by six advocates-general who help investigate cases before the court and express opinions on the issues involved in the litigation, but have no vote in deciding the cases. The advocate-general assigned to a case will study the issues involved before the judges begin their deliberations, and submit a lengthy written opinion. The judges may well be influenced by the advocate-general's point of view and adopt his decision as their own, but they are not required to do so.

Powers of the Bodies. The Commission initiates legislation (including the annual budget) and enforces the law of the community. The Council makes the final legislative and policy decisions that the Commission enforces. The Assembly is a consulting agency, with no legislative power except for the budget, though it has the power to remove the commissioners from office by a two-thirds vote. (It cannot remove individual commissioners, however; it can only remove the entire body.) The Court of Justice interprets the community law and decides cases involving it.

With respect to legislation other than the budget, the Commission makes a proposal that is submitted to the Assembly. The Assembly debates the matter and makes its opinion known to the Council and to the Commission. The Commission may then amend the proposal based upon the Assembly's recommendations, but it is not obligated to do so. The Council will then enact the Commission's proposal, amend it, or refuse to enact it. Amendment of a Commission proposal can be done only by unanimous vote. Approval requires fifty-four affirmative votes. If the proposal does not receive fifty-four Council votes it is rejected. Should the Council pass the proposal, the Assembly has a second chance to debate it, and may then amend or reject it. The Council may then override the Assembly, but only by unanimous vote.

With respect to the budget, the Commission proposes a preliminary budget and sends it to the Council. The Council may amend this budget if it wishes and then sends the draft budget to the Assembly. The Assembly may amend the draft and send it back to the Council. The Council may accept or reject the Assembly amendments and send the revised draft back to the Assembly. The Assembly may then reject the draft by a two-thirds vote; if it does not do this the budget is accepted.

Thus the Assembly has a veto power over the budget.

The Court of Justice acts as an umpire in disputes between the other three bodies, having the power to annul acts of Council or Commission that are contrary to the community basic law. It may act on behalf of private persons or organizations under three circumstances: (1) in claims by community servants (employees) against the community; (2) to assess penalties against community organs for wrongs done to private individuals; and (3) to issue interpretations of community law in cases before national courts involving this law.

Much community law (such as antitrust law) is binding upon private parties. Where there is a conflict between community law and national law, the commuity law naturally prevails. Court of Justice interpretations of community law are naturally binding throughout the community. Cases involving arguments over proper application of community law may be appealed from the highest national courts to the Court of Justice.

Community Financial Resources. Customs duties throughout the community are levied by the community; the revenue is community revenue. As of now there is no other community taxation power.

Much community revenue is therefore contributed by community governments according to an agreed formula. There is argument among the members as to the fairness of the formula; the British in particular argue that they contribute more to the community than they take out.

The Common Market. The twelve nations of the community by joining entered into a common market. Within this Common Market there will eventually be:

1. Free movement of goods
2. Free movement of persons
3. Freedom of establishment
4. Freedom to provide services
5. Free movement of capital
6. Free movement of payments

Eventually goods will be movable across any frontier between Common Market members without delay or taxation. Intracommunity customs barriers have almost ceased to exist. Some restrictions on importation of agricultural produce from other members and border taxes based upon value-added tax differentials between the members, however, continue to exist.

In the Single European Act adopted by the community and its members the organization has committed itself to completion of the Common Market by 1992. Theoretically, that year should mark the end of barriers to the passage of goods, services, capital, and people across the frontiers between community nations.

Citizens of the member nations already have the right to settle and live anywhere within the community, subject to a few restrictions. Each nation still retains the right to exclude citizens of other community nations on grounds of public policy, public security, or public health.

A business organization from one member nation must not be forbidden to set up a branch or the like in another because of its nationality. However, where the local law sets up organizational requirements for business organizations, a firm from a member nation that does not meet these could be denied entry.

In theory no restrictions should exist upon the movement of capital across the national frontiers of the community members for investment purposes and the like. But the theory has yet to be put into full practice. Member nations reserve the right to enact exchange controls and to impose other restrictions on the free flow of capital when the state of their domestic economies seems to require it.

No barriers now exist to the movement of money across frontiers of community nations in payment for goods and services. This is one dream that has been realized.

Professionals and licensed tradespeople should in theory be able to practice their trades or professions anywhere within the community. However, since professions — such as law and medicine — and trades — such as auto mechanics and beauticians — are licensed in all member nations, problems with respect to mutual recognition of such licenses continue to impede compliance with this ideal. Some nations set higher standards for licensees than others, and are therefore reluctant to admit foreigners licensed under lower standards to practice. Efforts are in progress to harmonize these licensing requirements, but they are proceeding slowly. Thus, freedom of establishment remains to a large extent a dream rather than a reality.

Community Policies. The community has established policies to unify approaches regarding aggravating problems. Thus there is an agriculture policy intended to promote the well-being of the agricultural sectors of all of the national economies while promoting free trade in agricultural produce. A fisheries policy is intended to do the same for that industry. A transport policy is intended to harmonize national regulations of trucks, railway trains, and inland waterway barges, etc., so that border delays caused by differing regulations are eliminated.

The community antitrust laws are enforced as a part of the competition policy of the organization. These will be discussed later.

The tax policy requires every member nation to levy a value-added tax, but at the moment each member nation is free to set its own tax rates. A long-term objective in this area is harmonization of indirect taxation throughout the community. At the moment the tax policy is not applicable to direct taxes, such as income taxes. In that area the member nations are free to do as they please.

Economic policy is intended to formulate a common approach to problems in this area throughout the community. Since the economies of the member nations are so very different and since each member has some unique problem areas, harmonization here will be difficult.

Monetary policy foresees monetary union within the community in the near future. Already a common monetary unit for the community exists: the European Currency Unit (ECU). At present the ECU is a unit of account only, though Belgium has issued some bills and coins denominated in ECU. Ultimately English pounds, French francs, and Spanish pesetas will cease to exist and the ECU will circulate as money throughout most of Western Europe.

Social policy is concerned with harmonizing the welfare state programs of the various member nations and fighting unemployment. A distant goal is to make all community citizens eligible for the same government benefits no matter where they live and work.

The community is obligated to create an energy policy, but very little has been done in this area. The members still primarily look out for number one here. Environmental policies are in the works, but not much has been done.

Spadework has been completed on a consumer protection policy to harmonize national laws in this important area.

Thus the European Community has become an international organization of considerable power. In some respects it has the attributes of a nation. Over the long term it may well become a United States of Western Europe, one of the most powerful nation-states on earth.

Other International Organizations

Organization for Economic Cooperation and Development (OECD). This organization consists of most of the nations of Western Europe plus the United States, Canada, Japan, Australia, New Zealand, and Yugoslavia. Its members cooperate to carry out the objectives in the organization's title. It operates through a council, to which all member nations belong. Decisions must be unanimous. One of its most useful functions is the collection and dissemination of statistics on the economic status of its members and of the world.

The Council of Europe. This organization, not to be confused with the European Community, has twenty-one members. The nations of the European Community are members, plus such countries as Norway, Sweden, Iceland, Switzerland, Austria, Liechtenstein, Malta, Cyprus, and Turkey. It has a Committee of Ministers composed of representatives of the governments of the twenty-one member states, and a Consultative Assembly consisting of members of the national parliaments. These two organs are primarily debating societies where problems affecting Western Europe are discussed.

The one area where organs of the council exercise some real power is with respect to the enforcement of the European Convention on Human

Rights. This convention guarantees to the people of the member nations a wide assortment of human rights — not only those contained in the Bill of Rights of the United States Constitution but some additional ones, such as the right to marry and found a family. Any citizen of any member state who is denied any basic right guaranteed by the convention may complain to the European Commission on Human Rights, which consists of twenty-one members, one from each member nation. The complaint will be considered only if the person complaining has exhausted all remedies provided by the law of the country he is complaining against.

The commission investigates the complaint, and if it proves well-founded tries to work out a settlement between the complainant and the country involved. If this effort fails the case may be brought before the Court of Human Rights.

This court consists of twenty-one judges, chosen by the Consultative Assembly for nine-year terms on a basis of one judge per member nation. Its decisions are binding upon the parties. It has become one of the more important world enforcers of human rights.

The Organization of American States (OAS). This Western Hemisphere organization has thirty-two members, comprising most of the independent nations of North and South America and the Caribbean Basin. It has a General Assembly in which each member has a vote. The General Assembly elects a secretary-general. It is essentially a collective security organization. It has no law-making authority, and its decisions are not binding upon its members.

Like the Council of Europe, however, the OAS is now involved in the task of preserving human rights. Through its Inter-American Commission on Human Rights, consisting of seven persons elected by the General Assembly for four-year terms, it hears complaints of violation of the American Convention on Human Rights, a document very similar to (but not identical to) the European Convention. Like the Court of Human Rights, this body's decisions are binding upon the parties.

The Andean Common Market. The Andean Common Market consists of five countries located on the west coast of South America: Chile, Bolivia, Peru, Ecuador, and Colombia. The members are making a serious effort to integrate their national economies. They have not eliminated customs barriers between themselves as yet, but the organization has promoted trade relationships between the members.

The Central American Common Market. The Central American Common Market, including Guatemala, Honduras, El Salvador, Costa Rica, and Nicaragua, was formed in 1960 with the intent to integrate the Central American economy. Though much progress was made during the 1960s, advancement has now stopped. The virtual civil war in El Salvador, the endemic guerrilla warfare in Guatemala, and the unsettling effects of the

Sandinista revolution in Nicaragua have virtually destroyed the political stability of the area. Without a restoration of tranquillity in these countries further progress is out of the question.

The Arab League. This organization of Arabic-speaking nations provides a forum for discussion of problems common to its members. Its Council is the league's primary organ. It also has a Secretariat and a secretary-general. It has no law-making authority. It has engaged in peace-keeping activities, most notably in Kuwait and Lebanon.

The Organization of African Unity (OAU). This is an organization of independent African nations. Its primary organ is the Assembly of Heads of State and Governments. Its meetings are essentially summit conferences of the heads of the member states. It has no law-making authority.

Its actions are primarily political. It seeks, among other things, the end of apartheid in South Africa and the true independence of Namibia.

Association of Southeast Asian Nations (ASEAN). This is an association of the non–Communist nations of southeast Asia, dedicated to promoting economic and political co-operation between them. It has annual ministerial conferences and a permanent Standing Committee. It makes no effort to enact law binding on its members.

Council for Mutual Economic Aid (COMECON). This is in a sense the Soviet bloc equivalent of the European Community. Its members include the Soviet Union and its loyal European satellites. It has not developed the elaborate organization of the European Community, probably because the fraternal co-operation of the Communist parties of the member nations makes possible a high degree of co-ordination between the respective national economies.

Chapter 9

Nature of International Law

First among the multiple sources of international law is *Custom.* European nations have had dealings with each other as long as they have existed, and over the centuries unwritten conventions have come into being to make these dealings smoother. National courts do not hesitate to cite international custom as the reason for decision in appropriate cases. A second source is *Treaties,* agreements between national governments. These may be international agreements involving many nations, bilateral agreements involving two nations, or regional agreements. Examples of international agreements involving many of the world's nations are the Hague Conventions of 1899 and 1907 on the law of war and the Genocide Convention of 1948. Other sources of international law include *General Principles of Law, Judicial Decisions,* and *Writings of Experts.*

Principles of International Law

Treaties. The United States Constitution provides that treaties are the supreme law of the land. However, whether or not a treaty becomes the supreme law of the United States depends in part upon whether or not it is self-executing. If it is self-executing it becomes part of the law of the land without supplemental congressional legislation. If it is not self-executing Congress must enact legislation to implement it. Most treaties are not self-executing. The major exception is treaties that end wars; upon Senate ratification, the state of war between the United States and the other nation ends. Thus, an international agreement in the form of a treaty will not bind the United States, even if ratified by the Senate, unless Congress enacts legislation to execute it.

If a conflict arises between a treaty and national law, the rules for resolving it under American law are complex. If the conflict is between the treaty and the United States Constitution, the Constitution usually prevails because the government of the United States has no right to change the

Constitution by treaty. However, the federal courts might well uphold the treaty by changing their interpretation of the conflicting constitutional provision. If the conflict is between a treaty and federal legislation the solution will depend upon priority of enactment. If the enabling legislation of the treaty came after the conflicting statute the treaty prevails. If the conflicting statute came after the enabling legislation of the treaty courts will try to harmonize the two enactments to keep both in force. However, if the later legislation repeals the enabling legislation expressly or by implication the later legislation prevails. If the conflict is between a treaty and state or local legislation, the treaty prevails.

The position of treaties in the law of other nations is not necessarily the same as in American law. In Great Britain, international agreements duly ratified do not become part of English domestic law unless made a part of domestic legislation by act of Parliament. Treaties alone are generally not a part of the law of the land. In France treaties become domestic law only if ratified in the form of enactment of ordinary legislation. Once a treaty has been so ratified, it cannot be "repealed" by subsequent conflicting legislation. Treaties are thus superior to all ordinary legislation, but not to the national constitution. In the Netherlands a duly ratified treaty becomes the law of the land and is superior to even the national constitution. Thus the Dutch cannot repeal a treaty even by constitutional amendment.

Sovereign Immunity. A principle of law that is as old as law itself is *The King Can Do No Wrong.* Even in those monarchies in which the king was theoretically subject to law and thus could not do as he pleased, an unhappy subject had no right to sue the monarch in his own national courts. Republican governments adopted the same principle, now transformed into *The State Can Do No Wrong.*

Only in modern times has the principle been somewhat abrogated. In France the state is almost as responsible for its wrongdoings as is any private party. Other national governments have accepted liability for some, but not all, of their acts. Thus in the United States persons who have contracts with the federal government may make claims for breach, but in most cases these claims are heard by administrative agencies rather than by the regular courts. Those who are the victims of torts committed by federal employees may sue in the regular courts under the provisions of the Federal Tort Claims Act. Most state governments have also accepted liability for torts of their employees and for breach of contract.

If a monarch would not allow himself to be sued in the courts of his own country, he would be much less likely to tolerate being sued in a foreign court. On the principle that every monarch should be master in his own kingdom and not be called to account for his acts in another realm, the principle of *Sovereign Immunity* became universally accepted; this principle holds that a sovereign may not be sued in a foreign court.

Republican governments had no difficulty in accepting the principle. It mattered not what form the foreign government had assumed: it could not be sued outside its realm without its own consent.

As national governments began accepting responsibility to residents of their realm for their wrongdoings, they began to reconsider the notion of absolute immunity of foreign governments from suit in their courts. The notion began to gain ground that it is only proper to immunize a government against suit in another country's courts if the government is acting as a government. If the government is acting as a business (engaging in commercial activity), it should be held as responsible for its acts as any other business. As the United States shifted from the absolute theory of sovereign immunity, which holds that a foreign government cannot be sued here under any circumstances, to the theory of limited immunity, which holds that a foreign government could be sued for its wrongful commercial acts, the courts allowed the executive branch of the federal government to decide when a claim of sovereign immunity should be allowed. This was a pragmatic solution to the problem, but it allowed considerations of diplomacy and international politics to take precedence over considerations of legal right and wrong.

To give the courts more authority in this area Congress enacted the Foreign Sovereign Immunity Act (P.L. 94–583, 90 Stat. 2892, 28 USC 1330, 1332(a), 1391(f), 1441(d), 1602–1611) in 1976. This statute provides that foreign states may not be sued in American courts and their assets may not be seized by creditors unless authorized by law. This statute, and the positions taken by other governments on this sensitive issue, will be discussed in Chapter 16, the chapter on transnational law enforcement.

Act of State Doctrine. If a monarch was to be free to rule his own subjects as he saw fit, no other monarch would have the right to question the lawfulness of his acts. This notion came to be generally accepted, giving birth to the *Act of State Doctrine*. The principle is simplicity itself. The acts of governments are to be considered lawful within their own boundaries.

Unlike the notion of sovereign immunity, the act of state doctrine has never become a principle of international law. It is rather a matter of comity, or good manners between nations.

How this principle influences international business will also be discussed in the final chapter.

Recognition of States. A potential state must meet four criteria to qualify for recognition from other states. These are (1) *Territory,* (2) *Population,* (3) *Government,* and (4) *Independence.*

A national *territory* need not be large. The smallest nation state on earth is Vatican City, with an area of less than a square mile. The European microstates of Monaco, San Marino, Liechtenstein, and Andorra each contain less territory than a small American county. The frontiers of a new state need not be definite and certain. For instance, the borders of Israel were most uncertain when she was recognized as a state in 1948, and they remain somewhat uncertain to the present day. Is all of Jerusalem legitimately Israeli? What should be the status of the Golan Heights? What should be the fate of the Gaza Strip, and of the West Bank of the Jordan?

The national *population* need not be large. The Republic of Nauru has less than ten thousand inhabitants. Andorra, Monaco, San Marino, and Liechtenstein each have less than fifty thousand.

A *government* may take any reasonable form. The main requirement is that it have some control over the territory and people of the nation. It should be located on the territory and among the people it is supposed to govern.

The government must be *independent,* able to conduct its foreign relations free of the dictation of other nations, and must have the intent and the capacity to carry out its international obligations.

The decision whether or not to recognize the existence of a state is the decision of individual national governments. It is to a large extent a political rather than a legal decision. For pragmatic reasons, an entity possessing the four requisites of statehood will usually be recognized — after all, it is there — private business may be done with its citizens, and it makes sense to deal with it as is.

Sometimes the question arises whether members of a federation are entitled to the privileges of a nation. The answer will depend in part upon the constitution of the federation. The cantons of Switzerland may enter into treaties with other nations when these do not infringe upon the sovereignty of the Swiss federal government. The states that comprised the pre–World War I German Empire could do the same. The states of the United States and most other federal nations do not have such power. An entity with treaty-making authority has at least some of the attributes of national existence; one without that authority does not. Thus most members of federations are not recognized as nations.

Dependencies and Colonies. Many nations claim sovereignty over the lands that are not attached to their home territories — islands, for example, or portions of another continent, or perhaps just nearby enclaves surrounded by the territory of a neighbor. An example of such an enclave is Campione d'Italia, on the shore of Lake Lugano a few miles south of Lugano, Switzerland. Campione is part of Italy, but it is entirely surrounded by Swiss territory.

These more or less distant possessions may be treated as integral component parts of the homeland, or as political entities separate and distinct from the homeland. France has incorporated many of her overseas possessions into herself, treating them as part of herself. Thus the Caribbean islands of Martinique and Guadeloupe, the Atlantic islands of St. Pierre and Miquelon (off the coast of Newfoundland), the Indian Ocean islands of Mayotte and Reunion, and French Guiana on the South American coast are French departments. Their residents vote in French national elections and elect deputies to the French Parliament. The Spanish flag flies over the Balearic Islands in the Mediterranean, the Canary Islands in the Atlantic, and the towns of Ceuta and Melilla on the coast of Morocco. These are all legally a part of Spain.

Great Britain does not choose to incorporate her distant possessions into the United Kingdom. Queen Elizabeth II is their sovereign, but they have local self-government, do not elect members of the House of Commons, and are not governed by legislation enacted in London. Thus the Channel Islands of Jersey, Guernsey, and Sark (off the coast of Normandy), the Isle of Man (in the Irish Sea, between Great Britain and Ireland), Gibraltar (at the southern tip of Spain), Hong Kong, the Cayman Islands (in the Caribbean, not far from Jamaica), Bermuda (a few hundred miles off the North Carolina coast), the Falkland Islands (in the south Atlantic, site of war between Great Britain and Argentina in 1982), the south Atlantic islands of Ascension, Tristan da Cunha, and St. Helena, and the island of Pitcairn (isolated in the far Pacific) rule themselves under the British Union Jack.

The Dutch flag flies over the islands of the Netherlands Antilles in the Caribbean (Curaçao, Aruba, Bonaire, and some others), but the islanders govern themselves. The Danish flag flies over frozen Greenland, but the handful of islanders enjoy local self-government. One of the oldest colonies of the world is Macao, the Portuguese possession on the Chinese coast a short boat ride from Hong Kong. This and the island chains of the Azores and Madeiras in the Atlantic enjoy self-government under the red and green Portuguese flag.

The fact that some dependencies of major nations enjoy local self-government makes them of potential interest to international businessmen, because their economic and legal environments are not necessarily the same as that of the country whose flag is seen on all flagpoles there.

Recognition of Governments. Sometimes two or more groups claim to be the legitimate rulers of a nation. The world's other nations must then decide which group to recognize as the true government. The decision may be important, for the acts of the unrecognized national government may not be recognized as valid under the act of state doctrine, it may not be able to use the defense of sovereign immunity to protect itself against suits in the courts of other nations, and agreements with it may not be recognized as lawful treaties.

The general rule in the world community is that if a government effectively controls the territory and people of the nation it is entitled to recognition. If it exercises control but its tenure is uncertain, *De Facto* recognition is conferred. Such recognition may be revoked later if conditions change. If its control is certain, with no challenges in sight, *De Jure* recognition will be conferred. This is theoretically permanent and irrevocable, as long as the government holds power.

The United States no longer makes the distinction between de facto and de jure recognition of foreign governments. All American recognitions are essentially de jure.

If there is constitutional continuity between one group of rulers and another, no question of denial of recognition will arise. George Bush succeeded Ronald Reagan as president of the United States through constitutional processes; the change of government was unchallengeably legitimate. Adolf Hitler lawfully succeeded Kurt von Schleicher as chancellor of Germany through another constitutional process, appointment to the post by President Paul von Hindenburg. Though the world knew that Hitler intended to destroy the constitutional basis of the German Weimar Republic, no one could doubt the lawfulness of his assumption of power.

Even when there is no constitutional continuity between a government and its successor (as in the recent changes of government in Haiti, Paraguay, and Burma), the successor will normally be recognized if it is able to control the nation's territory.

Continuity of States. A state is generally held responsible for the acts of preceding governments of that state, even if the successor government claimed its predecessor was unconstitutional. A revolutionary government often seeks to repudiate the obligations of its predecessor, as the Bolsheviks did with respect to obligations of the czarist government of Russia. In the days of gunboat diplomacy the great powers might have tried to crush such notions by the use of military force, but this happens no longer. If the revolutionaries have any staying power at all, their efforts succeed.

A change of government in a state will have no effect on claims belonging to that state. The successor may prosecute claims acquired by the predecessor. Thus, Americans damaged a ship belonging to the French government in 1869. Before the government of Emperor Napoleon III got around to filing suit on its claim, it was overthrown as a result of France's defeat in the Franco-Prussian War. The successor provisional republican government filed suit on the claim. Though the American defendants argued that the claim had died with Napoleon III's regime, the United States Supreme Court did not agree. The new republican government was said to have "inherited" all claims of the old imperial government intact.

When a state annexes another, the position will depend upon whether the annexation was voluntary or involuntary. When voluntary, the annexing state becomes a successor government, acquiring all of the assets and liabilities of the annexed state. Such was the case when the United States annexed Texas in 1845 and Hawaii in 1898. Both of these were accomplished by treaty, at least in theory with the consent of the annexed.

When a state acquires territory from another, the law of the annexed area is not automatically changed by the annexation. Thus when the United States purchased the Louisiana Territory from France, the pre-existing French law remained in force in that vast area. American settlers quickly replaced it with American law everywhere except in the present state of Louisiana, where the French-speaking majority decided to retain their French legal system.

Wars, coups, and revolutions play havoc with the orderly mundane affairs of humanity. International law seeks to maintain a semblance of order when these occur, but often the legal consequences of these catastrophes depend upon the power of the gun and the vagaries of international and domestic politics. One cannot be sure about the legal effects of these upheavals until all of the dust has settled. Anyone owning valuable investments in such areas will pass many sleepless nights until this has occurred (and maybe for a long while thereafter).

Nationality. Nearly all people, things, and organizations possess nationality in that they are thought of as "belonging" to a nation.

Individuals may acquire nationality by birth or by naturalization. How is a matter of national law. There are two principles in use for determining nationality by birth. Those nations using *Jus Sanguinis* hold that the children of parents who are nationals acquire their parents' nationality, no matter where they are born. This is the oldest and most commonly used principle. Those nations making *Jus Soli* part of their laws hold that a person born on the nation's soil is a national, regardless of the nationality of the child's parents. This principle is used most often by nations whose populations are composed to a large extent of immigrants from abroad.

The United States uses both jus soli and jus sanguinis. Thus if a Mexican mother-to-be living in Ciudad Juarez, Mexico, crosses into El Paso, Texas, to give birth to her child, the child will be an American citizen, even if both parents are Mexican. The child born in Ireland to an American father and an Irish mother will also be an American citizen due to the father's American citizenship. If even one of a child's parents is an American citizen, the child may claim American citizenship.

Great Britain also uses both jus soli and jus sanguinis. As with us, if one of the parents of a child born outside Great Britain has United Kingdom citizenship the child may claim UK citizenship. The Soviet Union too uses both jus soli and jus sanguinis. However, for a child to acquire Soviet citizenship by jus sanguinis both parents must be Soviet citizens.

Switzerland uses only jus sanguinis. Thus, the child born on Swiss soil to Italian parents will not be a Swiss citizen. However, the child born on American soil to an American mother and a Swiss father will be able to claim Swiss citizenship. Israel uses an extreme form of jus sanguinis, its Law of the Return. Any Jew from anywhere in the world may claim Israeli citizenship by coming to Israel and settling there.

All of the world's nations use jus sanguinis as a determiner of nationality. Those using jus soli use it only in combination with jus sanguinis. Some of the nations using jus sanguinis only grant citizenship through the child's father, not through its mother, though the number doing this diminishes as the nations granting equal rights to women increase in number.

It is possible for a child to be born with two or even three nationalities. The child of Mexican parents born in an El Paso, Texas, hospital will acquire American citizenship by jus soli and Mexican citizenship by jus sanguinis. The child born in the United States to a Swiss father and an English mother would acquire three nationalities: American by being born here, Swiss through its father, and British through its mother.

Naturalization may be *Voluntary, Derivative,* or *Involuntary.* Virtually all nations have established procedures for allowing aliens to voluntarily acquire their nationality. The procedure varies from nation to nation. Under American law the alien must reside here for five years as a permanent resident (three years if married to an American citizen), be a person of good moral character, be fluent in English, and pass an examination in American history and government.

Derivative naturalization may occur in numerous ways. Generally minor children are naturalized along with their parents, without any necessity for them to apply for naturalization in their own names. In a few nations a woman acquires nationality by derivation when she marries a male national. This was the law of the United States until 1922, and of Switzerland until 1988. The alien woman who marries a Frenchman does not automatically become French, but she may at once claim French citizenship by filing required documentation with the proper French authorities. Hardly ever does this principle work in reverse; nations will not grant their nationality to the alien male who marries a female national. In a few nations, such as Austria, one acquires nationality by derivation when one becomes a university professor in the country.

Involuntary naturalization occurs when territory of one nation is annexed by another. Thus, when Austria was incorporated into Germany in 1938 Austrians involuntarily became German citizens. When Austria became a nation again in 1945 her residents ceased to be German and became Austrian once more, though those Austrians who had moved to Germany and wanted to remain German were allowed to do so.

Naturalization may cause a person to acquire dual nationality. It will not for the American born with only American nationality, because such a person who undergoes naturalization in another land is automatically expatriated; he loses his American citizenship. (There is one exception to this rule. The American Jew who goes to Israel and accepts Israeli citizenship rights under the Law of the Return will not lose his American citizenship on the basis that he has not been naturalized as an Israeli.)

The Soviet Union holds that its citizens will not lose their nationality through naturalization abroad. Its rule is: once a Soviet citizen always a Soviet citizen, unless the Soviet government decides otherwise. Switzerland takes a similar stand. Thus the Swiss citizen who becomes an American through naturalization may choose to remain Swiss by filing the required documents with the proper Swiss authorities.

A person may lose nationality through expatriation. This may be voluntary; an American may choose to renounce his American citizenship by following a simple procedure. Before 1922 an American woman suffered automatic expatriation by marrying a foreign national (under the law of a few nations female citizens may still suffer expatriation in this way). Until the 1960s Americans would suffer expatriation by enlisting in the armed forces of another state or by voting in a foreign election. This is no longer true.

The Soviet Union and some other nations may expatriate nationals by administrative action and banish them from their soil. The Soviet government may also expatriate its citizens who become naturalized citizens of other states, but it does not always do so.

It is possible for an individual to become stateless, to be a person with no nationality. The Soviet citizen who is expelled from the USSR and involuntarily expatriated will be in this situation. The American who renounces his American citizenship before acquiring another nationality will also be stateless. The refugee who has no documentary proof of his place of birth or of the nationality of his parents has been a common sort of stateless person during the twentieth century. The children of such refugees will be born stateless if born in a nation that does not recognize jus soli.

Nationality confers a package of rights and duties upon an individual. Among the rights are the following: (1) the right to come "home" whenever the national desires; (2) the right to assistance from his country's diplomats when he has difficulties abroad; and (3) unlimited rights to vote, hold public office, and otherwise enjoy the benefits of membership in the national community. Among the duties are: (1) the duty to pay taxes, perhaps even if the national lives abroad and earns his income abroad; and (2) the duty to perform military service when such duty is imposed.

Ships, aircraft, motor vehicles, etc., also have nationality. A ship has the nationality of the nation where it is registered and of the flag it flies. This nation may not be the nation of the nationality of the ship's owners. Many American-owned ships are registered in Liberia, Panama, and other nations with lax regulation of ocean-going vessels. Aircraft and motor vehicles also have the nationality of the nation where they are registered.

Corporations also have nationality. Three tests are commonly used to determine the nationality of a corporation: (1) the nation of incorporation; (2) the *Siège Social,* that is, the nation where the corporation's headquarters are and where it does most of its business; and (3) the nationality of its controlling shareholders. The United States generally uses the first test. France and many other Romano-Germanic law countries use the second test. The third test is used for taxation purposes, and to identify enemy-owned assets in wartime.

Jurisdiction. A state has criminal jurisdiction over persons, or organizations when it has the power to subject such to its criminal law. States may claim jurisdiction on the following bases: (1) territoriality, (2) nationality, (3) security, (4) protective principle, (5) universality, and (6) crimes against international law.

Whenever a violation of a state's criminal law takes place upon its soil, it may prosecute the violator, whether or not he is a national of the prosecuting state, under *the principle of territoriality.* This is a universally recognized principle.

When a national of a state commits a crime abroad, under some circumstances he may be subject to prosecution in his home country. For instance, an American businessman may be prosecuted in a United States court for antitrust violations committed abroad under *the principle of nationality.* The United States does not apply this principle across the board. The American who murders another American in France could not be tried for the offense in an American court. The French, however, will try a French citizen for a crime committed anywhere on earth.

When a national commits an offense abroad that endangers his nation's *security* he may be tried in his home nation's courts. Thus the Englishman William Joyce, known as "Lord Haw Haw," was tried for and convicted of treason in an English court for broadcasting pro–Nazi propaganda from Germany during World War II.

When a person causes damage to a national of a country from outside that country, he may be prosecuted if he sets foot in the country of the person he injured under *the protective principle.* Thus a Texas newspaper owner who defamed a Mexican national in his Texas newspaper was prosecuted in a Mexican court for the offense, though the defamation was printed in Texas. The criminal law of the United States does not often recognize this principle. However, when a French firm and a Canadian firm made a bargain that defrauded minority American shareholders of the Canadian company, American authorities took action against a Canadian individual involved in the deal.

Most nations claim the right to criminally prosecute pirates for acts committed anywhere in the world under *the principle of universality.* It is argued that the universality principle should also be applied against terrorists and hijackers of ships and aircraft, though no agreement exists on that point as yet.

Most nations claim the right to try violators of *international criminal law* for injury to their nationals, even if the crime was not committed on the nation's soil. Thus Israel tried and executed Adolf Eichmann for crimes committed against Jews in Germany and elsewhere in Europe.

Extradition. When a person accused of a crime in Ruritania is known to be in Gerolstein, Ruritanian authorities may request the Gerolsteiner authorities to arrest him and send him back to Ruritania to stand trial. The Gerolsteiner are quite likely to do this as a matter of international comity, but, in the absence of an extradition treaty between the two countries, they are not obligated to do so.

Extradition duties may be spelled out in bilateral treaties between nations. Older treaties spell out in detail each extraditable offense. Newer treaties may simply state that crimes for which the permissible punishment is more than "X" (maybe two years' imprisonment) are extraditable. Acts that are serious crimes under the laws of both nations, for example, murder, theft, and rape, are covered in all such treaties.

If the offense with which our Ruritanian fugitive is charged is not a crime under the law of Gerolstein, Gerolstein will not extradite him. Political offenses, economic offenses, and tax offenses are generally not covered by these treaties. Thus, if our Ruritanian is wanted for slandering the prime minister of Ruritania, or for violation of Ruritanian exchange control laws, or for evasion of Ruritanian income tax Gerolstein probably will not extradite.

Many nations will not extradite their own nationals to stand trial abroad. The United States does not follow this policy as a general rule — occasionally the United States will extradite an American national. In some of our extradition treaties it is agreed that we need not do this. Germany and some other nations refuse to do this as a matter of course.

Civil Jurisdiction. The circumstances under which courts will accept jurisdiction over civil litigation vary from nation to nation and legal system to legal system. This problem will be discussed at length in the final chapter of this work.

Rights of Aliens. Theoretically every nation has absolute authority to keep aliens off its soil. No one has an absolute right in international law to visit a country of which he is not a national.

Few, if any, nations refuse entry to all aliens, but many will not allow certain aliens to visit certain places. Thus, no nation gives aliens (or even its own citizens) unrestricted access to its military installations.

Many western European nations allow other western Europeans to cross their frontiers without passports — a national identity card is sufficient for identification. For many non–Europeans, such as Americans, a passport is required.

During much of the twentieth century the United States has been more inhospitable. Not only do we require passports of most of our foreign visitors, we also require a *Visa* (official U.S. government permission to visit us). Of the nations of western Europe, only France presently requires visas of most foreign guests. A state may require *Transit Visas* of people crossing their states to reach another state; thus a person traveling from Japan to western Europe via the Trans-Siberian Railroad would need a Soviet transit visa permitting him to cross the Soviet Union on the journey.

Many nations restrict the right of their own nationals to travel abroad. Citizens of the Soviet Union need special permission to travel outside their country, and such permission is difficult to come by. Americans may travel to Canada and Mexico without passports, but need them to visit more distant places. Also, American passports are not valid for travel to Cuba, North Korea, Vietnam, and Kampuchea; he who goes to one of these lands without special government permission commits a criminal offense.

It is much easier to visit another nation than it is to establish permanent residence there. The United States limits the number of persons admitted per year for permanent residence, giving preference to close relatives of American citizens and those who have job skills in demand in the United States. Most other nations also impose such restrictions. During the 1950s and 1960s Australia had a very generous immigration policy because she wanted to increase her population. However, the global recession of the 1970s created unemployment problems even in "the land down under" and her government changed its policy, severely restricting immigration.

Citizens of member nations of the European Community have the right to establish residence in other member nations of the community. Great Britain is generous in allowing citizens of nations of the British Commonwealth to immigrate. France is similarly generous to citizens of former French colonies.

Most of the world's nations allow their people to emigrate without hindrance. The Soviet Union and other Communist nations are a major exception. Soviet citizens must receive an *Exit Visa* from their government before forsaking their homeland, and such visas are not readily granted.

Aliens have two basic rights in their host countries: the right to personal security and the right to basic justice. No country can guarantee an alien freedom from the attention of its criminals, but it can guarantee the same quality of police protection accorded its own citizens. It should not allow or encourage its own citizens to harm its guests.

The requirement that aliens be granted basic justice is not necessarily a requirement that they be granted due process of law American-style. It is simply that the courts of a nation must treat aliens as they treat their own citizens. Thus the Saudi Arab in the United States is indeed entitled to due process of law American-style. But the American in Saudi Arabia would be entitled to no more than due process of law Saudi-style, which could include amputation of the right hand for theft.

The argument is made that all national governments owe to all persons within their borders respect for basic human rights. In the best of all possible worlds this would be accepted without argument. However, many of the world's governments do not grant basic human rights to their own citizens. If a state treats its own citizens inhumanely, can it be expected to treat aliens any better?

Theoretically aliens should enjoy the same property rights as a nation's citizens. In practice this is seldom observed. Virtually all nations restrict alien ownership of property to a degree, especially the right of aliens to own land and to own business enterprises affecting the host nation's military and economic security. But the alien's rights to property he is permitted to own should be as secure as the property rights of the host nation's citizens. Thus in the United States aliens may not own broadcasting station or domestic airlines, and some states restrict their right to own land, but the right of the alien to property he may lawfully own is as secure as that of any U.S. citizen.

However, in time of war or national emergency alien property rights may be restricted in the name of national security. Property owned by enemy aliens was sequestered by the United States government during both world wars. In fact, Japanese assets in the United States — including Japanese-owned bank accounts and the like — were frozen in July 1941, five months before the Japanese attack on Pearl Harbor and American entry into World War II.

One of the burning questions of private international law in the latter half of the twentieth century is the right, or lack thereof, of governments to expropriate property owned by aliens without payment of compensation. In the days before Marxist-Leninist revolutions, opinion was virtually unanimous that expropriation without compensation was contrary to international law, because no government would expropriate the property of its own citizens without paying compensation. Since the Bolshevik Revolution of 1917 that reality has changed. The Soviet government expropriated virtually all property in Russia without paying a penny in compensation to its former owners. Many revolutionary governments have since followed in Lenin's footsteps. If a revolutionary government may confiscate the property of its own citizens without compensation, how can it be expected to treat aliens any differently? The problem of expropriation will be discussed in more detail in Chapter 15.

Virtually all nations restrict the right to vote and to hold public office to citizens. Many restrict the right to practice learned professions, particularly law, to citizens.

The right to live in another nation does not necessarily include the right to work there. No alien present in the United States has the right to work here unless his visa permits it. In this age of high unemployment this state of affairs is almost universal. Work permits for aliens are hard to come by everywhere.

Within the European Community, it is general policy that each member nation must treat citizens of all member nations as nearly alike as possible. The Spaniard should have the right to live and work in Belgium if he wishes; the Englishman should have the right to live and work in Portugal if he wishes. The German doctor should have the right to practice medicine in Greece if he wishes; the English lawyer should have the right to practice his profession in Denmark if he wishes. The Italian who has worked for twenty years in Italy, paying the Italian social security taxes, should be able to take his welfare-state entitlement with him to the Netherlands if he decides to accept work there. This ideal has not quite been reached within the community; the coordination of social security systems, requirements for professional licenses, etc., is a complex task. Eventually, however, the goal of equal treatment for all community citizens will be reached.

Asylum. Most nations will take in residents of other nations for humanitarian reasons despite their laws restricting immigration. This is the granting of asylum. Because of poor economic conditions, overpopulation, and other problems some nations are very reluctant to do this. Other nations have long traditions of being hospitable to the world's oppressed.

Rights of Citizens. The notion that citizens of a country should have rights in international law is a notion of recent origin. The traditional point of view has been that a government should be free to treat its citizens as it pleases, for otherwise it would not be sovereign within its own territory.

The Nations and Human Rights. Charles Humana graded most of the nations of the world on their respect for human rights as of January 1, 1987, in his book *World Human Rights Guide.* His criteria for evaluation included respect for the basic rights guaranteed by the Bill of Rights of the United States Constitution, a truly democratic political system, absence of a state religion and compulsory religious education in schools, absence of sex discrimination, the right to travel inside and outside the country, absence of the death penalty for crime, freedom to use contraceptive pills and devices, and the right to practice homosexuality between consenting adults.

No country attained a perfect grade, but five (Denmark, Finland, the Netherlands, New Zealand, and Sweden) received a mark of 98. The German Federal Republic and Norway received 97s. Austria, Belgium, and

Canada received 96s. The United States was relegated to a 90, primarily because elements of racial and sexual discrimination still exist here and abuses of police power occur at the local level of government. Negative marks are also assigned to the United States because the death penalty for crime is still imposed in most states, and the practice of homosexuality is still frowned upon.

At the other extreme, Ethiopia received the lowest mark with 13, followed by North Korea with 17, Iraq with 19, and the Soviet Union and Romania with 20 each. The Republic of South Africa scores 22, Bulgaria and China 23, and Mozambique 25.

The world average is 55. Hungary is the only country with that score; Algeria is her nearest neighbor at 54.

Every scheme of evaluation of this sort is of course somewhat subjective. Most of Humana's criteria for evaluation would be accepted as valid by both liberals and conservatives — though the absence of the death penalty and state toleration of homosexuality might not be counted as human rights plusses by some.

In the best of all possible worlds, there would be no governmental or other disrespect for human rights. In the next best, there would be a world authority with the power to force the nations to recognize the rights of their own citizens. In our world, there is no such authority. The enforcement of human rights remains for the most part a matter of national law, though in Europe the Court of Human Rights has authority to enforce the European Human Rights Convention on behalf of persons who have exhausted their domestic law remedies in member nations of the Council of Europe.

Thus, when we choose to play the game of life in someone else's ballpark, we are indeed forced to play by his rules. If his are more brutal than ours, it is our problem — nobody is forcing us to play there.

Chapter 10

The Export Transaction

It is possible to export goods and services abroad without making any direct investment in the importing country. This chapter considers the practical and legal framework of such transactions.

The Basic Contract

General Considerations. The American exporter needs to know that unique problems exist in the making of transnational business contracts. First, there is the language problem. Even if the foreign importer is receiving shipment in an English-speaking country, there are differences between American English and the English spoken in Great Britain or Australia. For instance, what Americans call "cookies" the English call "biscuits." What Americans call "garters" the English call "suspenders." What Americans call "a pharmacist" the English call "a chemist." What Americans call "a truck" the English call "a lorry." What Americans call "gasoline" the English call "petrol."

If the importer's first language is not English more problems can arise. If he knows English he may have learned it from an English person or from a native of his country who learned it in Great Britain. The European who understands our language is very likely to use British English rather than American English. But the Japanese or Korean on the other hand may have learned his English from an American or someone who learned English in this country; therefore he will understand American English.

If the importer's knowledge of English is imperfect or nonexistent other problems may arise. Some words look the same and mean the same in many languages, for example, English *coffee,* French *café,* German *Kaffee.* Others look the same in two languages but have different meanings. The German equivalent of English *gift* is *Geschenck. Gift* in German means *poison. Poison* has identical meaning in both English and French, but the very similar French *poisson* is English *fish.* What Americans call gasoline,

German speakers call *Benzin,* and German benzin bears no relationship to the petroleum distillate Americans call *benzine.*

If the exporter's knowledge of his customer's language is imperfect this can cause problems. German and Swedish both contain the noun *oel,* but the American who assumes that *oel* means the same in both languages could receive a rude awakening: German *Oel* is *oil,* Swedish *oel* is *beer.*

The maxim "say what you mean and mean what you say" applies in the negotiation of any contract, but it goes double in the transnational context. If the written bargain is to be in English, be certain that it means the same thing to your customer that it does to you. If it is to be written in your customer's language, be sure it means the same to you as it does to him.

In bargains involving large sums of money, the contract may be prepared in both languages. In such a case, one of the two versions should be designated as the official version because documents written in two languages are never completely identical — it is impossible to translate one language precisely into another.

If the importer is in a non–English-speaking country, he will be using the metric system of weights and measures. Thus he will weigh solids in kilograms, measure liquids in liters, and measure length in meters. Even if the importer is in an English-speaking country, if it uses the British Imperial measure for liquids its gallon will be larger than ours.

Currency of Payment. Thought should be given to the currency in which the price is stated, because in this era of floating currency exchange rates the value of one currency in terms of another may change by the hour. If the U.S. dollar is rising in world money markets it would be advantageous for the American exporter to state his price in dollars, because if it is stated in the importer's currency the exporter would receive fewer dollars on payment than he expected due to the depreciation of the importer's currency. But if the U.S. dollar is depreciating against the importer's currency it might be wise for the exporter to state his price in the importer's currency. He could thus earn a few dollars on the continuing dollar depreciation before payment.

The contract should also state the currency in which the price is to be paid. This is not necessarily the currency in which the price is quoted. Unless a contract says otherwise, the general rule is that the buyer pays in the currency of the state where payment is made. If this is not the currency in which the price was set, the buyer uses the exchange rate between the currencies on the date he pays to determine how much he pays.

It is possible for the exporter to *Hedge* his exchange-rate risk in the world money markets. One may buy or sell a currency for virtually immediate delivery in the *Spot* market; or one may buy or sell for delivery thirty, sixty, or ninety days in the future in the *Forward* market. Suppose that an American exporter sells goods to a Ruritanian importer for 160,000

Ruritanian glotnies (RG) payable in ninety days. The current exchange rate is RG 160 = U.S. $1. This means that anyone wanting to sell RG 160,000 for dollars right now would obtain U.S. $1000 for them, less brokerage commissions. This would be a spot transaction.

Our exporter probably has not got RG 160,000 to sell right now, but he should have RG 160,000 to sell ninety days from now. He could make a contract now to sell this quantity of glotnies ninety days from now in the forward market. This forward transaction will be at a rate very near the current rate of RG 160 per U.S. $1. He is thus protected against depreciation of the glotny over the next ninety days. (If the glotny appreciates in terms of the dollar, though, the exporter might regret making this forward transaction.)

If the Ruritanian importer agreed to pay U.S. $1000, he would assume a foreign exchange risk in case the glotny depreciates in terms of the dollar over the next ninety days. He could hedge by buying a forward contract for delivery of U.S. $1000 in ninety days, paying somewhere near RG 160 per dollar. His exchange rate would be locked in regardless of near-term fluctuations in the currency markets.

Governing Law. The exporter should also give thought to the law governing the contract. If the parties do not specify which law governs the contract, the question will be answered according to the rules of *Private International Law (Conflict of Laws)*. Most of the considerations to be taken into account here will be discussed in the last chapter of this work.

Before January 1, 1988, the law applicable to virtually all transnational contracts for sale of goods governed by American law was the Uniform Commercial Code. Its provisions were discussed in Chapter 2. On December 11, 1986, the United States ratified the *United Nations Convention on Contracts for the International Sale of Goods,* effective January 1, 1988. From that date on, this convention has controlled all transnational contracts governed by American law unless the contract itself provides otherwise.

To date only Argentina, Austria, China, Egypt, Finland, France, Hungary, Italy, Lesotho, Mexico, Sweden, Syria, the United States, Yugoslavia, and Zambia have adopted the convention, but other nations are certain to do so.

If both parties to the bargain are from nations that have adopted the convention, the convention governs unless the parties agree that some other law governs. Thus a contract between an American exporter and an Italian importer will be governed by the convention unless the contract provides otherwise. If the importer is in, say, Belgium, the convention will not automatically apply. If the rules of conflict of laws state that American law applies, the convention applies. If the rules state that Belgian law applies, the convention does not apply. Thus, it is vital that American exporters be aware of the provisions of the convention.

The rules regarding duration of offers are essentially Romano-Germanic. An offer is irrevocable if it says that it is, or if the offeree reasonably believes that it is, even if it is not put into writing (Art. 15).

With regard to acceptances, an acceptance of an offer must be received to be valid (Art. 18); this adopts the German rule.

A purported acceptance that varies the terms of the offer is a counteroffer, not an acceptance. The purported acceptance that adds terms to the offer without changing the fundamentals of the offer is, however, a valid acceptance. Silence by the offeror is agreement to the additional terms, as it is under the UCC (Art. 19).

The convention contains no provisions on mutual assent, consideration, capacity, or legality.

No contract of sale need be in writing (Art. 11).

A contract may be orally modified or terminated (Art. 29).

If either party commits a fundamental breach (such as nondelivery by the seller or nonpayment by the buyer) the victim may declare the contract avoided, relieving himself of further performance obligations (Art. 25).

The victim of a breach may fix an additional time of reasonable length for the breaching party to perform his obligation. The victim may not file suit for breach during this period, but he will have a claim for damages for delayed performance (Arts. 47, 53).

In case of breach a court may order the breaching party to perform his obligation unless the court sits in a country whose law does not provide for specific performance under the circumstances (Art. 28).

The seller's warranty obligations are very similar to those under the UCC. It is easier for a seller to recover lost profit from a breaching buyer than it is under the UCC.

The convention does not govern consumer sales, auctions, sales of securities, or certain other transactions mentioned in Article 2. It also does not govern service contracts.

It lacks rules to determine when title passes to the goods sold. It does contain rules for determining passage of risk of loss, but when the contract contains a shipping term in common usage passage of risk will be governed by the shipping term. The convention also lacks rules governing liability of sellers of goods for death or personal injury caused by defects in said goods. The ordinary product liability law will still govern here.

Force Majeure. The exporter should consider including a *Force Majeure* clause in the contract because transnational contracts for the sale of goods are much more subject to frustration than are domestic contracts. Such a clause will protect the exporter against happenings that could gravely interfere with performance of such contracts. If the importer's country and the exporter's country go to war, for example, performance of the contract will become illegal under the law of both nations. If one of the countries involved goes to war, its government may restrict imports and exports as a wartime emergency measure. If the two countries involved in the contract get into diplomatic difficulties, one may impose an embargo on trade with the other (as the United States has done with regard to Iran, for instance). A force majeure clause can also protect against changes in government licensing and quota policies. The parties may have anticipated that the importer could easily obtain an import license for what he agreed to buy, but a new government policy might make it very difficult or impossible to get the license. The clause also guards the exporter against imposition of exchange controls. These may make it difficult to impossible for the importer to pay as per the contract.

The parties need to decide whether they want unforeseen circumstances such as those named above to discharge the contract, or whether they would rather have these serve as an excuse for delayed performance. In the absence of a force majeure clause, changed circumstances making the performance of a contract illegal will discharge it, as will circumstances making performance impossible. If the circumstances merely make performance very difficult the agreement will continue in effect.

The well-drafted clause will list the circumstances that will constitute force majeure and then add a catch-all provision such as "and any other circumstances beyond the control of the parties," or words to that effect. It will then spell out what the effect of these happenings will be—discharge, excusable delay of performance, or whatever. (Subsequent illegality will probably make the contract unenforceable regardless of what a force majeure clause says, however.)

The parties may choose the law to govern their contract if they wish. They may also choose the forum in which any litigation will be heard. This forum could be some sort of arbitration tribunal rather than a court.

Foreign Import Controls. It will not do a would-be American exporter much good to contract to sell his goods to a foreign importer if controls imposed by the importer's government make it unprofitable or impossible to perform the contract. Among the difficulties that may arise are: (1) taxes, (2) quotas, (3) licensing requirements, (4) exchange controls, and (5) product standards.

Imported goods will almost certainly be subject to customs duty. In most nations this is assessed on the CIF value of the goods, not the FOB value that is used under our system. In short, the cost of transporting the goods to the importing country is included in their value for customs purposes.

If the importing country levies a value-added tax within its borders, it will probably impose an equivalent border tax on imports, to make the cost of the import equal to the cost of domestically produced equivalent products. Variable levies and tariff surcharges may also be imposed. These are sometimes used as a means of "fine-tuning" imports — raised to discourage imports at one time, lowered or abolished to encourage them at another.

A quota is a limitation upon the quantity of a product that may be imported into a country. Quotas can be global — no more than X quantity of product Y may be imported into the country per year. They can also be national — only X quantity of Y may be imported from country Z in any year, while Q quantity may be imported from country P. The American exporter would have to have his export fitted into the applicable quota to be able to make it; if it would not fit, it would be unlawful.

The United States does not require much licensing of imports. Other nations do much more of it. Some licensing is for statistical purposes, to make it easy for a government to monitor imports. More often, the purpose is restrictive. The more red tape the importing country requires license applicants to cut through, the more restrictive is the system.

Exchange controls make it difficult for exporters to be paid for their product. These are found in countries with severe balance of payments problems, and countries with chronic shortages of hard currencies. They may take the form of allocations of hard currency by the national bank; if your customer cannot get an allocation, he cannot pay you in U.S. dollars as he agreed. They may also consist of controls on taking currency out of the country. In such a case, your Ruritanian customer would have no trouble paying you for your export in Ruritanian glotnies in Ruritania, but you would not be permitted to take the glotnies out of the country. As an exporter you would then have to decide how valuable glotnies would be to you in Ruritania.

Product standards may be used to protect the people of the importing land from inferior imported products, or to protect the environment of the country, or to protect domestic producers of the product, or for numerous other purposes. If a standard is similar to that imposed by other countries, or if it is similar to what is required of the product in the exporter's domestic market it causes no problems. However, if it is an odd sort of standard imposed nowhere else on earth it will most certainly discourage imports.

It is obviously much easier to export to a nation whose government encourages imports than to one whose government stringently regulates them.

Shipping Terms

The parties must determine who will have the responsibility for doing what in the process of getting the goods from exporter to importer. Each party may want to minimize his duties while maximizing the obligations of his opposite number. The shipping term agreed upon will normally determine the allocation of duties.

The International Chamber of Commerce has defined the duties of buyer and seller under the terms in common use. Though the rules set forth in these *Incoterms* do not have the force of law in most countries (though they do in Spain, for instance) the parties to an export contract may specify that one of these terms is a part of the bargain.

The American usage of some shipping term terminology differs from the English and continental European usage. The differences will be explained when necessary.

The common terms and their meanings follow:

1. *Ex Factory (Ex Warehouse, English Ex Works).* The exporter must prepare the goods for shipment and notify the importer. The importer must arrange for transportation. Thus the exporter is under no obligation to move the goods. The importer must pick them up, and must obtain both export and import licenses.

2. *FOB Shipping Point.* The exporter must prepare the goods for shipment and actually ship them, receiving a clean bill of lading from the carrier. The goods may be shipped "collect" unless the shipping contract provides otherwise; thus the importer pays freight charges on arrival. This term is typically American; it is not used in Europe. The exporter obtains the export license, as he does under all subsequent terms. The importer obtains the import license.

3. *FOR (Free on Board Railway).* The exporter must see to it that the goods are picked up by a vehicle belonging to a railway for transportation to the railroad yards for loading. The exporter pays for getting the goods on board the vehicle, while the rest of the shipping charges are borne by the importer. Export and import licenses are handled as in (2) above.

4. *FOT (Free on Truck).* This English terminology might be unfamiliar to Americans. A truck here is a railway car. The exporter must see to it that the goods are loaded aboard a freight car. Here the exporter pays the cost of getting the goods aboard the train. The other obligations of the parties are the same as in (3) above.

5. *FOA (or FOB Airport).* The exporter must get the goods to an airport (the name of which may be included in the term) and deliver them to the transporting airline, getting a clean waybill for them. The exporter is not responsible for getting the goods aboard an aircraft. Other obligations are as in (3) above.

6. *FOB Aircraft.* This term is uncommon. It is similar to FOA, except that the exporter must actually get the goods aboard an aircraft.

7. *C & F (Cost & Freight).* The contract price includes the price of the goods plus shipping charges. Exporter obligations are the same as in (2) except that he must prepay the shipping charges.

8. *CIF (Cost, Insurance, Freight).* The contract price includes the

price of the goods, shipping charges, and cost of transit insurance. Exporter obligations are the same as in (2) except that he must also obtain transit insurance upon the goods.

9. *FAS (Free Alongside) Vessel.* The term usually contains the name of the vessel upon which the goods will be shipped. Exporter must get the goods to the point from which they will be loaded aboard the vessel, and obtain from the shipping company a clean *Received for Shipment* bill of lading. The goods may be shipped "collect" unless the contract provides otherwise.

10. *FOB (Free on Board) Vessel.* This term, too, usually contains the name of the vessel. Exporter must see to it that the goods are loaded on board the vessel, and must obtain from the shipping company a clean *On Board* bill of lading. "Collect" shipment is acceptable unless the contract provides otherwise.

11. *Free Carrier (Named Point).* When the exporter will pack the goods in a shipping container of the sort that can be carried by truck, railway, or ship he may want to use this term. His duty is to pack the container and deliver it to a carrier at the named point. Once the carrier takes charge of the container and issues a clean bill of lading (or whatever other document is appropriate) the exporter has fulfilled his obligation.

12. *Ex Vessel.* Again the term usually contains the name of the vessel. Exporter must see to it that the goods are unloaded from the vessel in undamaged condition at the point of destination. The exporter must prepay shipping charges, but need not pay import duty.

13. *Ex Dock (Ex Quay, Franco Quay).* Here the term will contain the name of the city where the goods will leave the ship. Exporter must see to it that the importer can pick up the goods from the dock without difficulty and in undamaged condition. He must prepay the shipping charges and also pay the customs duty. He will also be responsible for obtaining any needed import license.

14. *Delivered at Frontier.* European exporters often use this term. It usually names the frontier and the point on the frontier where the exporter will deliver the goods (for example, Delivered at Italian-Swiss Frontier, Chiasso). The exporter must get the goods to the named point on the named frontier and pay for getting them there. The importer takes delivery on the exporter's side of the border and is responsible for customs duties and import licenses.

15. *FOB Destination.* Only Americans use such a term. The continental European equivalent is *Franco Domicile;* the English is *Delivered Free* (named destination) *Duty Paid.* Exporter must see to it that the goods are delivered to the importer at his residence or place of business, paying all shipping charges, import duties and the like. The exporter is of course responsible for the import license, too.

16. *No Arrival, No Sale.* This, too, is American. Exporter has the same obligations as with *FOB Destination.* The difference between the two terms is this: under *No Arrival, No Sale* the nonarrival of the goods discharges the contract of sale and the exporter need not try to make another delivery. Under *FOB Destination* the nonarrival does not discharge the contract; the exporter may well be liable for damages for breach of contract due to the nondelivery.

Carrier Liability, Insurance and Risk of Loss

The exporter will arrange shipment under all shipping terms except Ex Factory. He may contract for shipment with a carrier himself, or he may turn the goods over to an international freight forwarder and let it arrange for shipment. Though freight forwarders do not themselves move goods, they are treated by law as carriers and have all of the liability of carriers.

Ground Carriers. The liability of an American ground carrier is governed by the Interstate Commerce Act, 49 USC 1 et seq., and by judge-made law. An American ground carrier is an insurer of goods entrusted to it for shipment and is liable for loss of or damage to the goods unless loss or damage is caused by:

1. Acts of God. These are natural catastrophes such as tornado, earthquake, or flood. Fires are not considered to be acts of God.

2. Acts of public enemies. Public enemies are defined as the armed forces of a nation with which the United States is at war. Thus if a truck containing goods is hijacked by criminals the carrier will be liable for the lost goods.

3. Acts of public authority. Public authority is government. If a government agency delays or seizes a shipment the carrier is not liable for the harm done. Its one obligation is to inform the shipper as soon as possible of the government act.

4. Acts of the shipper. If the shipper improperly packages, labels, or marks the shipment the carrier is not liable for ensuing harm. Thus fragile goods must be packed carefully, shipping labels must be attached securely, and the like.

5. Inherent vice. Perishable goods may spoil no matter how carefully packed or cared for in transit. Thus when agricultural produce or the like spoils in transit the carrier will not be responsible unless it was negligent in caring for the shipment.

When loss or damage is caused by one of the above five causes plus carrier negligence, the carrier will be liable.

The carrier may limit its liability to a stated sum per package shipped in its bill of lading if it allows the shipper to obtain full liability by paying a higher shipping charge.

Under the Federal Bills of Lading Act (49 USC 90 et seq.) which applies to export bills of lading, anyone having a right of property or possession in shipped goods may stop them in transit or divert them. Included would be an unpaid shipper (unless the goods were shipped under a negotiable bill of lading of which someone else had become the owner).

The rules of liability for European ground carriers are contained in two international agreements. Truckers are governed by the *Convention on the Contract for International Carriage of Goods by Road (CMR)*, while railways are governed by the *International Convention Concerning Carriage of Goods by Rail (CIM)*.

Under both conventions the carrier is not liable for loss of or damage to a shipment under the following circumstances:

1. Defective packing, handling, loading, or unloading by shipper or recipient.
2. Inherent vice.
3. When shipment consists of livestock.
4. Circumstances beyond the control of the carrier.

Where a combination of one of the above and carrier negligence causes the loss or damage the carrier is liable.

Some significant provisions of CMR follow.

Evidence of the contract of carriage is the *Consignment Note,* which is not a bill of lading and not a document of title for the goods and is not negotiable. It is made out in three copies, of which the shipper gets one, the carrier keeps one, and one accompanies the goods. Normally the recipient does not get one until the goods arrive.

The shipper has control of the goods while they are in transit. He can (1) stop the goods in transit; (2) change the place of delivery; and (3) change the recipient. The shipper's right continues until the recipient receives a copy of the consignment note or until the recipient receives the goods.

The carrier's liability is limited to twenty-five French gold francs per pound (approximately $3.70) unless the shipper declares excess value and pays a higher shipping charge. CMR is in force in twenty-three countries, all of which are in Europe. If either the country of shipment or the country of delivery has adopted CMR, it applies to the contract of shipment.

CIM has been adopted by most European countries, and also by a few nations of Asia and Africa. It applies to rail shipments that will pass through at least two contracting countries. Significant provisions of it are discussed below.

The contract of carriage is contained in a *Consignment Note* which has the same attributes of such notes under *CMR*. Under *CIM* only one copy of the note exists, not three.

The shipper has the same stoppage and reconsignment rights as he does under CMR; these terminate, as under CMR, when the recipient gets either the goods or the consignment note.

The recipient also gets a limited reconsignment right. He may reconsign when the goods are in his country and he is obligated to pay the shipping charges through that country, unless there is a provision in the consignment note denying him that right.

The shipper may specify that the goods be shipped with *Grande Vitesse* (great speed), or *Petite Vitesse* (normal speed). A carload lot shipped grande vitesse should cover four hundred kilometers (km) in twenty-four hours, a less than carload lot three hundred km. The carload shipped petite vitesse should cover three hundred km in twenty-four hours, the less than carload lot two hundred km. The carrier is allowed twelve hours to dispatch a grande vitesse shipment, twenty-four hours for a petite vitesse one. If the railway takes more time for delivery than what is allowed above, it is liable to the shipper for damages.

Otherwise the railway has the same exemptions from liability as the truckline. Its minimum liability is greater, however; under the 1980 amendments to the convention minimum liability is seventeen Special Drawing Rights (SDR) per kilogram. (Special Drawing Rights are the "paper gold" of the International Monetary Fund, a world money of account. They are discussed in some detail later in this work. Since there are 2.2 pounds per kilogram, this amounts to about 7.7 SDR per pound, or perhaps U.S. $8.50 per pound.)

Air Carriers. The United States has no statute that spells out the liability of air carriers, either domestic or international. The law on domestic carrier liability is essentially bailee liability; if carrier negligence damages a shipment the carrier is liable, if there is no carrier negligence there is no liability. The carrier must prove lack of negligence in contested cases.

The liability of international air carriers is governed by the Warsaw Convention. The original convention was negotiated in 1929, and has since been amended. Probably a majority of the world's nations (such as Great Britain) have ratified the amended convention. Others (such as the United States) ratified the original convention, but not the amended version. Still others (such as Peru) have ratified neither version of the convention.

Under the unamended convention (which governs international air shipments out of the United States and is found in the form in which it was ratified by this country at 49 Stat. 3000 et seq.) the air carrier is liable for loss of or damage to cargo in its possession unless it can prove: (1) that it took all possible steps to avoid the loss or damage that occurred, or that it was impossible for the carrier to take such steps; or (2) that the loss or damage was caused in whole or in part by the negligence of the shipper; or

(3) that the loss or damage was caused by negligence by the pilot or crew members in the navigation and management of the aircraft.

The maximum liability of the carrier is limited to 250 French gold francs per kilogram of cargo, or a bit more than U.S. $8 per pound. The shipper could obtain more carrier liability by declaring extra value for the shipment and paying a higher shipping charge.

The shipper obtains an *Air Consignment Note* when he makes an international air shipment. Like the CMR and CIM consignment notes, this is not a document of title. Also like the CMR note, three copies are made; one for the carrier, one for the shipper and, one to accompany the goods.

The shipper has stoppage rights. He may, as long as he can produce the consignment note and pay necessary charges, (1) stop the goods at an intermediate landing place; (2) reconsign the goods to someone else; (3) have the goods returned to the airport of shipment.

The recipient may require the carrier to hand over the consignment note and the goods on their arrival, if he pays all outstanding charges.

Notice of claim for damage to a shipment must be made within seven days of the arrival of the shipment. Notice of claim for loss must be made within fourteen days of the estimated time of arrival of the shipment.

Under the amended convention carriers are not exempt from liability because of pilot error in navigation and management of the aircraft. The shipping document is called an *Air Waybill,* but is essentially the same document as the air consignment note. Time limits for filing claims are fourteen days for damaged shipments and twenty-one days for lost shipments. An air shipment from, say, Great Britain to the United States would be governed by the amended convention because Great Britain, the point of shipment, is a party to the amended convention. The British Parliament has enacted a Carriage of Goods by Air Act which has incorporated the amended Warsaw Convention into British law. Other national parliaments have enacted similar legislation.

Shipments between two nonconvention countries would be governed by the domestic law of the countries involved.

Water Carriers. The rules of liability for American domestic water carriers are governed by the Harter Act, 46 USC 190 et seq.

The liability of international water carriers operating from American ports is generally governed by the Carriage of Goods by Sea Act (COGSA), 46 USC 1300–1315, of 1936. The act generally codifies the Hague Rules, an international agreement governing liabilities of international water carriers drawn up in 1920.

During the 1960s the Hague Rules were amended at a conference held at Visby in Sweden. The resulting Hague-Visby Rules were submitted to the nations for consideration by the Brussels Protocol of 1968. Great Britain amended her Carriage of Goods by Sea Act in 1971 to incorporate the Hague-Visby Rules; many other nations (but not the United States) have done likewise. The Visby amendments to the rules have not appreciably altered the basic liability of water carriers, so they will not be discussed.

Another international conference at Hamburg in 1978 rewrote the Hague-Visby Rules; under the resulting Hamburg Rules liabilities of water carriers would be considerably increased. However, as yet no nation has enacted the Hamburg Rules into law.

The following discussion of water carrier liability applies specifically to the American COGSA of 1936; but it also applies in general to liability under the Hague-Visby Rules also.

International water carriers have two primary responsibilities: (1) to furnish a seaworthy ship; and (2) to carefully stow the cargo. In order for the ship to be seaworthy it must: (1) be in good mechanical condition when it leaves its home port; (2) carry sufficient supplies to get it to its destination; and (3) be manned by enough competent officers and seamen to get it to its destination. If the ship is seaworthy when it leaves its home port, it or its owners will not be held responsible for its becoming unseaworthy later on in the voyage. The cargo must be carefully secured aboard ship because spells of rough weather are to be expected at sea. If cargo breaks loose during a storm and damages other cargo the ship and its owners will be held responsible for the consequences.

If the owners furnish a seaworthy ship and stow the cargo properly they probably will not be liable for any harm to the shipment. COGSA contains a lengthy list of occurrences for which ship and owner are not liable, including:

1. The five occurrences for which land carriers are not liable
2. Perils of the sea (high waves, icebergs, and the like)
3. Theft by officers or crewmen
4. Piracy
5. Acts of war
6. Delay in unloading caused by longshoremen strikes and similar problems
7. Deviation from course for any reason other than the unscheduled loading or unloading of passengers or cargo

The Hague-Visby Rules state that the carrier is not liable for harm caused by *Reasonable* deviations, but that it is liable for *Unreasonable* deviations.

Ship and owners will be liable for fire damage to cargo, if the fire was caused by the negligence of officers or crewmen.

It is possible for the owner of cargo aboard a ship to become liable to the owners of other cargo aboard the same ship. This can happen because the cargo is a danger to other cargo and causes harm. It can also happen because of *General Average*. Sometimes a vessel gets into difficulty at sea and it becomes necessary to lighten it by throwing cargo overboard. If this sacrifice of part of the cargo saves the ship and the balance of cargo the owner(s) of the sacrificed cargo have a claim against the owners of the ship and of the saved goods.

Suppose that Jones ships $100,000 worth of goods aboard the *USS Rustbucket*. The ship is worth $5,000,000. The owners earned $200,000 in freight from shippers of the cargo aboard. The cargo itself is worth $4,800,000. Though *Rustbucket* was seaworthy when it left its home port, it gets into rough weather at sea and is in danger of sinking. The captain orders that Jones's cargo be thrown overboard to lighten the ship. The sacrifice saves the ship; it reaches its destination intact. Jones has a general average claim against ship, its owners, and owners of the spared cargo. The entire *Rustbucket* venture on this voyage was worth $10,000,000 (value of ship, value of cargo, plus freight revenue). Jones owned 1 percent of the venture. The sacrifice of 1 percent of the venture saved the other 99 percent, so Jones has the right to recover $99,000 from the other venturers. Each of the other venturers is liable to Jones for 1 percent of his interest in the venture.

COGSA provides that ship owners may limit their liability to shippers to the sum of five hundred dollars per package if they allow shippers to claim total liability by paying a higher shipping charge.

Under the Hague-Visby Rules the liability of ship owners for lost or damaged cargo is the value of the goods, if declared by the shipper to the carrier before shipment and included in the bill of lading. Otherwise it is 666.67 SDR per package or two SDR per kilogram of gross weight, whichever calculation produces the greater sum.

Sometimes ship owners rent out their vessels to charterers. Such arrangements are called *Charter Parties*. There are three types of charter parties: (1) the *Demise* or *Bareboat* charter; (2) the voyage charter; and (3) the *Time* charter.

Under a *Demise* or *Bareboat* charter, the charterer rents the entire ship and may operate it as if it were his own. If he hires his own crew and otherwise controls the ship during the charter, he has the liability of an owner to those who ship cargo aboard the vessel. Sometimes the charterer hires the owner's crew along with the ship; in such case the owner will be liable to shippers for lost or damaged cargo, not the charterer.

Under a *Voyage* charter the charterer hires the ship to make a single voyage, or a consecutive series of voyages. The ship is operated by the owner's crew. Usually the charterer furnishes the entire cargo. If so, the owner issues no bill of lading and the ordinary law of water carrier liability does not apply. However, the owner is obligated to furnish a seaworthy ship and to stow the charterer's cargo properly. If the charterer causes the ship to take on cargo belonging to shippers other than himself (as he has the option to do) the owner issues the required bills of lading to these shippers for their cargo, and the owner assumes all of the liabilities of the issuer of an ocean bill of lading.

Under a *Time* charter the charterer hires the vessel for a stated time period, along with its crew. For the duration of the charter the charterer controls the vessel's movement. During the charter the vessel may carry only the charterer's cargo, or it may carry cargo belonging to other shippers at the charterer's option. As with voyage charters, the owner issues bills of lading to shippers other than the charterer and assumes all of the liabilities of the issuer of an ocean bill of lading.

To make a claim against an international water carrier a notice of claim must be filed within three days of the delivery of the cargo to the recipient.

A shipper who has a claim against a water carrier may make it either against the ship carrying the cargo or against the ship's owners or both. Admiralty law (the law of the sea) regards a ship as a legal entity. A ship owner is liable for cargo damage and the like only to the extent of his ownership interest in the ship. Thus, if the *USS Rustbucket* is worth $5,000,000 and Sanders owns a 5 percent interest in her, Sanders is liable for no more than $250,000 to persons having claims against ship and owners for cargo damage.

Goods are often transported by hovercraft between Great Britain and European Channel ports. The British Parliament has chosen to treat hovercraft as watercraft; they are specifically governed by the British Carriage of Goods by Sea Act. Logic should cause other nations to treat hovercraft in the same way.

Container Carriers. At present there is no special law or international agreement fixing rules of liability for container carriers. The liability of these for loss of or damage to a shipment depends upon whether the damage took place on land, in the air, or on the sea.

A United Nations *Convention on International Intermodal Transportation of Goods* has been submitted to the world's nations for ratification and will some day apply uniform liability rules to this type of carrier. However, the convention has not received enough ratifications to go into effect.

Container operators may issue a *Combined Transport* document to shippers upon receipt of a shipment. These may be negotiable or nonnegotiable and are very similar to bills of lading. The International Chamber of Commerce has promulgated uniform rules to govern such documents. These may be incorporated into container transport contracts by agreement of the parties.

Insurance. Because of the limited liability of carriers, it is wise to insure goods against loss or damage in transit. Insurance of land and air shipments will generally protect against acts of God, theft, and the like. It will not protect against acts of the shipper, acts of governments, or inherent vice — though broader coverage than the standard may be negotiated for a higher premium.

Ocean marine insurance will protect water shipments against acts of God, perils of the sea, general average claims, etc., but it will not protect against war risk. War risk insurance is obtainable only through the United States government (under some circumstances) or from foreign insurers such as Lloyd's of London (again, only under some circumstances). Moreover, any one of the following circumstances will automatically cancel ocean marine insurance coverage: (1) the unseaworthiness of the ship at the beginning of its voyage; (2) deviation of the ship from its course for any purpose other than the saving of lives and property at sea; or (3) illegality of the shipment (under either the laws of the exporting nation or those of the importing nation).

Risk of Loss. International shipment of goods is still a somewhat risky business, even in our modern age. Goods may be lost or damaged in transit under circumstances where no carrier or insurer may be made to pay for the harm. In such a case, who takes the loss? The risk of loss is allocated in the contract of sale. Generally its passage is determined by the shipping term used.

Under Ex Factory terms the importer gets risk of loss when he is notified that the goods are ready to be picked up.

Under FOB Shipping Point, Free Carrier, C & F, CIF, FOR, FOT and FOA the importer gets the risk when the goods are loaded aboard the first carrier.

Under Delivered at Frontier the importer gets risk of loss when the goods arrive at the named point on the frontier.

Under FAS Vessel risk passes when the goods reach the point at which they will be loaded aboard the vessel (usually the appropriate dock).

Under FOB Vessel risk passes when the goods are loaded aboard.

Under Ex Vessel risk passes when the goods leave the ship's tackle at the port of destination.

Under Ex Dock risk passes when the goods are picked up from the dock.

Under FOB Destination or similar terms the importer does not get risk of loss until the goods arrive.

If harm comes to the goods while risk of loss is on the importer, importer must pay the entire contract price. If the goods are insured importer must file the insurance claim. If a carrier may be liable the importer must deal with it.

If harm happens while risk of loss is still on the exporter the importer is under no obligation to pay anything. Under American law, if the exporter can replace the lost or damaged goods he must do so or be liable for breach of contract. If exporter cannot replace the lost or damaged goods the contract may be discharged. If the contract is governed by the law of another nation the result may be different.

Chapter 11

Payment and Guarantees

Payment

There are five possible ways for payment to be arranged. These are (1) payment in advance by the importer, (2) sale on open acount, (3) payment against documents, (4) payment by letter of credit, and (5) consignment.

Payment in advance is the best arrangement from the point of view of the exporter, and the worst from the importer's viewpoint. If the importer pays in advance but the exporter does not ship the goods, the importer must sue in a foreign land to get his money back.

Open account is risky from the exporter's point of view. In addition to harm from the normal perils of selling on credit (a personal check of the buyer being dishonored, the buyer becoming insolvent, etc.), the exporter could be damaged by exchange controls imposed by the importer's nation, adverse movement of currency exchange rates, war or civil disorder in the importer's country, etc. Moreover, if the importer does not pay he still has the goods and the exporter must sue in a foreign land to try to collect the account. Government will assume some of the credit risk in these transactions, however. How this is done will be discussed shortly.

Since payment will almost inevitably be made in some form of commercial paper, I shall take up this topic before describing the more complex methods: payment against documents and by letter of credit, and consignment.

Introduction to Commercial Paper Law. There are three basic types of commercial paper used in commercial transactions: the *Check,* the *Promissory Note,* and the *Draft.* The United States law governing these is contained in the Uniform Commercial Code. English commercial paper law is found in the Bills of Exchange Act; most common-law nations other than the United States have modeled their commercial paper law on the English enactment. The huge majority of the non–common-law nations base their law in this area on the Geneva Conventions of 1930–31, though a few nations of Latin America use American or English law as their model.

Commercial paper circulates through the world economy as a substitute for money; therefore the law governing it seeks to give it some of the aspects of money. It may be *Negotiable* or *Nonnegotiable.* Non-negotiable commercial paper has virtually none of the aspects of money. It has the legal status of an account receivable. Anyone accepting it as payment of an obligation has the same right to collect it as his transferor had and no more. He who accepts negotiable commercial paper in payment of an obligation may obtain better rights to collect it than his transferor had if he qualifies as a *Holder in Due Course.*

Under the Uniform Commercial Code, an item of commercial paper must meet the following requirements to be negotiable:

1. It must be in writing
2. It must be signed by the maker or drawer
3. It must contain a promise or order to pay
4. The promise or order must be unconditional
5. The promise must be payable in money
6. The sum payable must be certain
7. It must be payable at a definite time
8. It must be payable to order or to bearer

The requirements for negotiability under the English Bills of Exchange Act are substantially identical. The Geneva Conventions omit the eighth requirement above and add three additional requirements: (1) the paper must contain a designation of its type—check, bill of exchange, or promissory note; (2) the date of issue must be stated; and (3) the place of issue must be stated.

The requirements for becoming a holder in due course are substantially identical under the American, English, and Geneva Convention regimes. As stated in the Uniform Commercial Code the holder in due course must:

1. Give value for the paper
2. Act in good faith
3. Have no knowledge that:
   a. The paper is overdue
   b. The paper has been dishonored
   c. A defense to payment exists
   d. An adverse claim (a claim of ownership by a third party) exists

Checks. There are three types of checks in common use in the United States: *Personal, Certified,* and *Cashier's.*

There are three parties to a check: the *Drawer,* the *Drawee,* and the *Payee.* With respect to *personal checks,* the drawer is the debtor. The drawee is the bank where the drawer has the account upon which the check is being written. The payee is the creditor for whose benefit the check is written. The drawer delivers the check to the payee. The payee collects it either by presenting it for payment at the drawee bank, or by depositing it in his own bank. In the latter case the drawer's bank (the *Depositary Bank*) sends it through banking channels to the drawee.

The drawee has no liability upon its customer's checks. When these are dishonored the payee's recourse will be only against the drawer or endorsers.

The most common reasons for dishonor of personal checks are: (1) insufficient funds in the drawer's account; (2) the drawer stops payment upon the check; (3) the drawer has no account in the drawee bank.

A certified check begins life as a personal check. It becomes certified when the drawee bank stamps upon its face evidence of certification. At this time the drawee debits the drawer's account the face value of the check, which now becomes a primary obligation of the certifying bank. In most jurisdictions the drawer may not stop payment upon a certified check. The only circumstances under which dishonor may occur are in the event the certifying bank becomes insolvent after certification and before honor, or if the check is reported to the certifying bank as lost or stolen.

A cashier's check is a check drawn by a bank upon itself, or upon another bank. A debtor may purchase these from his bank for use in payment of an obligation. Since the purchaser of such a check is not a party to it, he generally may not stop payment upon it. As with certified checks, the only reasons for dishonor are the insolvency of the issuing bank, or reporting to the bank that the check is lost or stolen.

Under the Uniform Commercial Code a check is deemed to be overdue when not presented for payment within thirty days of issuance. Under the Geneva Convention a check should be presented for payment within the following time limits: (1) eight days if payable in the country where issued; (2) twenty days if payable in another country on the same continent as the place of issue; and (3) sixty days if payable in a country on another continent from that of the place of issue.

Under the Uniform Commercial Code a check is considered to be a form of written contract; therefore a holder may bring suit against a party within four years after issuance. Under the Geneva Convention such suit must be commenced within six months of the deadlines for payment.

Since checks are completed by filling in blanks in prepared forms, they are virtually always negotiable; the forms are drafted so as to contain all requisites of negotiability. In common-law countries a drawer may render a check nonnegotiable by writing on the face of it "Nonnegotiable" or words to that effect, though this is rarely done. In countries with Romano-Germanic law the same may be accomplished through the use of the words "Not to Order" or equivalent.

In common-law nations the payee may limit the rights of subsequent holders of checks through the use of restrictive endorsements, the most common of which is "For Deposit Only." Such an endorsement is intended to prevent the drawee paying the holder the face value of the check in cash.

In Geneva Convention countries drawers, payees, and subsequent holders may accomplish a similar objective by the use of *Crossed* checks. A check is crossed when the front bears two parallel lines. A *General* crossed check bears no writing between the lines, or only the word *"Banker"* or word of similar meaning. The drawee may honor such a check only for one of its customers or for another bank.

A crossed check is *Special* when the name of a bank is written between the lines. The drawer may honor such a check only for the account of the named bank.

In Romano-Germanic lands the drawer or subsequent holder of a check may write on its face the words "Only for Settlement" or words of similar meaning. This limits the use of the check to settlement of the account the drawer intends to pay. The drawee bank may not cash such a check; it must honor it only when deposited.

Checks are most often used in domestic commercial transactions; their employment is less common internationally. They travel through international commercial channels only at the speed of international mail. In case of dishonor of international checks, the payee usually must sue to collect in the drawer's country. Therefore the exporter should use caution in accepting payment from the importer in the form of a personal check. Among the disadvantages to their use from the seller's point of view are the long transit time from buyer to seller and back to buyer's bank, and the risk of dishonor.

Drafts. A payment against documents deal and a letter of credit deal are going to involve the use of a draft (or, as the English say, a *Bill of Exchange*). This specialized item of commercial paper may not be familiar to nonbusinesspeople. There are two basic types of draft; the *Sight Draft,* payable on demand, and the *Time Draft,* payable at a future date.

There are three parties to a draft. The *Drawer* (the seller) writes up the document, which orders the *Drawee* (the buyer) to pay money to the *Payee* (who may be the drawer or some third party).

Drafts, too, are prepared by filling in the blanks in already prepared forms containing all requirements of negotiability. Thus they are virtually always negotiable.

Under the Uniform Commercial Code and under the law of every other country, no one is liable on commercial paper if he has not signed it himself or through an authorized agent. Therefore, as of the time a draft is drawn the drawee has no liability on it, because he obviously has not signed it.

A person who signs commercial paper incurs either *Primary* or

Secondary liability, depending on the capacity in which he signed. A party with primary liability is expected to pay commercial paper when it matures without being asked. If he does not pay at maturity he may be sued immediately. A party with secondary liability is expected to pay only if someone else does not. The drawer of a draft incurs secondary liability at the time he signs; he may be called upon to pay if the drawee does not.

Ultimately the payee will present the draft to the drawee. If it is a sight draft he will demand that the drawee pay. If the drawee pays, there are no problems. If he refuses to pay he is not liable on the draft itself, because he has not signed it. He has probably breached the contract of sale by not paying, however, and will be liable for that.

Nonpayment by the drawee is dishonor. This triggers the secondary liability of the drawer; if the payee is someone other than the drawer he may now demand that the drawer pay.

If the draft is a time draft the payee will present it to the drawee for acceptance. The drawee may accept simply by signing the paper. Normally, though, he will write "Accepted" on the draft, followed by the date of acceptance and his signature. He has now become an *Acceptor* and assumed primarily liability on the draft. When it matures he will be responsible for paying it unless he has some legally sufficient excuse not to pay (a *Defense to Payment*).

Should the drawee choose to accept but change the terms of the draft (maybe it is drawn payable thirty days after acceptance but he wants to accept payable sixty days after acceptance; or the face value of the draft is U.S. $10,000 but he wants to accept for U.S. $8,000) he may do so, and is liable on the draft only as per his acceptance. Such a *Draft-Varying Acceptance* discharges the drawer if done without his consent, and also discharges everyone who indorsed before the acceptance. (It may of course be a breach of contract on the drawee's part; if so, he is liable for the damage caused thereby.)

Nonacceptance does not make the drawee liable on the draft, because he has not signed it. Again, however, it may make him liable for breach of contract. Nonpayment by an acceptor gives the payee the option of holding the acceptor liable on his primary liability or of pursuing the drawer on his secondary liability.

The payee of a draft may negotiate it to a third party (very often a bank) either before or after acceptance. When the third party takes the draft for value; in good faith; before maturity; without knowledge of dishonor by drawer, drawee, or acceptor; without knowledge of any defenses to payment; and without knowledge of claims to the draft by third parties, he is a *Holder in Due Course* and will be entitled to collect its face value despite the existence of some defenses to payment.

A defense to payment is a lawful reason not to pay commercial paper at maturity. Defenses may be *Real* (good against anyone, even a holder in due course) or *Personal* (good only against nonholders in due course). The most common defenses (breach of contract, fraud in the making of the contract, lack of consideration, etc.) are personal. Real defenses include forgery or unauthorized signature (the signature in question is not genuine or signed by an authorized agent), material alteration (the draft has been altered since the person claimed against signed it), bankruptcy of the signer, illegality of the draft or the underlying contract, or the like.

When the ownership of a draft is transferred the seller is usually required to indorse, to sign his name on the back of the draft. Indorsers incur secondary liability. If the drawee does not pay, the owner may be able to collect from them. The indorser may escape this liability if he indorses *Without Recourse,* however.

The seller of a draft makes certain warranties to the buyer whether he indorses or not. When he indorses he makes the warranties to all future owners. These are: that he had title or the right to transfer the instrument when he transferred; that all signatures on the paper are genuine; there has been no material alteration; that no defense to payment is good against him (that is, he could collect on the paper if he held it to maturity); and that he knows of no insolvency proceeding involving the acceptor or drawer.

The indorser incurs both indorser liability and warranty liability, normally. Liability for breach of warranty may be enforced as soon as the breach is discovered; indorser liability does not come into play until after the paper matures.

Indorsers are not liable on their indorsements on international drafts until four things occur:

1. Presentment. The owner must ask the drawee to pay the sight draft or accept the time draft; or ask the acceptor to pay at maturity.

2. Dishonor. The drawer or acceptor must refuse to do as he was asked.

3. Timely notice of dishonor. The indorser must be given this by midnight of the third business day after dishonor (Saturdays, Sundays, and holidays do not count as business days). It can be done orally or by mail; if done by mail and sent to a proper address the notice is good when sent. Late notice discharges the indorser.

4. Protest. The owner must present the draft for protest before a notary public or consul and swear before that person that the draft was presented for acceptance or payment as the case may be and was dishonored. The sworn statement is reduced to writing, signed by the protestor, and stamped by the official with his seal. The resulting document is the protest.

He who indorses without recourse does not escape warranty liability. The only way to accomplish that is to indorse "Without recourse and all warranties disclaimed."

Sometimes a third party will sign the draft drawn in an international transaction as an accommodation to the buyer (perhaps because the seller is unwilling to trust the buyer completely). The buyer might draw the draft himself on the accommodation party payable to the seller; he then obtains the accommodation party's acceptance and sends the draft on to the seller. The accommodation party then honors the draft and the buyer reimburses him.

Or the draft is drawn by the seller on the accommodation party and sent to him for acceptance. The accommodation party accepts, obtains the signature of the buyer on the draft as an indorsement (subjecting him to secondary liability), and returns the draft to the seller. At maturity the acceptor pays it and obtains reimbursement from the indorser buyer.

Or the draft is drawn by the seller on the buyer in the usual way. Buyer accepts it and obtains the indorsement of the accommodation party before returning it to the seller. In such case the accommodation indorser has only secondary liability, unless he indorses *Payment Guaranteed.* If the acceptor does not pay at maturity in such a case the guarantor of payment is immediately liable; the owner need not make presentment, give notice of dishonor, or protest. An ordinary indorser on the other hand will not be liable unless the four prerequisites of liability are met.

Accommodation indorsers of both sorts make the warranties that were described above.

The English law governing *Bills of Exchange* is very similar to that decribed above, though not identical. The English drawer of an unaccepted draft has primary liability upon it; his responsibility becomes secondary if and when the draft is accepted. It is virtually impossible for a dishonoring drawer or acceptor to escape liability to a holder in due course in the absence of forgery or the like. Even when the holder is not a holder in due course, English law allows the defaulting party only the defenses of fraud, illegality, and (sometimes) failure of consideration. An ordinary breach of contract is not failure of consideration; the breach must be of such magnitude that the defaulting party got nothing in exchange for his bill. Suits on bills of exchange are heard under a simple summary procedure that awards the holder his judgment very quickly.

English law provides that notices of dishonor must be received by secondary parties located in the same city as the creditor on the day after dishonor; they must be sent to more distant secondary parties by the day after dishonor.

Under the Geneva Convention the drawee may not make a draft-varying acceptance. He must accept the draft as drawn, or not at all. A draft-varying acceptance is a dishonor.

He who acquires a draft after maturity may become a holder in due course under the convention, unless he acquired it after protest was made.

Since consideration is not a requirement for the existence of a valid contract in Romano-Germanic law, it is not essential for validity of commercial paper either. Furthermore, Romano-Germanic law holds that commercial paper justifies its own existence; therefore lack of causa is never a defense to payment.

Protest is required to fix the liability of secondary parties to all commercial paper in Romano-Germanic law.

Notice of dishonor to secondary parties must be given by the holder within four workdays of the day of protest.

Indorsers are individually liable under English and American law, as are the drawer and acceptor; but under the Geneva Convention drawer, acceptor, and indorsers share joint and several liability. An owner of a dishonored draft could file suit against acceptor, drawer, and indorsers all at once if proper protest has been made.

The Geneva Convention allows a type of accommodation indorsement which is not recognized by the common law, the *Aval.* One who indorses as aval makes none of the warranties of an indorser. He essentially guarantees in full or in part the obligation of one of the parties to the draft. His indorsement should state that it is an aval (to avoid warranty liability) and should state the name of the person whose obligation is being guaranteed. If the name of this person does not appear, the guarantee is that of the obligation of the drawer of the draft.

The making of an aval subjects the indorser to liability *even though the obligation of the guaranteed person is void.* Thus the maker of the aval cannot use defenses to payment available to the party guaranteed.

The Islamic law of some of the nations of the Arabian Peninsula accords no protection to a holder in due course. Under the law of these countries, if the drawer, acceptor, or indorser of a draft is a victim of a breach of contract or otherwise did not get value for his promise to pay he need not pay, no matter who is trying to collect.

Payment Against Documents. A payment against documents transaction may be either a form of cash deal, or a form of credit deal. The cash deal works in the following way. The exporter ships the goods and obtains from the carrier a clean negotiable bill of lading. He then draws a sight draft on the importer for the agreed price. He attaches to the draft the bill of lading (which usually makes the shipment consignable to the order of himself), an invoice showing what was shipped, an insurance certificate if he was obligated to insure the goods while in transit, and any other documents required by the contract or by the importer's government. Other documents may also be required by the parties or governments involved.

A *Certificate of Origin* proves the country of origin of goods. The importer's government may well require such a document to insure that the goods are not coming from an embargoed country. Shipments of nickel ore destined for the United States must be accompanied by a Certificate of Origin proving that the ore does not come from Cuba, for instance. The certificate may also entitle the importer to tariff preference, as when a Swiss exporter sells Dutch cheese to an Italian importer. Since the cheese originates in a country of the EC, it is entitled to tariff preference upon entry into Italy (another EC nation) if its Dutch origin can be proven.

Certificates of Inspection, Quality, Quantity, and the like signed by experts other than the exporter may be required by the importer as a guarantee that he is getting what he paid for. In the absence of such a certificate the buyer will not be able to check quality before he pays, since he is paying against documents.

A *Packing List* is drawn up by the seller. Since in a sense it duplicates the invoice, it is only required when the importing nation will not admit shipments of imports unaccompanied by such a document.

When a shipment consists of live animals the exporter may have to furnish *Veterinary Certificates* showing proof of required vaccinations and the like.

Certificates of Carriage may be required when the importer's nation requires imported goods to be transported by carriers registered under its flag only, or when it refuses to accept goods carried under the flag of unfriendly nations.

The seller indorses the draft and the bill of lading to his bank. The package of documents then goes through banking channels to a bank in the importer's area. The importer then pays the draft and receives the documents.

When the shipment arrives, the buyer exchanges his bill of lading for it. Meanwhile the proceeds of the paid sight draft go back through banking channels to the seller. (Very likely they will be remitted by cable to minimize delay.)

The biggest disadvantage to the seller of payment against documents is that the buyer might choose to breach the contract and dishonor the draft. If the draft is a sight draft the buyer cannot dishonor the draft and at the same time get his hands upon the goods; but since the goods are in transit the seller will have to go to some trouble and expense to recover them.

The disadvantage to the buyer is that he pays the draft before he gets to inspect the goods. If the goods are nonconforming the buyer has to deal with a seller who already has his money.

The buyer must carefully inspect the documents before paying the draft. If the documents disclose a breach by the seller but the buyer pays anyway, he cannot later complain about it.

Four sorts of breaches that will show on the documents are these:

1. A required document is missing.

2. The invoice shows that the seller shipped nonconforming goods. In other words, the seller did not ship what buyer ordered.

3. The packing list (when required) and the bill of lading do not jibe; the exporter has not shipped what he has billed the importer for.

4. The bill of lading is *Foul,* or, as the English say, *Claused.* If the bill shows that the goods were received by the carrier for shipment in damaged condition, it is foul. It is a breach by a seller to ship under a foul bill.

If the deal is a credit deal the seller will draw a time draft on the buyer for the price, payable thirty, sixty, or ninety days after acceptance. The buyer is entitled to the bill of lading and other documents when he accepts the draft, not when he pays it.

The goods will arrive before the accepted draft matures; thus the buyer knows whether or not he got comforming goods before he pays. However, if the accepted draft gets into the hands of a holder in due course before maturity buyer will be obligated to pay it even if seller shipped nonconforming goods; breach of contract is not a good defense against a person with holder in due course rights.

The seller naturally prefers the sight draft variant of this kind of transaction. The buyer will prefer the time draft variant.

All of the above transactions will involve sending negotiable commercial paper from one country to another for collection. Though the commercial paper law of all trading countries is similar, it is not identical, as stated earlier. Problems may arise to bedevil the careless or unlucky exporter.

The International Chamber of Commerce has devised Uniform Rules for Collection which may be included in all transnational contracts involving collection of commercial paper. The courts of all nations will recognize these when they are included in appropriate contracts. The use of these eliminates problems that can be caused by the differing commercial paper law of the countries involved.

Letters of Credit. A letter of credit transaction is very similar to a payment against documents transaction. Under such a transaction the buyer must obtain a letter of credit from a bank in which the bank agrees to honor the seller's draft.

There are three parties to a letter of credit. The *Customer* is the buyer of the goods. The *Issuer* is the issuing bank. The *Beneficiary* is the seller of the goods and the drawer of the draft(s) to be honored under it.

Letters of credit may be *Revocable* or *Irrevocable.* The issuer may revoke a revocable letter of credit at its option, for any reason. An irrevocable credit may not be revoked without the consent of the customer and the beneficiary. Thus, when a contract calls for payment by letter of credit, an irrevocable credit is meant unless the contract specifies otherwise.

Letters of credit may also be *Confirmed* or *Advised.* A credit becomes confirmed when a bank in the beneficiary's financial market agrees to assume liability on it. It is advised when such a bank simply takes the beneficiary's draft for collection and forwards it to the issuing bank. Thus, two banks are liable on confirmed credits, but only one on advised credits. The buyer is not obligated to obtain a confirmed credit unless the contract specifies it.

Under an advised credit the seller does not ship the goods until he has been notified that the credit has been issued. He then draws his draft upon the issuing bank, attaches to it invoice, bill of lading, and other required documents, indorses the bill of lading to his bank, and the documents begin their journey to the issuing bank. Upon arrival the issuer checks the documents to be sure they comply with the contract. If they do the issuer pays the draft (if a sight draft) or accepts it (if a time draft) and notifies the buyer of the arrival of the documents. The buyer then reimburses the bank for what it paid out in exchange for the bill of lading. When the goods arrive buyer exchanges the bill for them while the draft proceeds are remitted to the seller.

Under a confirmed credit the seller draws his draft on the confirming bank, which will pay or accept. The confirming bank is then reimbursed by the issuing bank, which is in turn reimbursed by the buyer.

Credits may also be *Transferrable, Nontransferrable,* or *Straight.* The beneficiary of a transferrable credit may assign the right to draw drafts under it. The assignment does not become binding upon issuing or confirming banks until they are notified of it.

The beneficiary may not assign the right to draw drafts on a nontransferrable credit, but the payee of such drafts may be someone other than the beneficiary. So long as the beneficiary is the drawer, the payee may be anyone.

The beneficiary of a straight credit may not draw drafts payable to anyone other than himself. Thus, the beneficiary must be both drawer and payee of the drafts drawn.

Credits may be *Lump-sum* or *Installment.* The beneficiary of a lump-sum credit is limited to drawing one draft. The beneficiary of the installment credit may draw as many drafts as he chooses, so long as the total amount drawn does not exceed the face value of the credit.

Suppose that Ace Company of the United States contracts to sell goods to Deuce Company of Great Britain, Deuce to pay with a confirmed letter of credit. Ace needs to acquire raw materials for performance of the contract from Trey Company of Canada. Ace may pay Trey by obtaining a letter of credit from the confirming bank (a bank in Ace's financial market) in favor of Trey, giving his bank a security interest in the proceeds of the Deuce credit as collateral. These credits are *Back-to-Back* credits.

In the Ace-Deuce bargain above, suppose that Ace wanted Deuce to obtain a credit it could draw upon before shipping the goods to help finance their manufacture or packing or whatever. *Anticipatory* (or *Packing*) credits serve this purpose. The issuing or confirming bank in such a case will require documentary proof from Ace that it has begun a performance of the Ace-Deuce contract before granting the advance. The documentation required will be spelled out in the letter of credit.

If Ace and Deuce regularly do business by letter of credit they and their banks may establish a relationship under which the banks will honor drafts drawn by Ace on Deuce up to a stated amount over a stated period of time. Deuce thus has a semipermanent line of credit with the banks for purposes of buying goods from Ace. Each time the banks honor a draft from Ace the credit available is reduced; each time Deuce reimburses the bank for what was paid the credit available is restored.

Banks in the Far East often issue authority to purchase credits. Under these the issuing bank instructs the advising bank to purchase the draft drawn by the exporter against the seller at face value. The advising bank then negotiates the draft to the issuing bank which presents it for acceptance or payment to the importer. If the importer accepts or pays it everyone is happy; if he dishonors it the issuing bank must proceed against the advising bank on its secondary liability as indorser, and the advising bank must do the same to the exporter on his secondary liability as drawer.

A bank's obligation to honor a draft drawn under a letter of credit is not absolute. If the documents do not comply with the seller-buyer contract and the terms of the credit the bank must dishonor. If the documents do so comply the bank must honor. Thus the buyer cannot stop payment on a letter of credit as he could on a check.

The documents accompanying a letter of credit would not be in order in the following situations, among others:

1. A required document (insurance certificate, certificate of origin, etc.) is missing.

2. The packing list shows that the shipper did not ship what is listed on the invoice.

3. The goods listed on the invoice are not the goods called for by the exporter-importer contract.

4. The bill of lading is foul.

5. The drawer of the draft is not the beneficiary of the letter of credit and the honoring bank has not been notified of any assignment of the right to draw drafts (which would not be valid anyway unless the credit is a transferrable credit).

If the seller insures that the documents accompanying his draft are in order he is virtually certain to be paid by the issuing or confirming bank. If the goods are not in order (though the documents are) the buyer must reimburse the honoring bank and try to recover his loss from the seller.

The seller's risk is small in such a transaction. If the credit is confirmed the risk is minimal, because seller will collect the contract price in U.S. dollars from a bank in his financial market soon after the goods are shipped. If the credit is only advised the seller will be collecting from a foreign bank, probably in the currency of that country. Exchange controls and the like in the buyer's country might hinder collection; fluctuations in exchange rates could influence the exporter's dollar receipts.

The buyer is to a large extent at the seller's mercy. The seller may obtain payment from an issuing or confirming bank even though he has breached his contract with the buyer. He could send nonconforming goods while assembling a package of documents showing the shipments to be conforming goods. The documents will be in order though the shipment is not. Or he could send a package of forged documents through banking channels in the company of a genuine draft, while shipping no goods. If the forgery is not apparent on the face of the documents the banks could justifiably honor the draft and require the defrauded buyer to reimburse them. Or dishonest employees of the seller could prepare a package of forged documents (including a forged draft) and send these through banking channels before the seller ships the goods. The bank honors the forged documents because they appear to be genuine. The seller then ships the goods and sends a package of genuine documents through banking channels. The bank dishonors the genuine draft because it has already honored the seemingly genuine forged draft. In such a case both buyer and seller have been victimized by the forgers, but the buyer comes off decidedly worse. If he wants his goods he must pay for them twice; once to reimburse the bank for the forged draft and once to pay the seller.

The courts of virtually all trading nations apply the above-described rules to letter of credit transactions. Almost all such are governed by the Uniform Customs and Practice for Documentary Credits (UCP) promulgated by the International Chamber of Commerce. These do such an effective job of regulating letter of credit transactions that they are almost the equivalent of law.

Since consignment arrangements involve the hiring of an agent, they will be discussed in the next chapter.

Export Financing. Unless the exporter's customers pay in advance, some of his capital is bound to be tied up in various sorts of receivables. The sooner these are reduced to cash the more healthy is the exporter's business.

Open account terms in export transactions are rare in the United States;

they are more common in Europe. English and other European exporters often turn their accounts receivable into cash by engaging in *Factoring.*

Factors essentially purchase the accounts receivable of the exporter, relieving him of credit and collection concerns. In *Disclosed Factoring* the exporter assigns his accounts to the factor for consideration, making the factor the owner of the account. The factor informs the importer of the assignment, so that the importer pays the factor. The exporter must offer all accounts receivable to the factor for purchase. Those the factor approves are bought on a nonrecourse basis, so that if they prove uncollectible the factor may not charge them back. Those not approved are purchased on a recourse basis; if these prove uncollectible the factor may charge them back.

The American factor needs to file a financing statement in the proper place (usually the office of the secretary of state of the state where the assignment takes place) to protect himself against double assignments and the like.

In undisclosed factoring the exporter discounts his invoices with the factor, receiving an agreed percentage of the invoice price less a service charge in return. The exporter then collects the accounts from the importer and deposits the proceeds in a trust account for the benefit of the factor. From here the advances made by the factor are repaid.

The exporter collects quickly when payment is by confirmed letter of credit; the confirming bank will pay him one hundred cents per dollar of the face value of his drafts. When payment is by advised letter of credit or payment against documents by sight draft he may have to wait longer, unless he chooses to discount the drafts drawn against the issuing bank or the buyer (as the case may be) with his local bank. If he discounts he gets less than one hundred cents per dollar of face value.

When the contract terms call for payment by acceptance of a time draft against documents the accepted draft is known as a *Trade Acceptance.* The seller may hold this until maturity, or he may discount it with a bank. Again, if seller discounts he will receive less than one hundred cents per dollar of face value.

When the contract calls for payment by time draft drawn against a confirmed letter of credit the duty of the confirming bank will be to accept the draft if the accompanying documents are in order. This results in the creation of a *Banker's Acceptance,* which may be sold in the appropriate commercial paper market at a small discount. If the time draft is drawn against an advised letter of credit the banker's acceptance will be created by the issuing bank. In such case the seller could have the draft sold in the buyer's financial market, or have it returned to him so he may sell it in his.

The exporter will of course have the secondary liability of a drawer upon both the trade acceptance and the banker's acceptance. The risk of this ripening into true liability on the banker's acceptance is in effect nil, though trade acceptances are occasionally dishonored at maturity.

An exporter may grant long-term credit to an importer buying valuable capital goods or the like. The importer in such a case will probably pay in the form of a promissory note or notes maturing years into the future. Such notes could be immediately discounted by banks for cash, but the discount upon such long-term paper could be large.

American exporters must realize that certain common provisions used in negotiable promissory notes drawn in this country will render notes drawn abroad nonnegotiable.

Promissory notes payable in installments are very common in our country, and are considered negotiable. Under English law installment notes are negotiable only when the due dates of the installments are stated specifically. Under the Geneva Convention installment notes are nonnegotiable.

American installment notes commonly provide that if the maker defaults on his loan contract the entire unpaid balance of the note becomes immediately due and payable. English notes may contain such acceleration clauses; under the Geneva Convention such a clause renders a note nonnegotiable.

American installment notes often give the maker the right to pay his obligation before maturity. Such a provision in an English or Geneva Convention country note renders the paper nonnegotiable.

European exporters often require importers who are granted long-term credit represented by promissory notes to make the sale a *forfait* transaction. In such a bargain the importer draws the promissory notes by which he promises to pay off his obligation. Before he transmits these to the exporter he agrees to have them avalized by a bank in his financial market; the bank indorses them with avals, thus guaranteeing payment regardless of any defense to payment on the importer's part. The exporter then sells the notes to a bank in his financial market without recourse, at a small discount.

The avalized notes are almost as safe an investment as a banker's acceptance, because they are essentially bank obligations. The buying bank has bought the obligation of the avalizing bank and runs only a small risk of dishonor. The exporter has obtained cash for the notes without any danger of the notes being charged back to him in case of dishonor.

Guarantees

The exporter may not be willing to completely trust the good will of the importer in these transactions, nor may the importer completely trust the exporter. Either party may want a bank or other reputable institution to guarantee the other's performance of his duties.

There are three parties to a guarantee: (1) the *Principal*, whose obligation is being guaranteed; (2) the *Beneficiary*, for whose benefit the obligation is being guaranteed; and (3) the *Guarantor*, the party doing the guaranteeing (usually a bank).

The principal is responsible for arranging these guarantees.

The sort of guarantee required of a buyer is a *Payment* guarantee. The purpose of it is to assure the seller that, if the buyer does not pay as obligated, the guarantor will. The seller wants assurance that he is going to be paid by a reliable paymaster.

A *Standby Letter of Credit* will serve rather well as a guarantee of payment and is probably the most commonly used such device in the United States. Such a credit is issued by a bank in the same way as are other credits. They are documentary credits, but the documents required to trigger the issuer's obligation to pay are not the traditional invoice, bill of lading, and insurance certificate. Because the issuer agrees to honor drafts drawn under the credit only if the buyer is in default on his obligation to pay for the goods, the document required to trigger the issuer's obligation will usually be some proof of the buyer's default. In Europe such guarantees may be non–letter-of-credit bargains between the principal and the guarantor for the benefit of the beneficiary.

Payment guarantees may be *Conditional* or *Unconditional* (or *Demand*). Under a conditional guarantee, the guarantor agrees to pay on condition that the beneficiary produce a specified document or documents (a statement that the buyer is in default on his payment obligation, a certified copy of a judgment obtained by the seller against the buyer, or whatever). Under a demand guarantee the beneficiary simply demands payment of the guarantor, and guarantor is obligated to oblige. Banks prefer demand guarantees, because there can be no question of whether they should have paid or not. Under a conditional guarantee the principal might refuse to reimburse the guarantor because the document produced by the beneficiary was improper or the like.

The stand-by credit may in essence become such a guarantee when the only document required is a statement of the buyer's default.

Three sorts of guarantee may be required of sellers by buyers: the *Performance* guarantee, the *Repayment* guarantee, and the *Tender* guarantee. In a performance guarantee the guarantor agrees to pay the beneficiary damages in case the seller does not properly perform his contract. In the repayment guarantee the guarantor agrees to repay advanced payments made by the buyer to the seller in case the seller does not properly perform. Tender guarantees may be requested when the principal bids on a procurement or construction contract to be let through competitive bidding. The guarantor agrees to pay the beneficiary damages if the principal is awarded the contract and does not perform.

These types of guarantees may be conditional or unconditional (demand). Middle Eastern and African buyers are very likely to require demand performance guarantees of their suppliers.

The seller who agrees to a demand performance guarantee runs something of a risk. If the buyer gets nervous and doubts the seller's ability to perform he may make a demand under the guarantee. Since the guarantor is obligated to pay on demand he will do so, even if the seller really is not in default. The seller may find himself obligated to reimburse the guarantor and perform his contract with the beneficiary at the same time though he was never in default.

Performance, repayment, and tender guarantees are governed by the Uniform Rules for Contract Guarantees (URCG) of the International Chamber of Commerce. These rules are very often included in contracts creating such guarantees.

Clive Schmitthoff discusses two special types of guarantees in his work *The Law and Practice of International Trade. Counterguarantees* are required in Egypt, Syria, and Iraq when local buyers are importing goods or services from abroad. The seller is required to obtain a guarantee from a bank in his financial market. The beneficiary of the guarantee will not be the buyer, however; it will be a local bank in the buyer's financial market. The local bank then grants the buyer the counterguarantee. The advantage of this is that the buyer may make his claim against the local bank on the counterguarantee rather than against the foreign bank on the guarantee, thus obtaining satisfaction very quickly. (The buyer's bank then claims against the seller's bank on the guarantee, and the seller must then reimburse his bank.)

A buyer might also demand a *Superguarantee* of a seller who obtains a guarantee from a small local bank in his area. The buyer will demand that the guarantor obtain a guarantee of its obligation from a large well-known bank. If the buyer wants to make a claim under the guarantee, then, he may claim against the large bank under the superguarantee rather than against the local bank under the guarantee.

The URCG provide that a claim under a performance or repayment guarantee must be made within six months of the date specified for delivery of the goods or completion of the contract. Time limits under tender guarantees may vary. This time limit may also be varied if the parties agree to do so. Middle Eastern buyers want these time limits expressed in years rather than in months.

The URGC apply only to guarantees of the obligations of sellers; they do not apply to guarantees of obligations of buyers.

Government Supported Export Credit. An American exporter selling on credit to his foreign customer may be able to obtain insurance on his credit risk through the Foreign Credit Insurance Association (FCIA). This private organization operates in cooperation with the Export-Import Bank (Eximbank), an instrumentality of the U.S. government, and will insure both the credit and political risks of the venture; but it will generally require the exporter to coinsure from 5 to 10 percent. If the importer cannot pay for reasons covered by the insurance, the exporter suffers only a small loss.

The insurance will not cover losses caused by the importer canceling his order. It also will not cover loss covered by the importer's insolvency unless a special indorsement to the policy is purchased for an additional premium. What is covered is refusal to pay on the part of the importer or refusal to accept the goods by the importer. (If the exporter breached his contract with the importer and this caused the importer's default the exporter of course has no claim under his insurance.)

Political risk coverage is fairly comprehensive. The exporter is protected if after shipment an export or import license is canceled; if a change in the law of the importer's country makes the import unlawful; if the voyage of the vessel carrying the shipment is interrupted or the vessel is diverted; if war, revolution, or confiscation makes performance impossible; or if transfer or nontransfer of a currency deposit is delayed.

The exporter may obtain a master policy from FCIA covering all of his export sales for a five-year period, or he may obtain specific policies for individual transactions.

The commercial bank financing export transactions may obtain loan guarantees from the Export-Import Bank (Eximbank). The commercial bank makes a Master Guarantee Agreement with Eximbank spelling out the general terms of all loan guarantees to be made under the arrangement. Each guarantee of a specific loan must be specifically authorized by Eximbank. These guarantees are unavailable for loans for shorter terms than six months or longer terms than five years. They are also not available for transactions involving export of goods not made in the United States.

The guarantee will cover an unpaid exporter loan if the default is due to insolvency of the importer, arbitrary nonacceptance of goods by the importer, cancellation of export license, cancellation of import license, currency inconvertibility, war, revolution, expropriation, and the like. Not covered are defaults caused by repudiation of a contract by a public buyer (an agency of a foreign government), natural catastrophe outside the United States, or currency exchange rate fluctuations.

Eximbank will also grant direct loans to foreign buyers of American goods if the term of repayment is more than five years and the foreign buyer meets other Eximbank terms. The agency will also guarantee loans to foreign buyers by commercial banks under the same circumstances.

Exporters of American agricultural products and foreign importers of the same may arrange government guarantees of loan arrangements through the Commodity Credit Corporation of the Department of Agriculture.

A commercial bank lending funds to a small business to finance export transactions may also obtain government guarantees on the loan through the Small Business Administration.

Lastly, for long-term arrangements where commercial bank financing is hard to come by, the exporter may obtain what he needs from the Private Sector Export Funding Corporation (PEFCO), another organization working in close cooperation with Eximbank.

Many other nations have competing export financing programs. The services offered by all of these, and the terms and conditions of the offer, are substantially the same, though differences in the various programs exist.

Countertrade. An exporter may arrange with his importer customer to take payment in goods of the importer's country rather than in currency. Bargains of this sort are most often made with Communist nations, but they are becoming increasingly popular with trading partners outside the Communist bloc.

There are four ways of arranging these transactions.

In *Counterpurchase* deals the importer pays for what he buys from the exporter in his own currency. The exporter agrees to spend this currency within the importer's country over a short period of time (generally not to exceed five years) on products available for export contained on a list furnished by the importer's government. The exporter here has a choice as to what products to accept in payment for his export. Generally the products appearing on the permissible purchase list are items in oversupply in the importing nation's economy or products the importing nation wishes to stimulate export of.

In *Reciprocal Sales* arrangements what the exporter will buy from the importer's country is specified in the importer-exporter contract. Often the contract is worded so that the importer is not obligated to perform his obligation to buy until the exporter has performed his parallel obligation. These are not barter deals because each party pays in money for his purchases. Since the prices of the parallel purchases will not balance out to the penny, someone will owe someone else a small cash balance after performance.

In *Compensating Purchase* deals the exporter sells equipment, technology, or an entire plant to the importer and is paid in the importer's currency. In return the importer agrees to sell and the exporter to buy and export a stated percentage of the output of the plant in which the equipment or technology was installed. A bargain of this sort may be very long-term — ten years or more. The price the exporter pays for the product he buys in compensation is negotiated; generally he pays a price below world market price.

In *Barter* deals the importer pays for the exporter's product with another product. Generally no currency changes hands.

The advantages to the importer in countertrade transactions are the following: (1) he conserves hard currency because he pays either in his own currency or in goods or services; (2) he does not aggravate his country's balance of payments problem (if it has one); and (3) he hopefully assures himself of a market for products he has had difficulty in exporting.

The advantages to the exporter include: (1) he may be getting access to a market he could not invade in any other way; (2) he may be getting around bothersome exchange controls in the importer's country since he is not bringing any funds out of that country; and (3) he obtains additional sources of revenue through the sale of the products he acquires in the countertrade, perhaps establishing him in new product markets in the United States or elsewhere.

The main disadvantage to the exporter of such deals is that he may have no organization to market what he obtains in the countertrade. He may well have to dispose of it through another firm specializing in the sale of the product or commodity.

Chapter 12

Doing Business Abroad

Selecting a Foreign Agent or Distributor

The American exporter desiring to penetrate a foreign market *may* want to have a native representative on the spot in that market to deal with potential customers. The native knows the local language and culture; he can advertise and promote the product on the spot; and he can serve as the contact man for the local customers. In some countries a resident agent or distributor *must* be a local citizen; this is true in Egypt, Indonesia, Iraq, Jordan, Burma, and Saudi Arabia, among other lands.

The foreign representative may be either an *Agent* or a *Distributor*. The agent will simply act as an order solicitor and contact man, making any contracts with his customers in the name of his principal. The distributor will generally maintain its own inventory of his principal's product, make contracts in its own name, collect payment in its own name, and in general assume the risks of distribution of the product.

The principal will usually send inventory to the distributor on consignment. Under this arrangement the exporter ships the goods to the importer to see if the importer can sell them. The exporter gets paid if and only if the importer sells the goods. The goods remain the exporter's property until sold. The exporter assumes most of the risk in this arrangement. If the goods are harmed due to the importer's negligence the exporter could recover damages, but he would have to sue in the importer's country to collect. If the goods are not sold the exporter would probably have to pay the cost of having them shipped back here, though that would be governed by the consignment contract.

The agent is generally an individual rather than a business organization. Depending on his contract with his principal, he may be either an employee or an independent contractor. If he is an employee the principal may closely control what he does. However, the agent will then have all of the rights of an employee under the law of his country. This means that the principal will be responsible for making social security contributions for him. The agent may have the right to severance pay on the termination of his employment and he may have something resembling job tenure. If he is an independent contractor the principal will have less control over him, but the principal will also be free of the burdens of an employer-employee relationship.

The agent who sells his principal's goods on credit is not normally liable to the principal for the unpaid accounts of his customers. If the customer does not pay the account the principal must collect from him. However, principal and agent may agree that the agent will in essence guarantee payment of customer accounts. Such an agent is known as a *Del Credere* agent. The del credere agent will charge a higher commission for his services because he assumes a greater risk. It may well be worth the expense to the principal to be certain that he will be paid for what his agent sells.

Romano-Germanic law recognizes two types of agent: *Direct* and *Indirect*. The direct agent makes contracts with his customers in the name of his principal. The indirect agent is similar to what the common law calls an agent for an undisclosed principal, who makes contracts with his customers in his own name. French law calls such indirect agents *Commissionaires*.

One significant legal difference exists between the common-law agent for an undisclosed principal and the Romano-Germanic commissionaire. The undisclosed principal may sue to enforce contracts made for his benefit, but the commissionaire's principal may not.

Thus, Ace Company of Dallas hires Bloggs of London as its English agent. Bloggs sells Ace goods to his customers in his name, but Ace ships the goods to the buyers direct from Dallas. Chutney of Oxford does not pay Bloggs for what he bought on credit. Ace could sue Chutney to collect the account; the Bloggs contract with Chutney could be enforced by Ace, because Ace was the true seller of the merchandise. By the same token, if the goods Ace shipped to Chutney were defective, Chutney would be able to sue Ace for breach of contract since common-law undisclosed principals are responsible for breaches of their contracts.

Ace also hires Sucre of Paris to act as its French agent, the contract specifying that Sucre is a commissionaire. Sucre sells Ace goods to his customers in his name, but again Ace ships the goods to French buyers direct from Dallas. Cafard of Lyons does not pay Sucre for what he bought on credit. Ace could not sue Cafard to collect this account, because under French law Ace is considered to have no contract with Cafard. Only Sucre, the agent, may sue to enforce this bargain. And if the goods are defective Cafard will be unable to sue Ace, because Ace and Cafard have no contract. Cafard's only recourse is against Sucre.

The commissionaire of course must account to his principal for the profit he earns, and is entitled to the agreed commissions on his sales.

Many nations have special laws governing termination of agents; in such countries the principal must use care in ending the relationship. Among such countries are Austria, Brazil, Finland, West Germany, Spain, Sweden, and Switzerland.

The distributor, being an independent contractor, will usually also be a business organization. The relationship between it and its principal will be a matter of contract.

Many countries have special laws governing termination of distributorships and agents; in these, too, the principal must be careful. Such countries include Colombia, the Philippines, Saudi Arabia, Thailand, and North Yemen.

U.S. Antiboycott Legislation. Under the Antiboycott Law U.S. persons and firms are forbidden to participate in boycotts unauthorized by the United States Government. The legislation was originally enacted to prevent U.S. businesses from participating in the Arab world's boycott of Israel. This boycott still remains the main potential violation of this legislation. Foreign subsidiaries, affiliates, or establishments controlled in fact by a U.S. citizen or corporation are covered by this law; therefore, the more control an exporter exercises over his agent or distributor abroad, the more likely it is that he will be held responsible for the agent or distributor's participation in an unauthorized boycott.

The American firm with an agent or distributor in the Middle East runs the greatest danger of violating this legislation. The agent will probably be a Muslim and a local patriot, sharing the hatred of his countrymen for the Jewish state. Though there would be almost no potential for an agent in, say, Iraq to do business in Israel, it would still be wise for the American principal to exercise the minimum control consistent with the effectiveness of the agency over his local representative.

The Foreign Corrupt Practices Act (FCPA). The FCPA prohibits any person subject to United States jurisdiction from making payments to any foreign government official, political party, or candidate for public office to influence any act or decision of the official, party, or candidate in order to gain or retain business. The act forbids only payments to high-level personnel in foreign lands intended to influence government policy. It does not forbid payments to low-level bureaucrats (such as customs inspectors) to ensure performance of routine administrative duties.

Not only are American businesspeople themselves forbidden to make such payments. Making payments to agents and employees abroad that will be used for unlawful purposes under the act is also forbidden. Thus, if an American firm has an agent or distributor operating in a country where such payments occur, it must make certain that the agent or distributor does not use money received from the principal for such unlawful purposes.

If unlawful payments are being made by the representative, and the principal knows or should know what is happening, the principal will be held responsible. In a sense, the less the principal knows about his agent's activities the better. The best policy for the principal to follow is to forbid his agent to engage in conduct that violates FCPA, whether or not it is consistent with local custom.

For violation of FCPA, a corporation may be fined up to $2,000,000. Officers or directors of the same may be fined up to $100,000 or imprisoned up to five years or both.

Licensing Transactions

The American producer of a product may decide that his market for it in another country will be improved by producing it in that country, but he does not want to go to the trouble and expense of establishing production facilities in that country. A solution to the problem may be the granting of a license to a native firm in the target country.

The granting of a license will almost inevitably involve the granting of permission to the licensee to use intellectual property — patents, trademarks, copyrights, or trade secrets — belonging to the licensor. The licensor will want to make as certain as possible that his intellectual property will not get into the hands of competitors who will use it to his disadvantage.

In order to better understand the problems of international licensing, we shall now consider the law governing the various forms of intellectual property.

Patents. A patent grants an inventor a monopoly upon the use of an invention for a stated period of time. Under United States law a patent may be granted for a new and useful machine, a process, a manufacture, or a composition of matter. The patent holder obtains a monopoly upon the use of his invention *within the United States* for seventeen years. A United States patent confers no rights upon the patent holder outside the United States. He who wishes to acquire patent protection upon an invention in more than one country must therefore obtain a patent in each country in which he desires protection.

The United States is a signatory, along with some eighty other nations, of the Paris Convention for the Protection of Industrial Property. This convention grants to inventors two important rights. First, signatory nations must accord the same rights to alien inventors as they do to their own citizens. Second, when an inventor files for a patent in a second country after filing in his own country, his second application is predated to the date of his first application, so long as he files for the second within twelve months of his filing for the first.

Thus, an American inventor files for a U.S. patent upon an invention on June 1, 1987. On March 1, 1988, he files for an English patent upon the same invention. His English application will be dated June 1, 1987. This is important because when two or more inventors file for a patent upon identical inventions, the first inventor to file may well be granted the patent.

Should he wait longer than a year to file in the second country, he will probably lose his right to a patent there. Under most national laws one must file within one year of filing in another country. In countries such as Australia, India, Pakistan, Switzerland, and Greece late filing will not disqualify the applicant if the invention has been given no publicity in the country of application, but such countries are a small minority.

Under the Patent Co-Operation Treaty, an applicant may make one filing for a patent that will be valid in all signatory countries. The one filing will not be sufficient for him to obtain a patent in all of these lands, however; he must prosecute his application in all countries in which he desires a patent under the national law of each.

There exists a European Patent Office, created by the Convention on Grant of European Patents. One may file for a patent there and obtain a grant that is valid in all member nations for twenty years if one is a national of one of the member nations. The protection granted by this patent, and what constitutes infringement, is governed by the national laws of the member nations. At present eleven nations have ratified the convention: Austria, Belgium, France, the German Federal Republic, Italy, Liechtenstein, Luxembourg, the Netherlands, Sweden, Switzerland, and the United Kingdom. An Englishman could file for a patent under this convention and obtain one that is valid in all eleven nations. An American could not do this because of the limitation of the privilege to nationals of member nations.

Under the Libreville Agreement a citizen of, say, Senegal could obtain a patent that would be valid in most of the African nations that at one time were French colonies (Gabon, Togo, the Ivory Coast, Benin, Burkina Faso, etc.). The Industrial Property Organisation for English-Speaking Africa does the same for citizens of Uganda, Zimbabwe, Ghana, Malawi, and Sudan.

The nations of the EC have negotiated a Community Patent Convention which has not yet come into force. When it does it will be possible for a citizen of an EC member state to obtain a patent valid in all twelve member nations of the community.

Under some national laws (mainly those of the Soviet bloc and other Communist nations), certain sorts of inventions may not be patented. Instead, the inventor receives an inventor's certificate that entitles him to royalties, but does not give him a monopoly upon the use of the invention. Communist ideology does not approve of private ownership of rights in inventions, since only the state would have the capacity to make use of it. Why should the inventor be able to profit at the expense of the people? (China is an exception to this rule. It is now possible for individual Chinese inventors to obtain patents.)

In the United States and some other countries an inventor may suppress a patent for its life by not producing the patented product and not licensing others to produce it. Some other nations will not allow this procedure. If the inventor refuses to produce the invention himself he may be compelled to license others to produce it.

In the United States one must pay a fee to the Patent Office every four years in order to keep a patent in effect. In other lands one must do this on an annual basis.

Trademarks. A trademark is any word, name, symbol, device, or combination thereof used by a merchant or manufacturer to identify its goods and distinguish them from goods produced by others. In the United States one may acquire rights in a trademark by registering it with the Patent Office, or by simple use.

One may perfect ownership rights in a trademark in the United States through registration, but the effort to register will be defeated if another can prove he was the first to begin using the mark in interstate commerce.

Prior to November 16, 1989, American trademark registrations were valid for twenty years, and were renewable for an indefinite series of twenty-year periods for as long as the mark continued in use. The Trademark Law Revision Act of 1988 shortened this period to ten years.

Trademark protection laws vary throughout the world. According to Clive Schmitthoff's *The Law and Practice of International Trade* three systems exist: (1) ownership based on priority of use; (2) ownership based on priority of registration; and (3) ownership based on uncontested registration for a specified period.

Perhaps a majority of the world's nations use the first method. One should register a trademark used in these countries with the proper authority, but registration merely creates a public record that as of a certain time the registrant was using the mark. Anyone who can prove that he was using the mark before the registrant's registration can establish ownership and thereby charge the registrant with infringement. In short, the first user of the mark is the true owner, whether or not he is the first registrant.

Under the second system, he who first registers a mark is recognized as the owner. He has the right to take action for infringement against all other users—even those who used the mark before his registration. Most Communist and South American countries use this system, as do Japan, West Germany, France, Spain, and Sweden.

Under the third system, in use in the United States, he who obtains registration of a mark may have his ownership challenged by a prior unregistered user for a period of time after registration. As explained above, a mark registered in the United States may be contested for five years after registration. In the United Kingdom the registration may be contested for seven years. Most of the countries that use the third system are English-speaking (Canada, India, Ireland, and New Zealand, for example). Other users include Indonesia, Israel, and Switzerland.

The old twenty-year validity of American trademark registrations was relatively long. In many other nations, reregistration every ten years or less is required. The United States has joined the mainstream in this regard.

As with patents, trademark registrations are valid in only one nation. Under the Paris Convention, second and subsequent applications for registration of a trademark made within six months of an initial application for registration are dated as of the original registration application.

Under the Madrid Agreement, to which the United States is not a party, one may register a trademark in up to thirty-five nations simultaneously through an application to the World Intellectual Property Organization in Geneva.

Under the law of the United States and of most other nations, a trademark holder may charge a fee for licensing others to use his mark. In a few nations the charging of such fees is unlawful, however.

The American exporter who markets goods under his trademark in a country using the first system of trademark protection runs no great risks, unless he knows that someone else is already using the mark in that country. As long as he is the first to use it there it is safe, whether his use is registered or not.

The exporter doing business in a country using the second system must be careful. Before using his mark in that country he must make sure that no one else has registered the mark there. If anyone has, he owns the mark in that nation; for the exporter to intrude lays him open to infringement liability. If there is no prior registration, the exporter should register his mark as soon as possible. He thus makes himself the owner of it in that country.

The above considerations also apply to doing business in a country using the third system. One should register one's mark as soon as possible in these countries also (assuming no prior registrations), but the registration might be contested later by a prior user. One's ownership is not secure until the mark becomes incontestible (five years after registration in the U.S., seven years thereafter in the U.K.).

Copyrights. One protects intellectual property rights in printed matter, computer software, and the like through copyright registration. In the United States this is done through applications to the Copyright Office of the Library of Congress. Generally an American copyright registration grants protection to the registrant for the life of the author plus fifty years.

Under the Berne Convention, of which the United States is a signatory, the registration of a copyright in one member nation grants rights in all member nations. Thus the copyright is the only sort of intellectual property in which a sort of international registration is possible.

The length of copyright protection under the convention is a matter of the national law of its signatories.

Trade Secrets. Most know-how that is the subject matter of international licensing agreements is not protected by patent, copyright, or trademark. This sort of information is protected by the law of trade secrets.

There is no mechanism for registering a trade secret and acquiring ownership rights in it. The only way to keep the secret a secret is through stringent security precautions and by contracts with users that forbid disclosure to unauthorized persons.

He who acquires a trade secret through licensing will be restricted in his use of the information acquired. He who acquires the information by accident or through independent discovery or reverse engineering may use the information as he pleases.

Technical Data Export Licensing. Under the Export Administration Act exports of technical data are subject to licensing. General licenses for most data available to the public exist, as do general licenses for export of other sorts of data to Country Groups T, V, and Canada (see Chapter 1).

A validated license may well be required to export technical data to Communist countries, or to Libya and South Africa.

Host Country Licensing Restrictions. Some governments impose restrictions upon technology imports. These might include:

1. Registration of the licensing agreement
2. Restrictions on the type of technology that may be imported
3. Limitation of the amount payable for technology
4. Foreign exchange controls
5. Taxes, registration fees, and the like

Underdeveloped countries are most likely to impose such restrictions.

Where registration of the licensing agreement is required, the registry office may well have the right to deny registration of agreements inimical to the national interest. Thus the licensor may be required to negotiate with the national registry office as well as with the licensee. Mexico in particular can be difficult to deal with in this regard.

Licensing agreements involving a Japanese party must be submitted to the Japanese Fair Trade Commission for determination that they do not violate Japanese antitrust law.

Agreements involving parties from nations belonging to the European Community must not reduce competition within the community.

Royalty payments by the licensee to the licensor may be subject to taxation by the host country. Mexico and other nations require withholding of the tax from the royalty payments at the source.

An American licensor will naturally want his royalties to be paid in U.S. dollars. However, if the host country has balance of payments problems and has imposed exchange controls the licensee could have difficulty in obtaining the necessary dollars.

In Communist countries the licensee will be a state enterprise. In these cases the licensor is to a great extent at the mercy of the host government, because in essence it is the licensee.

American Antitrust Considerations. A licensing agreement must not cause injury to American competitors of the licensor. Provisions that attempt to restrict the access of American competitors of the licensor to the licensee's market and the like may cause the licensor difficulties in this country.

Joint Ventures

Occasionally the American firm wishing to penetrate a foreign market is unwilling to do so through host country agents or licensees. It may also be unwilling or unable to invest in wholly owned branches or subsidiaries. The solution may then be an enterprise owned in part by the American firm and in part by persons or organizations of the host country.

The *Joint Venture* may be a voluntary partnership between the foreign firm and a host country firm, such as the General Motors–Toyota arrangement here in the United States. It could also be a somewhat coerced arrangement required by host country legislation. In Mexico, for instance, foreigners may not control a business enterprise; only Mexican citizens can own the controlling interest. The same is true in the Philippines and India.

In Communist countries direct foreign investment is generally forbidden. Some of these nations, notably Romania, Hungary, Yugoslavia, and China, do allow the establishment of joint ventures, co-owned by the foreign investor and the state enterprise authorized to participate in the venture.

A bit less than two years ago the Soviet Union ventured into these waters. Here, too, the venture is co-owned by a state enterprise and the foreign party. The foreign joint venturer may not own more than 49 percent of the venture, thereby allowing the Soviets to retain control. The ultimate management authority lies in Soviet hands. Acquisitions of raw materials and the like within the USSR will be a matter of dealing with other

Soviet state enterprises. Employees will essentially be employees of the Soviet state.

If the venture proves to be profitable, the foreign investor will pay heavy taxes on its share of the profit. However, it may be permitted to repatriate at least some of what remains to the home country.

Direct Foreign Investment

The foreign business desiring to make a direct investment in the economy of a host country may do so by establishing a *Branch* or by establishing a *Subsidiary*.

The branch is less desirable. Legally it is a part of the foreign investor. It is thus subject to legislation regarding the privileges of alien corporations to do business in the host country, and it may be discriminated against as an alien. Moreover, the foreign investor will be totally responsible for the branch's liabilities. Thus all of its assets will be subject to the jurisdiction of the host country's courts. If the country subjects the world-wide income of its residents to its income taxation, in theory all of the investor's income would be taxable there, too.

It will be necessary to hire an agent to manage the foreign branch. Since such an agent will require very broad authority much thought must be given to his appointment.

The laws of some Romano-Germanic nations provide for two basic but different types of agency: the *Mandate* which exists in all countries of this legal system, and the *Procura* which was originally defined by the German BGB and has since been recognized in Japan, Switzerland, Italy, and the Scandinavian countries—among others.

A *Procurist* has extremely wide powers. Under German law he can do anything on behalf of his principal that the BGB does not forbid him to do. He is forbidden to do only the following: (1) to make someone a partner in his principal's business; (2) to sell or otherwise dispose of the entire business; (3) to appoint another procurist; and (4) to sell or dispose of land, buildings, and other immovable property. Thus a firm doing business in a country that recognizes the procura could grant to its manager extremely wide authority with a relatively simple document. It goes without saying that the manager given such power must be extremely trustworthy.

Any restrictions upon a procurist's power will not be binding upon third parties; the procurist has the apparent authority to do anything his principal can with the exception of the acts listed above. Such restrictions will be binding between procurist and principal, however, rendering the agent liable to the principal for violations.

If the branch manager is to be appointed via mandate, the document appointing him will be long and complex. Under the common law an agent exercises three major types of authority: *Express,* that which his appointment authorizes him to exercise; *Implied,* that which he must be able to do in order to carry out his express authority; and *Apparent* (or *Ostensible*), that which a third party dealing with him would assume he has.

Common-law managers have wide implied authority and even wider apparent authority. It is assumed that certain types of managers may do certain things; if they are to have less than the usual authority firms and persons dealing with them must be notified of their limitations in order to narrow down their apparent authority. The nearer the manager's authority is to that which is normal for that sort of manager, the less detail is necessary in the document (or oral understanding) appointing him.

The Romano-Germanic mandate is different. Most of such an agent's authority is express. The authority he has is what has been delegated to him — no more, no less. Thus the mandate appointing the Romano-Germanic agent must be detailed indeed.

It is assumed that the common-law manager may delegate certain duties to underlings, such as hiring and firing employees or purchasing supplies and inventory. The Romano-Germanic manager has no implied or apparent authorization to delegate authority. If he is to have the authority to delegate his duties, the extent of it must be spelled out to the last detail.

The appointment of any Romano-Germanic business manager must be made in writing. The document must be recorded in the Commercial Register of the locality where the manager will exercise his authority. Thus, anyone wishing to know the extent of the manager's power may learn it simply by consulting the register.

A subsidiary will be organized under the law of the host country. Almost always it is organized in the corporate form as a host country citizen; thus it is not discriminated against as an alien. Furthermore, since it is a legal entity separate and distinct from its parent, only its income is subject to host country taxation, and only its assets are subject to host country jurisdiction.

Corporate Forms. In most American states two types of corporation exist: the *Close Corporation* and the *Ordinary Corporation*. The close corporation is for small enterprises; its form and attributes vary from state to state.

In Great Britain there are *Private Corporations* and *Public Corporations*. The private corporation is for small enterprises; its reporting obligations and the like are less than those of public corporations.

The two major corporate forms in Romano-Germanic lands have already been discussed in Chapter 4. In situations where the parent plans total control of its subsidiary, use of the limited liability company form of organization (SRL, SARL, GmbH) is simplest. When shares will be sold to the public, use of the SA or AG form will be mandatory.

Financing the Foreign Subsidiary. The simplest way to accomplish this is by having the parent furnish all of the subsidiary's initial capital. The parent thus retains 100 percent equity ownership of the subsidiary, and the subsidiary owes no outside creditors. This may, however, put an undesirable strain on the parent's finances.

In developed countries financing could be obtained in the local capital market. Funds could be borrowed in host country currency from local banks, or securities denominated in host currency could be issued to local investors. In such cases the securities are usually debt rather than equity, so that the parent retains undisputed control over the subsidiary.

In underdeveloped countries local financing may be difficult or impossible to obtain. Even in developed countries management may not wish to become involved in the local capital markets. In such cases the best solution to the financing problem may be borrowing from foreign branches of American banks. The borrowed funds may well be Eurodollars—American dollars circulating abroad.

Interest rates on Eurodollar loans may well be lower than rates on U.S. dollar loans in the United States. Furthermore such loans are not directly subject to regulation by U.S. bank regulators.

Such financing could also be arranged in other Eurocurrencies: Swiss francs, deutschmarks, yen, and the like. Large quantities of all of these currencies circulate outside their home countries and may be lent by international bankers without controls by the currency's issuing government.

Employer-Employee Relations

Employment. Every nation regulates and to an extent restricts the employment of aliens on its soil. Most national labor legislation requires that employers use native employees in all jobs for which they are qualified.

Particularly in underdeveloped countries, alien businesses are happy to hire native skilled and unskilled labor because wage rates in such countries are low and the work discipline of the workers is high. Management personnel in these countries will at the beginning be almost totally foreign, because natives with the necessary management skills are scarce.

In many underdeveloped countries foreign employers are obligated to establish training programs to upgrade the job skills of native employees. This helps natives to rise in the organization and in the long run enables more natives to fill responsible jobs within it.

In developed countries skilled natives are available to fill almost all positions within the organization. Within a short time after the founding of the enterprise, virtually all employees may well be native.

The rights of employees vary greatly from country to country. Almost every nation has minimum wage laws. These wages may be very low in poor countries and very high in prosperous developed countries.

Laws providing for mandatory employee benefits will vary greatly from country to country. In most European countries employees are entitled to four or five weeks of paid vacation per year, plus several paid holidays. Many national laws provide for mandatory sick pay. In most countries employees who become mothers are entitled to paid maternity leave. In Sweden new fathers are entitled to a long period of paternity leave if they desire.

In Austria it is customary for employers to pay employees a thirteenth and fourteenth month of salary. The thirteenth month is generally paid at summer vacation time and the fourteenth at the end of the year. A similar custom prevails in Japan.

The European attitude toward job security differs from the American, the Japanese, and the Soviet.

The concept of employment at will has dominated American law until very recently; the employee may quit any time for any reason, and the employer may terminate at any time for any reason. Collective bargaining agreements, civil service and academic tenure, and antidiscrimination legislation have modified the concept over the last thirty years — and revolutionary new developments in employment law are narrowing it even more.

The notion of wrongful termination is taking hold in American law. An employee terminated under the following conditions may now have a legal claim against the employer in at least some American states when the termination: (1) violates an implied employer-employee contract (such as the provisions of an employee handbook); or (2) is contrary to developing concepts of good faith and fair dealing toward employees; or (3) is for refusal to perform an illegal act; or (4) is under circumstances that subject the employee to humiliation and embarrassment.

Since it has been the custom of Japanese employers to hire employees for life, terminations are rare in that country. As Japanese employers progressively alter that old custom, however, a law of wrongful termination may begin to develop there.

In the Soviet Union employment is guaranteed by law. There it is very difficult for an employer to terminate an employee, except for extreme misconduct, incompetence, or political unreliability.

European nations do not accept the notion of guaranteed employment, and neither do they accept employment at will. An employee is entitled to a notice several weeks before termination. In the Netherlands the employer must obtain permission for the dismissal from a District Labor Office before the termination can take place. In other nations the employee may complain to a government office if he feels the employer action is unjustified.

In cases of multiple termination (lay-offs and the like) clearance from a government agency will probably be required.

In Austria a terminated long-term employee may be entitled to as much as a year's salary in severance pay. Under the laws of several other nations, too, similar entitlements exist.

In Switzerland and some other nations employers are required to provide pension plans for their employees to supplement benefits paid by the national Social Security system. Switzerland also requires most employers to provide comprehensive health insurance for employees.

Union-Management Relations. The status of labor unions varies tremendously from country to country. In some undeveloped countries trade unions are unlawful. In other undeveloped countries they are lawful, but have no real power. This is also the case in Communist countries.

To some foreign managements, a great advantage of operating in Taiwan, Singapore, Sri Lanka, and Romania is the fact that no powerful unions exist to make employee relations "complicated."

In the developed world unions are recognized as legitimate and they do exercise power. How much power they have and how it is exercised vary from country to country.

The attitude of unions toward management varies from hostility to cooperation. In the United States the relationship is adversarial. The law forbids domination of the union by management, thus assuring union independence. To an extent there is a feeling that "what's good for the company is good for labor," but it does not run too deep. Strikes are common. But the interests of American unions do not go very far beyond the workplace; the political power of American unions is far less than that of their counterparts in some other nations.

The closed shop is illegal under federal law here; no person may be denied a job because he is not a union member. Union shops (in which nonunion employees may be hired, but must join the union within thirty days) are lawful under federal law, but unlawful in a minority of states.

A relatively low percentage of American employees are union members.

In Great Britain there is an extreme adversarial relationship between unions and management. British labor feels that management is the enemy and that no common ground exists between labor and management. The unions are deeply involved in politics, exercising much power within the Labour Party. A large segment of the party is hostile to private ownership of business. If a private employer cannot survive in the marketplace, the unions might well prefer to see it nationalized and placed in the public sector; the jobs of the employees are saved and a more sympathetic management may well take office.

British unions do not hesitate to strike—even against public-sector employers (such as the coal mines). They recognize disruption of the economy as a powerful weapon of strikers; if through such disruption they can force the public to bring pressure to bear on the government to make concessions to them, so much the better.

Closed shops are legal under British law; one may not obtain blue-collar work in many industries unless one belongs to the appropriate union. However, recent law has imposed restrictions upon the effectiveness of the institution.

A larger percentage of the United Kingdom workforce is unionized than is the case in the United States.

Swedish unions are among the most powerful in the world. They, too, are a powerful political force. They have much to say about the policies of the Social Democratic Party, which has governed Sweden for most of the last fifty years.

Though we consider Sweden to be one of the most socialist nations on earth, its economy has a very large private sector. Swedish unions have not exercised power through nationalization of the private sector, but by subjecting it to thorough public regulation.

Swedish collective bargaining takes place at the national level, between the unions, national associations of employers, and the government. In cases of disagreement between union and employers, the government uses its power to obtain agreement.

Only after agreement is achieved at the national level does bargaining take place at the local level on local problems.

Swedish law makes unions an equal partner in the operation of business enterprise. Employees are entitled to elect two members of the supervisory board of Swedish corporations, one to represent blue-collar employees and the other to represent white-collar employees. Though American law makes certain aspects of running a business "out of bounds" for collective bargaining (such as what the company will produce, dividend policy, and the like) all aspects of the operation of the enterprise are the union's concern in Sweden. Any change of any sort in management policy requires consultation of the union.

In addition, employers are required to contribute money to a fund that is used by the government to buy stock in employers' businesses in the name of the unions. Slowly Swedish employees are acquiring ownership equity in the businesses where they work. The long range objective of this policy is to place control of employers in the hands of their employees through the controlled operation of the corporate system.

A very large percentage of the Swedish workforce, white collar as well as blue collar, is unionized.

In Germany employees of employers with over five hundred employees are entitled to representation on the *Aufsichtsrat* of the employer. When the firm has over two thousand employees worker representatives comprise half of the board. These employee directors are chosen by the blue-collar workers, white-collar workers, and mid-management workers in proportion to their numbers and have all of the rights and privileges of directors elected by the shareholders. Thus the employee representatives know everything about company affairs that the other directors know.

In addition, German unions have the normal collective bargaining rights found in other developed countries. They also are a powerful force in the inner circle of the Social Democratic Party.

Strikes are relatively rare in West Germany. Traditionally German unions have not been militant in asserting their rights, believing in cooperation with management rather than opposition. The relatively high unemployment that has prevailed in the Federal Republic for the past decade has somewhat eroded labor belief in cooperation; some union people are beginning to ask what German labor is really getting from it. Still, cooperation is more prevalent in German labor relations than is confrontation.

Union membership is not as prevalent in the German Federal Republic as it is in Sweden or elsewhere in Scandinavia.

In Switzerland employees are not represented on corporate boards, and unions have no say in management policies outside the areas of wages, hours, and working conditions. Yet Swiss industrial wages are among the highest in the world and Swiss unemployment is among the lowest. The Swiss unions lost their militance after the unsuccessful general strike of 1918 and have collaborated with employers in building one of the world's most prosperous economies.

In Switzerland, as in other European countries, employee layoffs in hard times are rather rare. Instead of depriving some workers of their jobs so that others may continue to work full time, the work week of everyone is shortened so that the sacrifice is shared equally. Since those who do not work full time are entitled to partial unemployment compensation the real income of the employees drops little, if at all.

Compulsory unionism is unlawful in Switzerland. A relatively small percentage of the Swiss workforce is unionized.

In France and Italy the major unions are dominated by the Communists. These unions are more interested in political objectives than in the usual union concerns of wages, hours, and working conditions. The relationship between unions and management is extremely adversarial. Compulsory unionism is unlawful. A large fraction of the workforce is not unionized.

In Norway and Austria the employees are entitled to elect one-third of their employer's directors. In most other European countries the employees are entitled to elect work councils, with which managements must consult on matters of interest to employees.

In Japan most unions are enterprise unions. Because employment is traditionally for life in Japan, the workforce has a great stake in the economic well-being of the employing enterprise. Union-management relations mirror other Japanese relationships, emphasizing cooperation over confrontation.

Since Japanese management is in some ways less authoritarian than American, and since Japanese employers take a more paternal attitude toward their employees, there is not the understanding gap between management and employees that Western management systems foster.

Antidiscrimination Legislation. The United States possesses one of the more comprehensive systems of law forbidding employers to discriminate in hiring and the like on the basis of race, sex (including pregnancy), national origin, age (to an extent), physical handicap (with respect mainly to employing government contractors), and certain other grounds. Most industrialized countries have similar legislation, but coverage will vary from country to country. Virtually all countries with such legislation ban discrimination due to race and sex, but their laws vary otherwise.

Many countries (including Great Britain, Japan, and the German Federal Republic) allow age discrimination. Very few forbid discrimination on grounds of pregnancy (Italy and Japan have joined the United States in not allowing it). Very few forbid discrimination against the handicapped.

Most European countries forbid discrimination on the ground of family responsibility, social origin, or political opinion.

Canada is unique in banning discrimination on the ground of pardoned offenses. Canada and France forbid discrimination on the basis of sexual orientation.

Affirmative action programs to combat employment discrimination are rare outside the United States. Canada uses it to encourage increased employment of women. The United Kingdom is developing a few guidelines. The French government is in some areas paying subsidies to employers to encourage the hiring of more women. Elsewhere the concept is not a part of national law.

The American mechanism for enforcement of antidiscrimination law is probably the most highly developed on earth, helped by the propensity of American jurors and judges to award large sums in damages to discrimination victims. Elsewhere stringent burdens of proof and reluctance to award large sums in damages hinder enforcement efforts.

Chapter 13

Securities Regulation, Antitrust, and Product Liability

Securities Regulation

American Securities Regulation. Companies offering new issues of securities in American interstate commerce are required to register them with the Securities and Exchange Commission under provisions of the Federal Securities Act.

Domestic issuers are to an extent exempt from registration requirements when: (1) the issue is intrastate, to be sold only in the state where the issuer is incorporated; (2) the issue is a private offering, to be sold only to a limited number of sophisticated investors; (3) the issue will bring in $1,500,000 or less (*Regulation A* exemption), in which case a short-form registration statement must be filed.

A foreign issuer cannot claim the intrastate exemption. It may avoid American registration of an issue of securities sold to Americans only by taking advantage of the private offering exemption.

Companies whose shares are traded on American stock exchanges or in the over-the-counter market are required to register them under the Federal Securities and Exchange Act and to make periodic reports to the Securities and Exchange Commission.

The required reports consist of: (1) unaudited quarterly profit and loss statements; (2) audited annual balance sheets; and (3) reports of any corporate events that may affect the market price of the corporation's securities.

Any foreign firm whose shares are listed on an American stock exchange or are traded in the over-the-counter market must comply with these registration and reporting requirements. The financial reports so filed must be prepared in accordance with American generally accepted accounting principles, even though these do not apply in the firm's home country.

An American firm offering a new issue of securities only to persons outside the United States may escape Securities Act registration only if no offers are made to American nationals and steps are taken to ensure that no part of the issue will find its way back to the United States. Assuring that is so difficult that wisdom dictates registering all such issues—just in case.

Officers and directors of companies subject to Securities and Exchange Act reporting requirements, and holders of 10 percent or more of any FSEA-registered corporate security must file reports of purchases or sales of their company's securities with the SEC. These persons must not sell shares in their company short. All profits on securities held by these persons in their companies for less than six months must be paid over to the company.

These requirements apply as stringently to foreigners as they do to Americans.

A foreign firm buying shares of United States companies for investment will not subject itself to American securities regulation if it has no American shareholders and is not an investment company. However, so-called *Off-Shore Funds*—mutual funds operating outside the United States and selling no shares to American nationals—nevertheless subject themselves to minimal federal regulation when they invest assets in American securities through American securities markets. They render themselves liable, for instance, for violations of the antifraud provisions of American securities law.

Under SEC Regulation 10-b-5, anyone guilty of fraud in the sale of an FSEA-registered security is liable to the party he defrauded in damages.

Any foreign firm committing fraud within the United States that injures its shareholders may be held liable to said shareholders under Rule 10-b-5 even though few or no Americans are damaged. A firm committing fraud outside the United States that damages American shareholders would be similarly liable.

Officers, directors, large shareholders, and corporate insiders are forbidden by American law to take advantage of corporate information not available to the general public in order to profit from trading in their company's shares. This prohibition against *Insider Trading* applies to insiders of any company whose securities are registered under the Federal Securities and Exchange Act, including insiders of registered foreign companies.

It has happened that foreigners in possession of inside information about an American firm purchase its stock through a foreign bank, the price of the stock rises, and the insider sells out and realizes his profit. European banks buying securities for their customers usually make their purchases in their own names; if the banks do business in a country with stringent bank secrecy laws they refuse to disclose the names of their stock-purchasing customers because it is an unlawful breach of secrecy. Foreign governments have generally cooperated with the SEC in tracking down these secret purchasers and inducing the banks to disclose their names. One may not camouflage insider trading in the United States by conducting it through a foreign bank in the name of that bank.

Attempted takeovers of American firms are regulated by federal securities law. Any person or firm, American or foreign, acquiring 5 percent or more of a security issue registered with the SEC must report the acquisition within ten days of the making of it. If a firm intends to make a tender offer to the holders of a registered security issue it must inform the SEC before making the offer and disseminate certain required information about itself (including financial information, prepared according to American generally accepted accounting principles *even though the firm does not use American GAAP in its usual operations*) to the shareholders being contacted.

When a foreign firm attempts to take over an American firm the SEC requirements must obviously be met. When an American firm seeks to take over a foreign firm that has no American shareholders the requirement need not be met. When a foreign firm seeks to take over another foreign firm with American shareholders problems arise; if the tender offer is made to the American shareholders the offer must comply with American law. If the offer is not made to American shareholders but these are damaged in some way by the outcome of the combination the offering firm may be liable to them under American law.

For instancee, Grun AG, a Ruritanian corporation, makes a tender offer for the shares of Blau AG, another Ruritanian corporation, that is valid under Ruritanian law. Seven percent of Blau's shares are owned by Americans in the United States. Grun carefully makes sure that no offer is made to these American shareholders for their shares so that it does not, as it thinks, have to register its offer with the American SEC. Grun acquires enough Blau shares under the offer to obtain control of Blau. As a result most of Blau's remaining European shareholders sell their shares to Grun in private transactions, so Grun ends up with 80 percent of all Blau shares. The market for Blau shares now dries up due to lack of supply; the American Blau shareholders cannot sell out except at a large loss. Could they claim that Grun violated American securities law here? Though Grun deliberately did nothing in the United States to avoid American jurisdiction, the Blau shareholders were certainly damaged by what occurred. They may have a case.

Foreign Securities Regulation. Several capital and securities markets exist outside the United States. The countries where these exist have their own schemes of securities regulation. In general these are nowhere near as comprehensive as the American regulations.

Requirements for registration of new issues of securities are much more likely to be enforced by stock exchanges than by government agencies. Accounting standards tend to be looser and information reporting requirements less stringent. The annual reports of many foreign corporations are well-constructed public-relations pieces, containing little in the way of hard corporate information.

Most countries having securities markets have laws against insider trading, but they are not as rigidly enforced as the American law. Many are enforced by stock exchange officials rather than government agencies. Some countries, such as Switzerland, are only now in the process of enacting appropriate legislation.

The very nature of foreign securities markets lends itself to less stringent regulation, because in most countries only a small percentage of the general public own shares. In countries like West Germany, Switzerland, and Japan the primary owners of corporate shares are banks. Since these shareholders are very likely to also be creditors, they have access to all corporate information they desire, without the necessity for special protective legislation.

Antitrust Laws

American Antitrust Laws. These apply to American business operations everywhere in the world. The most important of these are the Sherman Act, the Clayton Act, the Federal Trade Commission Act, and the Robinson-Patman Act.

Section 1 of the Sherman Act forbids contracts, combinations, and conspiracies in restraint of trade. Section 2 of the same act forbids monopolization of, attempted monopolization of, or conspiracy to monopolize a market.

Section 7 of the Clayton Act forbids corporate combinations that tend to restrain trade or to create a monopoly.

Section 5 of the Federal Trade Commission Act forbids acts of unfair competition.

The Robinson-Patman Act forbids *Price Discrimination* under most circumstances; price discrimination is the selling of identical goods to two different buyers for two different prices.

Among the types of contracts considered to be in restraint of trade are price-fixing agreements, boycott agreements, tying arrangements, market division agreements, price discrimination, and exclusive-dealing and requirement contracts that tie up large amounts of a market.

The acts are written in broad general language. Nowhere did Congress define the meaning of *Monopoly* or *Contract in Restraint of Trade,* for instance. It has been left to the courts to provide the necessary definitions.

With respect to some types of contracts in restraint of trade the American courts have adopted a *Per Se* approach: it is a violation to do this no matter what the reason. Among the sorts of conduct considered to be per se antitrust violations are the following:

1. *Horizontal Price-Fixing.* Ace Company and Deuce Company, competitors, agree upon the prices they charge their customers for their products.

2. *Vertical Price-Fixing.* Spade Company tells retailers who market 100-tablet bottles of Spade Aspirin how much to sell it for — no more, no less. (If the product is one upon which Spade has a valid patent, vertical price-fixing is acceptable.)

3. *Horizontal Market Division.* Ace Company and Deuce Company agree that they will not compete against each other in certain markets.

4. *Horizontal Group Boycotts.* Spade, Clubb, and Hart companies agree not to have any business dealings with Diamond Company.

5. *Vertical Group Boycotts.* Black Company, a manufacturer, tells Pink, Blue and Redd companies, wholesalers, not to sell Black products to White Company.

6. *Tying Arrangements.* Ace Company refuses to sell its air conditioners to buyers unless they sign a three-year service contract with Ace for necessary repairs and maintenance, though any competent air conditioner repairman can service and repair Ace air conditioners. (If Ace equipment is so unique that only Ace maintenance people are competent to service it this arrangement would be lawful.)

With respect to exclusive dealing and requirements contracts, vertical market division arrangements (manufacturer territorial restraints on distributors), monopolization, corporate combinations, and the like, the courts use the *Rule of Reason* approach and consider why the questioned arrangement exists and what harm it does to competition.

Thus a firm like Standard Oil of New Jersey that controlled a huge amount of the petroleum industry and sought diligently to control more was found guilty of unlawful monopolization. United States Steel, which controlled much of the American steel industry but followed a "live and let live" policy with respect to its competitors, was found not guilty of monopolization. Bigness alone is not an antitrust violation, nor is possession of great power in the market. What the would-be monopolist does with its power is the determining factor.

To repeat, with respect to the per se violations it does not matter why the violator commits them: they are wrong. With respect to rule of reason violations motives and competitive behavior will be considered.

The following enforcement mechanisms exist:

1. Criminal prosecution
2. Civil suits for injunction filed by the Anti-Trust Division of the Department of Justice
3. Administrative action by the Federal Trade Commission
4. Private suits for injunctions and or for triple damages, which is the most commonly used mechanism.

Though the Webb-Pomerene Act exempts from the effect of the antitrust laws arrangements between American exporters that make it easier for them to compete in foreign markets against foreign competitiors, any act by an American firm abroad that injures another American firm operating abroad or injures competition within the American domestic market may well be ruled an antitrust violation.

Here are a few examples of problems that can arise.

Ace, Deuce and Trey are American firms exporting gizmos to Ruritania. They compete against non–American gizmo manufacturers there. They form a joint venture, ADT, to cooperatively market their gizmos in this market. This is perfectly lawful under the Webb-Pomerene Act, even if it damages ADT's non–American competitors.

However, if Ace and Deuce form AD as a joint venture but they do not allow Trey to participate this could be a violation if it damages Trey's position in the Ruritanian market; it is an attempted monopolization.

Salubrium ore is mined only in Guatador, and Perez S.A., a privately owned Guatador corporation, mines 80 percent of all the ore that is produced. Perez sells its output to six consumers, two of which are American: Spade and Clubb. Spade negotiates a contract with Perez under which Perez agrees not to sell salubrium ore to any American firm other than itself, Spade. This is unlawful if it damages Clubb; it is a vertical boycott.

If Spade and Clubb jointly contract with Perez to buy all of its salubrium output, this would be lawful. It shuts the non–American competitors of this pair off from supplies of the ore, but this is of no concern to American law enforcers unless it somehow influences the United States economy.

What if Spade obtains control over Perez and refuses to allow it to sell salubrium ore to Clubb? This, too, would be unlawful if Clubb is damaged thereby.

Bon Marche AG operates the largest department store chain in Ruritania. Hart produces a personal computer for which there is a huge demand in Ruritania. No other American firm produces a similar personal computer, but two Japanese firms do. Hart also produces video casette recorders, but Diamond and Clubb, two American competitors of Hart, produce similar VCRs that sell better in Ruritania. Hart informs Bon Marche that it will not allow it to market the personal computer unless it agrees to stock only Hart computers and VCRs. Bon Marche agrees to this demand. Diamond and Clubb may well be damaged because of the loss of access to Bon Marche's stores. If so, this bargain is unlawful. The Japanese firms may also be damaged because they will not have access to Bon Marche's stores as outlets for their computers—but, again, this is of no concern to American authorities unless, somehow, it has an adverse effect upon competition in the American economy.

Ace Co., an American firm, owns the most productive neptunium mine in Guatador. It sells all of the mine's production to its American producer of neptunium-alloyed steel. Deuce also produces neptunium-alloyed steel, but it has to obtain more expensive neptunium from the Ungarish People's Republic because it has no access to the Guatadoran ore. Deuce knows that political opinion in Guatador is hostile to foreign ownership of Guatadoran natural resources. It helps to lobby through the Guatadoran Congress legislation that expropriates Ace's neptunium mine. When the new management takes over, Deuce contracts with it to buy 50 percent of the mine's output. The management sells the other 50 percent of output to Ace. Ace claims Deuce's lobbying was unlawful.

Here there is no antitrust violation. The expropriation of the Ace mine was an act of the Guatadoran government, an act of state. Had Deuce bribed Guatadoran congressmen to vote in favor of the expropriating legislation, or had it contributed funds to the political party supporting the legislation, or had it paid bribes to the new management of the mine to gain access to the mine's production, it would have violated the Foreign Corrupt Practices Act. Had Deuce initiated the idea of expropriation and been primarily responsible for shepherding it through the Guatadoran Congress it would be guilty of attempted monopolization. Assuming, however, that Deuce's lobbying activity was of the sort that is normal in Washington there is no illegality in Deuce's actions at all.

Redd Co. produces whatzits in the United States and markets them throughout the Western Hemisphere. Blau AG produces whatzits in Gerolstein and markets them throughout Europe. Redd whatzits are not sold in Europe and Blau whatzits are not sold in the United States. Redd negotiates a merger with Blau.

American antitrust enforcers might well object to this merger, on the ground that if Blau remained an independent whatzit producer, it might some day decide to market its whatzits in the United States. The Redd acquisition of Blau is removing potential competition within the American market and is therefore bad.

American and Foreign Antitrust Philosophy. The European Community, Japan, and individual nations in Europe and elsewhere have enacted antitrust legislation. It is similar to the American legislation in that it is intended to restrict monopoly and promote competition.

Corwin D. Edwards states in his work, *Control of Cartels and Monopolies: An International Comparison,* that the American approach to antitrust is virtually unique. Americans have always distrusted concentrations of power, whether political or economic. The United States Constitution seeks to discourage concentrations of political power through federalism and separation of powers at the federal level. United States antitrust law similarly seeks to prevent concentrations of economic power. It acts on the assumption that the use of economic power for the benefit of the holder is evil, and that the power and majesty of the law should punish those who do this. It tends to act through compulsion and force rather than through negotiation, and seeks permanent solutions to problems of economic power—solutions that will endure forever (such as permanent court injunctions).

According to Edwards, the following notions dominate foreign antitrust policies:

1. There are moral obligations in economic affairs. Businesspeople should behave fairly toward competitors, suppliers, and customers. Cutthroat competition is evil. Forbearance in competition is a virtue.

Some Americans believe this, others do not. To many of us, business is a game that you play to win. If you cannot take the heat of competition, get out of the kitchen. Sure, the game has rules, but play strictly by the book—no Mr. Nice Guy! Nice guys finish last.

2. Distributive justice and equality of opportunity are more important then increasing productivity. The sort of market efficiency that builds productivity but eliminates competitors from a market is not necessarily good.

Americans tend to believe that efficiency is a great good, so long as it does not concentrate too much power in too few hands. Productivity increases both wealth and living standards. To us it does not make sense to impair productivity by protecting the inefficient.

3. Concentrated private economic power is not necessarily bad. In the European environment of the last four centuries, concentrated power of one sort or other has been a fact of life. If you do not concentrate as much as possible of it in your own hands, your neighbor may concentrate it in his and then subject you to his will. Power is the ability to defend yourself. Concentrated economic power is only bad when it is misused. The law's objective should be to discourage this misuse.

Because American history is so different from European, we have been able to afford the luxury of believing that concentrations of private economic power are bad in and of themselves. We are slowly learning that the rest of the world disagrees, and that it is quite willing to allow these concentrations to exist and to obtain power even in the United States of America.

4. Government should have broad discretionary power to deal with

antitrust problems. Every situation is different; government should have a free hand to deal with each as its unique nature demands. Adherence to former precedents and the letter of detailed laws and regulations may do more harm than good.

Americans state that we believe in a government of laws, not a government of men. We do not like arming government bureaucrats with broad discretionary powers because human holders of power cannot be trusted not to abuse them. If we enact detailed law and regulation for the bureaucrat to enforce we put him in a straitjacket, which is where he should be. He, like the rest of us, is subject to the law.

5. It is not wrong to grant regulatory power to representatives of private interests. Who better understands business than businessmen? Just as businessmen sit on commercial courts in European countries, they sit on government commissions that make and enforce antitrust policy.

American courts have said more than once that law-making and law-enforcing authority may not be delegated to representatives of private interests. Governments are created to govern, and the exercise of governmental power must be restricted to them. To allow private interests to exercise the powers of government is to delegate such authority to those who are not entitled to exercise it.

6. Freedom of contract should be preserved as much as possible. Let businesspeople regulate their own affairs by contract as long as they do it fairly.

Americans favor freedom of contract, too, but we know that contracts may be used by the powerful to increase their power. We do not trust them to be fair to the extent that others do.

The American approach to antitrust problems is far more legalistic and rigid than most. Others seek to be more flexible and pragmatic in dealing with them.

European Community Antitrust. The major non–American system of antitrust law is that of the European Community. It is found in Articles 85 and 86 of the Treaty of Rome, and is enforced primarily by the Commission of the community.

Article 85, section 1, forbids all contracts between undertakings and concerted practices of undertakings that affect trade within the community and that prevent, distort, or restrict competition within the community and which:

1. Directly or indirectly fix selling or purchase prices or other trading conditions (Horizontal and vertical price-fixing)

2. Limit or control production, markets, technical development, or investments (Conspiracy to monopolize)

3. Share markets or sources of supply (Horizontal market division)

4. Apply unequal conditions to parties undertaking equivalent engagements, so that some are at a competitive disadvantage (Price and other discrimination)

5. Making agreement to a contract subject to the acceptance of other obligations having no commercial relationship to that contract (Tying arrangements)

Section 2 declares all such undertakings to be null and void.

So far the prohibitions of Article 85 appear more stringent than those of Section 1 of the Sherman Act. Section 3, however, adds the European touch.

The provisions of section 1 may be declared inapplicable to agreements between undertakings, decisions by associations of undertakings, or concerted practices of undertakings that:

1. Help to improve the production and distribution of goods

2. Promote technical or economic progress

3. Allow consumers a fair share of the resulting benefit without: (a) subjecting the undertakings to unnecessary restrictions, or (b) enabling them to eliminate competition with respect to a substantial part of the goods concerned.

Thus there is no per se prohibition of any of the named practices; if an otherwise prohibited agreement benefits the public without eliminating competition it will not be disturbed. The result is a sort of rule of reason approach.

An individual enterprise cannot violate Article 85. Only two or more enterprises working in concert may do so.

Article 86 states that the exploitation by any undertaking or undertakings of a dominant position within the community or a part of it is prohibited. Exploitation consists of, among other things:

1. Imposing unfair prices or other trading conditions

2. Limiting production, markets, or technical development to the prejudice of consumers

3. Applying unequal conditions to parties undertaking equivalent engagements, placing some at a competitive disadvantage

4. Making the conclusion of a contract subject to acceptance of other obligations having no reasonable commercial relationship to the contract in question

One firm acting alone may violate Article 86, but only if it has a dominant position in a market. Two or more firms sharing such a dominant position may also violate this article.

It is not per se unlawful under Article 86 to have a dominant position in a market. A firm with less than a 30 percent market share cannot possibly have a dominant market position. Whether a firm with 30 percent or more of a market has dominant position depends upon the nature of the competition, how hard the firm strives to maintain its market position, and other factors.

A firm without dominant market position cannot violate Article 86. A monopolist who does not misuse his monopoly power also cannot violate the article.

A person or firm with a complaint under Article 85 or Article 86 will probably file it with the Commission of the community in Brussels. The Commission will conduct an investigation without any open trial-type hearings. If it finds the respondents guilty it may cease and desist orders, or fines of up to one million ECUs or 10 percent of the previous year's sales.

Commission decisions may be appealed to the European Court of Justice, which may increase as well as decrease fines.

The Commission may initiate its own investigations, which it does not often do.

Private plaintiffs may sue in national courts also. Triple damages are not recoverable for violations of Articles 85 and 86, however.

Often Commission investigations of community antitrust violations involve subsidiaries of non-community multinational enterprises. If the Commission is investigating Ace de France, a wholly owned French subsidiary of Ace of Chicago, an Illinois corporation, could the Commission claim jurisdiction over Ace of Chicago, even though it does no business within the community? It may well try. The Commission and the European Court of Justice use the *Single Enterprise Theory* to claim jurisdiction over parent corporations in these cases, the logic being that subsidiary and parent are one single enterprise.

If parent and subsidiary are both doing business within the community this causes no problems. In the case of Ace of Chicago, however, there are problems. First, the Commission will be unable to obtain evidence from Ace of Chicago's offices in Illinois. Second and more seriously, if the Commission finds the respondents guilty and fines them, it will be unable to collect anything from Ace of Chicago unless that firm has assets within the community.

On the other hand, Ace of Chicago will have every incentive to cooperate in the investigation, because the Commission's cease and desist orders could have adverse effects on Ace de France's operations within the community.

Most nations within the European Community have national antitrust laws. Where these conflict with community legislation and the conduct complained of has effect outside the nation the community law takes precedence.

Canada, Australia, and Japan are examples of non-community nations with rather stringent antitrust legislation.

Corporate Combinations in American Law. Corporate combinations are a special element of concern in American and some other antitrust laws.

Section 7 of the Clayton Act forbids corporate combinations the result of which would be to reduce competition and tend to create a monopoly.

The reaction of antitrust enforcers to a combination depends upon the relationship between the combining firms. There are seven possible types of combinations:

1. Horizontal, between direct competitors
2. Vertical, between a customer and a supplier
3. Geographic market extension, between two firms with the same product market that do not operate in the same geographical market
4. Product market extension, in which a firm expands its product line by acquiring the producer of an established product rather than by developing a new product
5. Reciprocal dealing, by which a firm coerces a supplier by acquiring a supplier of a product needed by its supplier
6. Joint venture, in which two firms join forces to penetrate a new market that neither wishes to invade alone
7. Pure conglomerate, which is a combination that does not fit into any of the above six categories

The job of enforcing Section 7 of the Clayton Act is divided between the Anti-Trust Division of the Department of Justice and the Federal Trade Commission. It is also possible for a private party to challenge the lawfulness of a corporate combination, but this seldom occurs.

Before the advent of the Reagan Administration horizontal combinations were very likely to be challenged by one or the other enforcer, and the courts tended to disallow the combination. Combinations between direct competitors obviously reduce competition to an extent; if the partners are very large the marriage may well tend to create a monopoly. However, during the 1980s the enforcers began to take into account the competitive state of the industry to which the combining firms belonged. If a combination would tend to make the American industry stronger in its battle against foreign competition the combination might get by unchallenged.

Challenges of vertical combinations have been rare; they have only occurred when both firms have been relative giants in their respective markets.

Geographic market extension combinations have traditionally been challenged only in the retail grocery industry and in the dairy product industry. Attempts to bring about such combinations internationally sometimes occur; such attempts will be discussed later.

Product market extension combinations have been unpopular with antitrust enforcers, especially when the acquiring firm is a giant generalist with many product lines while the acquired firm is a specialist producer of its small product line.

Reciprocal dealing combinations are carried out with a predatory intent. They are not tolerated.

Joint ventures and pure conglomerate combinations generally escape without challenge. It is very difficult to prove that these reduce competition or tend to create a monopoly.

Under the Hart-Scott-Rodino Act firms intending to combine must notify antitrust enforcers in advance when both operate in interstate commerce and when the larger firm has assets or annual sales of $100,000,000 or more and the smaller has assets or annual sales of $10,000,000 or more. If the combination is to be accomplished through a tender offer such offer cannot be made for fifteen days after the notification; if it is to be accomplished in another manner the parties must wait thirty days.

As mentioned earlier, attempted takeovers through tender offers must be reported to the SEC before the tender offer is made.

Horizontal combinations between an American firm and a foreign firm, or between two foreign firms, may be challenged by American enforcers. Thus a proposed combination between British Petroleum and Standard Oil of Ohio was challenged; since BP and Sohio both operated in the United States they were direct competitors. The challengers lost the case; the combination was approved. The combination between the giant Swiss pharmaceutical firms Ciba and Geigy was also challenged, because both did business and competed against each other in the United States through wholly owned subsidiaries. Obviously the United States authorities could not prevent the combination; that was a matter under Swiss jurisdiction. The American objections to the combination were resolved through a consent order; the antitrust enforcers were thus satisfied that competition in the American pharmaceutical industry would not be reduced.

An example of an international geographic market extension challenged by American antitrust enforcers was the combination between Gillette, the American razor manufacturer, and Braun, a West German razor manufacturer. Braun sold no razors in the United States, though it did market some other products that Gillette did not produce here. Gillette did not sell its razors in Europe, Braun did not sell its razors here. Gillette was seeking to invade the European razor market by acquiring Braun.

The antitrust enforcers challenged this combination on the ground that Braun might some day invade the American razor market in competition against Gillette if it were allowed to remain an independent company; Gillette was potentially reducing competition in the American market by acquiring Braun. The enforcers essentially won the case; Gillette's acquisition of Braun was hedged about by restrictions to make sure that competition in the American razor market would not be reduced.

One of the most aggravating aspects of American antitrust law from the foreign point of view is that it intervenes in foreign business transactions that are only peripherally connected with the United States. Thus, when Pilkington Glass Company, a British producer of float glass valves, combined with some of its Canadian and Mexican competitors, the U.S. Federal Trade Commission objected because this combination could reduce competition in the North American (including the American) float glass valve market. Pilkington could not ignore the FTC's concern without jeopardizing its access to the American market, so it modified the terms of its acquisitions to meet the American objections.

Foreign Law on Corporate Combinations. The European Community frowns upon the acquisition by a firm with a dominant position in the EC market of an EC firm; it matters not whether the acquiring firm is EC or foreign.

In certain industries the EC encourages corporate combinations on the basis that it is good to strengthen EC industry against foreign competition by eliminating productive overcapacity and encouraging efficiency.

West Germany has legislation similar to the American Hart-Scott-Rodino Act, under which corporate combinations between large firms must be reported in advance to the Cartel Office. The Cartel Office may halt a corporate combination if it will increase or create a market-dominating position.

Great Britain considers the situation in which a firm controls one-quarter or more of the United Kingdom market for a product or service to be a potential monopoly. Any corporate combination considered by the British antitrust authorities.

In the United States the tender offer makes it possible for one firm to acquire control of another despite the opposition of the target company's management. Outside the United States it is very difficult to complete such a maneuver because independent individual shareholders own much less corporate stock abroad.

In most western European countries the major shareholders in publicly held corporations are banks, which generally tend to support incumbent managements.

In Japan there is even less individual ownership of corporate shares; banks, competitors, suppliers, and customers own most of the shares of Japanese companies. All of these organizations favor the maintenance of the status quo within an industry; they will not support a change in control of a firm unless the incumbent management favors it.

Product Liability

Most American states have adopted strict tort product liability. Any merchant selling a product that is dangerous if defective is liable to anyone injured by a defect in the product without regard to negligence unless user misuse caused the harm. The liability extends to everyone in the distribution chain, from manufacturer through jobbers and wholesalers to the ultimate retailer, and may not be disclaimed. An injured party may recover not only actual damages caused by the defect but also damages for pain and suffering, and perhaps punitive damages.

The Uniform Commercial Code (effective in every American state except Louisiana) also imposes five implied warranties upon merchant sellers of goods:

1. Title—that the buyer is becoming the owner of what he has bought

2. Against encumbrances—that the buyer will not lose what he has bought because some creditor of the seller had an unsatisfied lien against it

3. Against infringement—that the buyer will not be subject to claims for patent infringement, copyright infringement, and the like because of buying the merchandise

4. Merchantability—that the product bought is fit for normal use

5. Fitness for buyer's purpose—that the product is fit for the use the buyer had in mind when he purchased it (if he had a special purpose in mind, seller knew of it, and seller chose the merchandise)

These may be disclaimed.

In countries with legal systems based upon French and Spanish law two implied warranties are imposed upon sellers of goods to consumers. These are: (1) quiet enjoyment—buyer is getting clear title to what he is buying, with no liens attached; and (2) no hidden defects—the product is in good working order and will remain that way for a reasonable time.

A directive of the Council of the European Community required all member nations to amend their laws to provide for strict tort product liability by June 30, 1988. Its important provisions follow.

The producer is to be held liable for defects in his product (Art. 1). The following are defined as producers:

1. The manufacturer

2. Producers of raw materials

3. Manufacturers of defective component parts

4. Those who allow use of their trademarks or trade names on products they did not produce

5. Importers of goods manufactured outside the community into the community

Suppliers of the product (retailers and wholesalers) are not to be held liable under this directive unless the producer cannot be identified; they may escape this liability by identifying the producer to the injured party (or by identifying their supplier) (Art. 3).

All movables are declared to be products except primary agricultural products (products of the soil, stock raising, or fisheries that have not undergone initial processing) and game (Art. 2).

All parties liable under this directive will share joint and several liability (Art. 5).

A product is to be deemed defective if it does not meet a person's expectations, considering: (1) the presentation of the product; (2) the reasonably expected use; and (3) the time when it is put on the market.

A product is not to be deemed defective just because a better product came onto the market (Art. 6).

The directive allows the following defenses to a liability claim:

1. The defendant did not put the product into circulation.

2. The defect probably did not exist when the product was put into circulation.

3. The product was not manufactured for sale or any other commercial distribution.

4. The product was defective because compliance with government regulations caused it to be defective.

5. The defect was unforeseen at the time the product was put into circulation because the state of scientific and technological knowledge was not advanced enough to spot it.

6. Component and raw material suppliers are not liable if the defect is due to the design of the manufacturer's finished product or to instructions given by the manufacturer.

The various nations have the option to eliminate the fifth defense from their legislation.

The producers will be liable for death, personal injury, and for damage of five hundred ECUs or more to personal property. There is no liability under the directive for damage to commercial property (Art. 7).

There is no ceiling mandated for personal injury damages, though individual nations may set such a ceiling if they wish. The ceiling must not be less than seventy million ECUs (approximately U.S. $65,000,000) (Art. 16).

There is no provision for punitive damages or damages for pain and suffering, except as allowed by national law.

The extent to which product misuse and negligence by the injured party will be defenses is left to national law.

The statute of limitation under the directive is three years after the discovery of the defect or ten years after the product was put into circulation, whichever expires first.

This directive will make the product liability law of the European Community closer to American law in philosophy than before. The European law will not be as sweeping as the American, however, because

(1) retailers and wholesalers are not covered by it, though rather comprehensive implied warranties are imposed on them by national law; and (2) no punitive damages are allowed.

Under French law, professional dealers in a product (including wholesalers and retailers) are liable for harm caused by a defective product sold by them without limitation of liability and without defense (except that they did not truly sell the product). The law of Belgium and Luxembourg is similar.

In West Germany, wholesalers and retailers can escape liability for harm done by defective products by proving lack of fault in the sale of it; if they cannot prove this they are liable for harm done by the product.

Denmark, too, assumes fault on the part of wholesalers and retailers; they must prove lack of fault to escape liability.

On the other hand the Netherlands and Italy stick to the principle of no liability without fault with the plaintiff having to prove fault.

In Great Britain and Ireland all sellers of goods make a warranty of merchantability similar to the American warranty of that name. However, these nations do not have anything in their law like American strict tort liability.

The non-EC nations of Europe are of course not bound by the EC directive. Austria and Switzerland do not recognize product liability without fault, forcing plaintiffs to prove fault by defendants in order to recover. The courts of these countries do lean over backward to give the plaintiff the benefit of the doubt in borderline cases, however. Norway and Sweden have gone the other way, making strict liability a part of their law.

Chapter 14

Accounting, Taxation, and Tax Havens

Accounting

Generally accepted accounting principles vary from country to country, and mandated disclosures in financial statements also vary from country to country. American law requires the most comprehensive, detailed financial statements of any nation on earth. Most other national laws require much less disclosure by managements.

Accounting practices will also vary from country to country. *Fixed Assets* are valued in the United States at cost less depreciation; this is the practice in West Germany, Japan, and some other lands, too. However, in Chile fixed assets must be written up in value every year to account for inflation, and in France these assets must appear on the balance sheet at appraised value. It is permissible in many countries to write up the value of these assets to account for appreciation, creating revaluation reserves. In Italy and South Africa such reserves may be used for payment of cash dividends.

In the Netherlands many companies value assets on the basis of replacement cost rather than historic cost or appraised value. Changes in replacement cost are debited or credited to a *Revaluation Surplus* account.

Depreciation is based in the United States on the cost of the asset being depreciated less estimated salvage value, usually over the estimated useful life of the asset. In most countries salvage value is disregarded in figuring depreciation. Many countries use the rates of depreciation allowed for tax purposes; American firms do not normally do this. A few European countries (Switzerland, France, Belgium, Denmark) allow extremely rapid depreciation of assets (over periods less than the estimated useful life). Great Britain and the Netherlands do not follow this practice. Sweden is probably the most generous in allowing rapid depreciation of machinery and equipment.

Dutch firms valuing fixed assets at replacement cost calculate depreciation as a percentage of this cost.

Research and Development Costs are written off as expenses when incurred in the United States. In most other countries they are deferred and amortized.

In the United States it is rare for large quantities of earnings to be appropriated to *Special Reserve Accounts.* In most other countries this is mandatory, and voluntary appropriation in excess of legal requirements is encouraged. Thus in Sweden a company may appropriate up to 40 percent of its net earnings for a period to an investment reserve account, thus sheltering that income from taxation. However, 46 percent of the amount so appropriated must be deposited in a non–interest-bearing account with the Swedish National Bank, which cannot be withdrawn for purchase of an asset without the consent of the Swedish Labor Board until it has been on deposit for five years.

Appropriated Funds are sheltered from taxation in all countries permitting this sort of thing. Funds "stashed away" in these reserves can amount to a large percentage of all firm assets.

In lean years it is possible for a management to appropriate in reverse, to transfer funds from reserve accounts to unappropriated income in order to increase reported income. This practice makes "income smoothing"— keeping profits relatively uniform despite variations in the performance of the company—possible.

In some countries, including Switzerland and Italy, movement of funds into and out of reserve accounts need not be disclosed; only the account balance itself is disclosed. In a few countries the very existence of reserves need not be disclosed.

In West Germany cost of goods sold and earnings per share must not be disclosed. In Great Britain many firms choose not to disclose the cost of goods sold.

The financial statements of a foreign subsidiary must of course be prepared in the currency of the host country according to the host country's generally accepted accounting principles.

Since what must be disclosed in financial statements is a matter of national law, only those disclosures that are required by the host country must be made. Detailed disclosure is required in Scandinavia, minimal disclosure in Switzerland, and other nations fall in-between.

Since the parent must account to U.S. government regulators and tax collectors for the operations of the subsidiary, the subsidiary's financial statements must be recast according to American accounting principles. Then it will be necessary to translate the statement from the host currency into U.S. dollars.

This raises the problem of the currency exchange rate to be used in making the translation. The general principle is that assets and liabilities carried at current prices (cash, accounts receivable, accounts payable, and the like) will be translated at the current exchange rate. Assets and liabilities carried at past prices will be translated using historical exchange rates (such as property, plant, equipment, inventory valued at cost, intangible assets).

If the subsidiary is operating in a highly inflationary economy (such as Israel, Mexico, or Brazil) financial statements in local currency may not accurately reflect the true condition of the subsidiary. It would essentially be required to keep two sets of statements at all times: one set in local currency to satisfy local regulators, and the other in U.S. dollars to allow management to keep its finger on the true pulse of company operations.

The consolidated statements of American multinationals must of course comply with the comprehensive disclosure requirements of American law.

Taxation

The taxation systems of the world's nations vary immensely. Probably the most commonly used taxes are the individual income tax and the corporate income tax.

Personal Income Taxes are inevitably progressive: the higher the taxpayer's income, the higher is his rate of tax. Also inevitably, a small amount of income is not taxed as a personal exemption. Usually it is permissible to deduct from taxable income certain personal expenses.

Some nations, the United States included, tax the income of citizens earned anywhere in the world. Others tax only the income of residents earned within the borders of the taxing nation.

• Some nations, such as Switzerland, consider the income of husband and wife as a unit, compelling the couple to file a joint return and pay a joint tax. Others, like the United States, permit this practice but do not require it.

Some nations, such as Japan, tax investment income (interest, dividends, and the like) at lower rates than ordinary income. Others, like the United States, treat investment income as ordinary income.

The United States now taxes capital gains income as ordinary income. Japan and some other nations do not tax capital gains at all.

Corporate Income Taxes are levied upon the net profit of the taxpayer. The United States and some other nations tax the worldwide net profit of the taxpayer; other nations tax only the net profit earned within the taxing nation.

In theory the United States considers the net profit of a foreign subsidiary to be the net profit of the parent, but also provides rules to mitigate the severity of the policy. Some other nations treat subsidiaries strictly as separate entities for income taxation purposes.

The United States taxes corporate net profits whether or not paid out to shareholders as dividends. Other countries tax profits paid out as dividends at a lower rate. Still others do not tax such distributed profits at all.

Nations wanting to encourage investment and economic growth allow very liberal depreciation, investment credits, and the like. Other nations, not so interested in stimulating investment, do not.

Many of the developed nations of the world levy a *Value-Added Tax.* This is a tax on all firms providing a product or service, on the value the firm adds to what it sells. Putting it another way, it is a tax on gross receipts less cost of raw materials.

The value-added tax rate in the nations of the European Community is between 10 and 20 percent, depending on the country. The rate may vary according to the classification of the product involved: necessities may be taxed at a low rate, luxuries at a high rate, and other commodities at an average rate. Though business firms pay the tax, they add it to the price they charge their customers. Thus the tax is passed on to the consumer in the form of higher prices.

The tax provides an appreciable part of the revenues of the governments that levy it. It is criticized as a consumption tax, hitting hardest those who can afford least to pay it. Yet it is easily administered, difficult to evade, and does not hinder capital accumulation (because funds saved or invested are not spent on goods or services subject to the tax).

In some states of the United States and in some other countries retail *Sales Taxes* are levied. This tax is levied on the sale to the final consumer as a percentage of the retail price. It is paid by the consumer and collected and paid over to the taxing government by the retailer. In the United States it is unlawful to add the tax to the price of the product; thus the taxpayer knows how much tax he is paying. In some other countries the sales tax is concealed in the retail price; the consumer pays the price tag price for the product and no more.

In Communist lands and a few others, *Turnover Taxes* are levied. These are taxes added to the selling price of a product whenever it is sold: on a sale of raw material to a manufacturer, on a sale of final product by manufacturer to wholesaler, and on every subsequent sale until the product reaches the consumer. Turnover taxes, too, will be passed onto the consumer in free-market economies.

Excise taxes are levied on specific commodities such as alcoholic beverages, tobacco products, automobiles, and the like. They are likely to be imposed on luxury items; on products harmful to the user; or on imported products the government wishes to discourage the consumption of.

The tax is usually concealed in the price of the product, and is paid by the consumer. Such taxes are almost universal.

Transaction Taxes are levied upon transfers of real estate, corporate securities, and the like. They generally apply to a transaction that must be recorded in a public record or otherwise be in writing. A stamp proving payment of the tax must be attached to a document before its recording becomes lawful.

Employment Taxes are paid by employers and employees. Examples of such taxes in the United States are the social security tax and the federal and state unemployment taxes. In the United States the old age pension system and the unemployment compensation system are financed by such taxes. In most developed countries a far more comprehensive welfare state exists which is financed by these taxes.

Among the benefits that may be financed by such taxes abroad are comprehensive health insurance for the employee and his family, maternity benefits (including paid maternity leave), free public education for the employee's children, family allowances for couples with minor children, and the like. Such taxes may add up to a significant percentage of payroll costs in developed countries. For instance, the Swedish employer's employment taxes may amount to as much as 36 percent of payroll. In Singapore they may amount to 46 percent of payroll.

Extraction Taxes are levied upon natural resources. Oil companies may pay these upon oil pumped, mining companies upon ore mined, and lumber companies on trees felled.

Property Taxes are popular in common-law countries. Widespread is the real property tax, assessed as a percentage of the market value of real estate. The tax is an important source of revenue for local governments in the United States, Great Britain, and some other countries.

The *Capital Tax* is a tax upon the net worth of the taxpayer. In countries where it is levied, it influences the decision of property owners as to whether to encumber their property. In Switzerland almost everyone has a mortgage upon his house. Since one normally is not required to repay the principal of a mortgage loan, no one pays off the mortgage. To do so would increase net worth and thus increase one's capital tax liability.

Estate and *Inheritance Taxes* are levied almost everywhere. Estate taxes are payable by the estate of the deceased before assets are distributed to heirs. Inheritance taxes are paid by heirs after they receive their shares of the deceased's estate.

International Taxation. A nation levying an income tax must make several decisions with respect to its international reach. Will it be levied on income earned within the taxing nation by citizens only, or on income earned by citizens and aliens alike? Inevitably it is levied against all income earned within the nation, whether the earner be citizen or alien.

Will it be levied only against income earned in the taxing nation by that nation's citizens, or against the worldwide income of the citizen? Most nations do as the United States does, taxing income earned by their citizens anywhere in the world.

Will it be levied against the worldwide income of resident aliens? Some nations do this, others do not. The United States does.

Will it be levied against the domestic income of nonresident citizens? Most nations do tax in this situation, since the income is earned within the taxing nation and is within the reach of tax-collecting authority.

Will it be levied against the worldwide income of nonresident aliens? The universal answer is "no." Even in the United States nonresident aliens pay income tax only on income earned in the United States.

Will it be levied on the income of nonresident citizens earned outside the taxing nation? Most nations do not attempt to tax this potential source of revenue. This explains why Ingemar Stenmark, the former great Swedish slalom skier, lives in Monaco rather than in Sweden. By living in Monaco he exempts himself from Swedish income tax on income he earns outside Sweden, but he still retains his Swedish citizenship. The United States, however, is the great exception to the above rule. The American citizen who earns no income in the United States and lives outside the United States is still subject to federal income tax on all of his income wherever earned (except that portion which Congress sees fit to exclude). The only way an American citizen can escape federal income tax liability altogether is to move outside the United States and renounce his American citizenship (unless he renounces the earning of income instead).

The resident of a country that taxes worldwide income who earns income outside his land of residence will face a double-taxation problem. The land where the income was earned will tax it, as will his land of residence.

There are various ways of handling the problem. The United States solution is the foreign tax credit. An American earns income in Ruritania, upon which he must pay Ruritanian income tax. He will report the income on his American tax return as taxable income, but he is allowed to deduct the tax paid to Ruritania as a credit against his United States tax. The credit of course may be no greater than the United States tax.

The Swedish solution has been to negotiate bilateral tax treaties with other income tax–levying countries. Each such Swedish treaty contains its own method of solving the problem. The Dutch solution is to allow deduction of foreign earnings from worldwide earnings, taxing the difference. Thus there is no need to calculate a foreign tax credit.

United States law only allows the taxpayer to claim a credit against his United States income tax for foreign income taxes paid. One may not claim a credit against U.S. income tax for foreign capital, turnover, or value-added taxes paid (though these will probably be allowable deductions from taxable income).

Taxability of Foreign Business Operations. As mentioned before, the income of a foreign branch is taxable to its owner. The American firm with a branch in Ruritania must count the branch's earnings as part of its taxable income, but it may claim credit against its United States income tax for Ruritanian income tax paid.

If the American firm operates branches in more than one country the situation becomes more complex. Suppose the firm has branches in Ruritania, Gerolstein, and Guatador. It will be required to add together the profits of the three branches. It will then be required to add together the income taxes paid to Ruritania, Gerolstein, and Guatador. It may then claim this one credit, up to the amount of American tax due against the consolidated profit.

Suppose that the Ruritanian and Gerolsteiner branches operated at a profit, but the Guatadoran branch suffered an immense loss. No tax was paid to Guatador, but tax was paid to Ruritania and Gerolstein. The Guatadoran loss is greater than the combined Ruritanian and Gerolsteiner profit. No United States tax is due on the net loss, so there is no United States tax to claim a credit against. Therefore there is no credit.

If the American firm incorporates a subsidiary under Ruritanian law to conduct its business there, a different situation prevails. The Ruritanian subsidiary is a separate entity. Its profits are not its parent's profits. Thus the subsidiary's profit is taxed by Ruritania, but not by the United States.

No part of the subsidiary's profit is taxable to the parent unless and until it is paid out by the subsidiary to the parent as a dividend.

However, *Subpart F* of the United States Internal Revenue Code provides that, under some circumstances, the profit of a controlled foreign corporation is taxable ratably to its American shareholders. Thus, the separate existence of the corporation is ignored.

A *Controlled Foreign Corporation* (CFC) is an entity incorporated under the law of a foreign jurisdiction in which Americans (individuals or organizations) owning 10 percent or more of the shares each own more than 50 percent of the shares in toto.

Thus, Ace Company, a Texas corporation, owns 100 percent of the shares of Ace Ruritania AG, its Ruritanian subsidiary. Ace Ruritania AG is a CFC.

Spade, Clubb, Diamond, and Hart, Americans, own 100 percent of the shares of Deuce Company. They cause to be incorporated under Ruritanian law Deuce Ruritania AG, of which Deuce Co. owns 20 percent of the shares, the four individual Americans own 10 percent each, and various Ruritanians own the other 40 percent. Deuce Ruritania AG is a CFC.

Trey Company organizes Trey Ruritania AG to do business in that country. Trey Company owns 50 percent of Trey Ruritania's stock, and various Ruritanians own the other 50 percent. Trey Ruritania is not a CFC, because Americans do not own over 50 percent of its shares.

King Company organizes King Ruritania AG to do business in that country. King Company owns 35 percent of King Ruritania. Six individual Americans each own 5 percent of the company. Ruritanians own the other 35 percent. King Ruritania is not a CFC, because Americans who own at least 10 percent of the company do not own over 50 percent of it.

The income of a CFC obviously is not always taxable to its American shareholders. Its income is taxable to the shareholders only to the extent that it is Subpart F income. The most important type of Subpart F income is *Foreign Base Company Income.* Foreign base company income consists of:

1. *Foreign Personal Holding Company Income.* This is passive investment income such as dividends, interest, rent, royalties, and gains from the sale of securities coming from the investment of funds not repatriated to the parent company or shareholders in the United States as dividends.

2. *Foreign Base Company Sales Income.* Ace Company organizes Ace Overseas Company under the law of Hooraw Island, which levies no corporate income tax. Ace owns 100 percent of the stock of Ace Overseas; thus Ace Overseas is a CFC. Ace sells its Made in USA products to Ace Overseas at cost. Ace Overseas then resells the products to customers in Europe and Latin America, but never remits any profits to the home company as dividends. These profits will hopefully accumulate untaxed in Ace Overseas bank accounts. The income of Ace Overseas is base company sales income.

If Ace Overseas sells any of these products to Hooraw Islanders, the profit on these sales will not be base company sales income. Only profit on sales of goods not made in the base country to nonresidents of the base country is tainted.

3. *Base Company Services Income.* If Ace Overseas in the above example earns income by servicing the products it sells to Latin Americans and Europeans and performs the services outside Hooraw Island, this income will be base company services income. Any income it earns servicing products it sold Hooraw Islanders on Hooraw Island will not be tainted.

4. *Base Company Shipping Income.* If Ace Overseas uses or leases aircraft or vessels in foreign commerce (hauling passengers or goods for compensation) the profit on these operations is base company shipping income. If the income is invested in other shipping assets, however, the tax due is deferred until the investment is withdrawn.

There is a good reason for the special rules regarding taxability of base company income. A jurisdiction like Hooraw Island, which has no income tax, is a tax haven. A company like Ace could theoretically substantially reduce income tax liabilities by causing most of its profits to be earned on the island by its Hooraw subsidiary and paying little or none of these funds to itself in dividends. Subpart F destroys this possibility.

These rules remove most of the advantages of locating base companies in a tax haven.

The other type of Subpart F income is CFC earnings that are invested in United States property, even if these are not any sort of base company income. The theory is that the CFC is essentially repatriating its earnings to the United States through the investment in United States property; therefore the earnings should be subject to United States taxation.

The Tax Reform Act of 1984 created another type of corporate entity that would enjoy tax advantages on income earned outside the United States. This is the *Foreign Sales Corporation* (FSC). A portion of the Foreign Trade Income of such a corporation is exempt from federal taxation. If such income is earned through dealings with unrelated foreign customers it is all exempt if at least 50 percent of certain export expenses were paid by the FSC. If the income is earned through dealings with a related entity it is partially exempt; complex transfer pricing rules determine how much. For a firm to qualify as an FSC the following requirements must be met:

1. It must have no more than twenty-five shareholders
2. It must be incorporated in an American possession outside the customs territory of the United States (such as Guam) or in one of twenty-nine approved countries
3. It must keep an office in the jurisdiction of incorporation
4. It must maintain accounting records in the United States
5. It must have at least one director who is not a United States resident
6. It must keep its major bank account outside the United States
7. Shareholder and director meetings must be held outside the United States

Tax Havens

Generally, developed countries with fairly large populations levy heavy taxes. The tax burden in European welfare states such as Sweden is higher than ours, while the burden in theoretically low-tax Switzerland is marginally lower. Generally, though, the tax differentials between developed nations are minimal enough that there is little advantage to be gained by multinational enterprises through tax shopping.

Microstates and dependencies offer more possibilities. The populations of Liechtenstein and Monaco are so small that their governments need little revenue. Populations of dependencies may be even smaller and the needs of their governments still less. In addition, the governments of a few not-so-small states structure their taxation and business regulation to attract foreign tax avoiders in the interest of economic growth.

Marshall Langer discusses the world's tax havens in his work, *How to Use Foreign Tax Havens*.

There are five tax havens located in the Western Hemisphere: (1) The Cayman Islands, (2) Bermuda, (3) The Netherlands Antilles, (4) The Bahamas, and (5) Panama. The first three are dependencies; the Cayman Islands and Bermuda are British colonies, while the Netherlands Antilles is a Dutch colony. The latter two are independent nations. The first two levy no income taxes. The Netherlands Antilles levies the highest taxes on foreigners of the five, but firms doing business there can take advantage of favorable Dutch tax treaties to reduce tax liabilities. Panama taxes its own citizens fairly heavily, but does not tax income earned outside Panama. The other three Western Hemisphere havens merit individual discussion.

Cayman Islands. The major island of the group is Grand Cayman, approximately two hundred miles northwest of Jamaica. The population of the colony is approximately 20,000.

The Cayman Islands levy no income or capital taxes. Under Caymanian law it is easy to incorporate companies that will not transact any business within the Islands. These companies need to have a local address and hold at least one meeting of the board of directors per year on Caymanian territory.

It is also very easy to incorporate banks and insurance companies under Caymanian law. Capital requirements are low, license applications are processed fairly rapidly, and regulation is minimal compared to that existing in more developed countries. For these reasons multinational firms establish captive insurers and banks here.

Caymanian law does not allow the formation of *Open-end Mutual Funds,* funds that sell unlimited numbers of shares and redeem them on demand. Closed-end investment companies, however, are permissible.

Bermuda. The Bermuda Islands lie about six hundred miles east of the North Carolina coast, and have a population of a bit under 60,000.

Bermuda has no income or capital taxes. Here, too, it is easy to incorporate companies that will transact no business on Bermuda soil.

The law of Bermuda makes it easy to establish insurance companies. Thus the islands offer the best climate for captive insurance companies of any jurisdiction on earth.

The government is not issuing new banking licenses — all banking in the colony is done by the three existing banks.

Open-end mutual funds are permitted to exist here.

The Bahamas. These islands stretch through the Caribbean from fifty miles east of Miami, Florida, to the vicinity of Haiti. The population is approximately 250,000.

Here, too, there are no income or capital taxes. Though there are restrictions on the right of foreign-owned businesses to participate in the domestic Bahamian economy, foreign businesses that will operate outside the country only are welcomed.

Two separate banking systems exist: the domestic system and the international system. It is difficult to get a license allowing participation in domestic banking, but the government welcomes new banks that operate in the international financial markets. Many large international banks have branches here, and many financial transactions in Eurocurrencies are consummated here. The Bahamas also provide a good location for captive banks of multinational firms.

The country also welcomes new insurance companies. The Bahamas are a popular place for establishment of captive insurers for the big multinational firms.

Mutual funds also flourish here.

European Tax Havens. European tax havens include the following: (1) The Channel Islands, (2) Monaco, (3) Liechtenstein, and (4) Switzerland.

The Channel Islands of Jersey, Guernsey, and Sark are British dependencies. The law enacted by Parliament does not apply there and the islands have their own taxation system. European corporations are able to reduce home country tax burdens by locating subsidiaries there.

Monaco levies no taxes on resident foreigners, which is why some high-paid European athletes have established residences there.

Switzerland and Liechtenstein merit more extended discussion.

Switzerland. Switzerland has been a country of bankers for at least two hundred years. Her location, her stable government and economy, and her success in escaping involvement in major wars have made her attractive as a place to preserve one's money.

The belligerents of World War I could transact financial business with each other in Switzerland. English shareholders in German corporations could collect dividends on their stock through Swiss banks; German shareholders in English corporations could do likewise. After the war knowledgeable Germans, Frenchmen, and others could convert their depreciating currencies into Swiss francs, deposit them in Swiss banks, and avoid being wiped out by the roaring inflation of the 1920s.

As Hitler's Nazis began striding toward power in the Germany of 1929–1932, many Germans, especially German Jews, began to stash away cash in Swiss banks — just in case. After Hitler came to power, he imposed rigid exchange controls on the German economy in order to conserve Germany's scarce foreign currency resources. It became very difficult to export reichsmarks from the Third Reich. Some Germans — including many Jews, for obvious reasons — evaded these prohibitions by smuggling cash across into Switzerland.

The Nazi state took action against some of its "enemies" by seizing bearer share certificates from their owners, as mentioned earlier (in Chapter 4). It also seized accounts in German banks and sought to reach similar accounts abroad. Through the use of third-degree methods many victims were forced to reveal the existence of their accounts in foreign banks. The secret police then forced the hapless account owner to sign a power of attorney appointing a police officer as his agent to withdraw funds from these foreign accounts. Much money disappeared from Swiss bank accounts and was withdrawn into Germany through these third-degree methods. It was to put a stop to this practice that the Swiss banking secrecy laws were enacted in 1934.

These laws in essence make it a serious crime for a bank employee to disclose information about an account or its owner to those who have no right to receive it. Release of the information is justified only in response to a government order, a court order, or the consent of the account owner. The banks assumed that the powers of attorney supposedly signed by German depositors were signed under duress. Therefore they refused to either recognize them or to disclose information to their holders. Thus the assets of the victims of Nazi tyranny held in Swiss banks became more secure.

When World War II began funds from all of the belligerent countries poured into Switzerland — including funds belonging to bigwigs of Hitler's Third Reich. All comers were entitled to the benefits of the bank secrecy legislation.

After the fall of France in 1940 Switzerland was entirely surrounded by Axis-occupied territory. After Mussolini fell from power and Italy was occupied by the Germans the country had German troops on every frontier. The Swiss were therefore forced to do business with the Third Reich in the interest of national survival. The Americans and British did not take kindly to this. In the middle of 1941 — before the United States had entered the war against Germany — President Franklin Roosevelt froze all Swiss assets in the United States. Ever since Roosevelt's action a bit of ill feeling and mistrust has existed between the Swiss and Americans.

A wartime incident added to the ill feeling. The German chemical combine I.G. Farbenindustrie owned a Swiss subsidiary, Interhandel. Interhandel owned General Aniline and Film (GAF), a competitor of Kodak in the American film and photographic products industry. After the United States entered the war against Germany the American Alien Property Custodian seized the properties of GAF as enemy assets. Switzerland protested, claiming that because a Swiss corporation owned GAF it should be regarded as Swiss property. The American position was that because

Germans owned Interhandel, GAF was German property; this position was based on the idea that a company's nationality should be determined by the nationality of its shareholders. When the war ended the United States refused to restore GAF's assets to their owners. Meanwhile most of the German shareholders of Interhandel sold their shares, feeling that they were about to become worthless. Swiss speculators bought them up dirt-cheap in the hope that Interhandel would be able, somehow, to get back control of GAF.

Interhandel's management went to court in this country to test the lawfulness of all that had transpired. The Justice Department of the United States served subpoenas on Interhandel's Swiss bank commanding that it produce records relevant to who really owned and in the past had owned Interhandel's shares. The bank refused to obey, claiming compliance would violate Swiss banking secrecy law. The trial court disagreed, holding the Swiss in contempt for refusal to obey the subpoena. The decision was naturally appealed. While the appeal was in process the Swiss government filed suit against the United States in the Court of International Justice to test the legality of what had happened. Before that case came to trial the United States Supreme Court reversed the lower court decision, holding that the Swiss bank secrecy laws did excuse the Swiss bank from obeying the American subpoena.

The Swiss now dropped their suit in the CIJ, and all the parties involved worked out a settlement of the Interhandel–GAF problem. The government eventually sold GAF to American buyers, and the proceeds were divided mainly among the shareholders of Interhandel, who by now were virtually all Swiss. GAF is now American-owned and controlled. The Swiss speculators who bought up Interhandel shares at the end of the war and had the patience to hang on until the lengthy dispute was resolved were handsomely rewarded. These people were very happy with the outcome, but the case did little constructive for Swiss-American relations.

While this struggle was beginning the victorious Allies also put pressure upon the Swiss to relax their bank secrecy laws in order to disclose Nazi-owned accounts. The Swiss resisted the pressure, claiming to be enforcing their law even-handedly. Eventually, however, they confiscated a large sum of money from Nazi-controlled Swiss accounts and turned it over to the victors. But it has been argued ever since that much of the Nazi money in Switzerland was left untouched.

Since the end of World War II foreign money has flowed into Switzerland to escape inflation, taxation, and expropriation at home. The owners of the accounts were happy with the anonymity provided by the bank secrecy laws. By the 1960s the money was flowing in in such quantities that the Swiss restricted the right of foreigners to open bank accounts in their country and began to charge negative interest on the accounts that already existed. Nevertheless, some foreign funds continued to come in. Foreign businesses naturally needed to maintain Swiss accounts to finance their Swiss affairs, and the authorities did not object to foreign accounts in currencies other than the Swiss franc.

Foreigners have expressed unhappiness with Swiss banking secrecy recently because it protects three sorts of undesirables: (1) national rulers who loot their people before being expelled from office (Claude "Baby Doc" Duvalier of Haiti, Ferdinand Marcos of the Philippines, and the late Shah of Iran are a few prominent examples); (2) organized crime members; and (3) tax evaders from all the world outside Switzerland.

The Swiss have always been willing to break the wall of bank secrecy concerning individuals suspected of acts that are criminal under the law of Switzerland. But they have been insistent upon receiving proof of probable criminal guilt before authorizing banks to release information. Mere suspicion has not been good enough.

What has aggravated American and other non–Swiss authorities the most is the fact that, until very recently, tax evasion was not recognized as a crime in Switzerland. Swiss law has given tax collectors such effective civil weapons against evaders that it has not seemed necessary to invoke criminal sanctions in this area. Thus foreign tax collectors got no assistance from the Swiss because they did not consider tax evaders to be criminals. (Under Swiss law an inaccurate tax return is not considered a false document in and of itself; investigators need to prove that someone had deliberately given tax authorities false documents with intent to mislead to demonstrate criminal intent.)

The United States and Switzerland have made two bilateral agreements with respect to the lifting of bank secrecy. The first is the Mutual Assistance Treaty of 1977. Under this agreement bank secrecy will be lifted in cases involving organized crime, securities law violations, and tax fraud of the sort that is a Swiss crime. The second agreement is the Memorandum of Understanding of 1982, under which the Swiss agreed to lift bank secrecy in investigations of insider trading in securities in the United States, although insider trading was not a crime in Switzerland (though it now is). Slowly, therefore, Swiss banking secrecy is yielding to the law enforcement needs of the national governments that demand more of their citizens regarding financial disclosure than the Swiss demand of theirs.

Though Switzerland has the reputation among the semiknowledgeable of having the most leakproof bank secrecy, the laws of the Cayman Islands and the Bahamas are just as strong. Indeed, they may be more effective because, so far, the United States has not applied similar pressure to these lands as on Switzerland to restrict bank secrecy as it is applied to Americans. How long this state of affairs will continue to exist, however, is anyone's guess.

The continued economic and political independence of Switzerland is in some danger. Three of her four large neighbors (The German Federal Republic, France, and Italy) are members of the European Community. As the national economies of the community nations become more integrated, the community will have more economic muscle to use against Switzerland. Should Austria decide to join (which is now at least a remote possibility) the community will surround Switzerland on all four sides.

The independence of Switzerland—particularly regarding regulations on weight and length of trucks using Swiss highways (which are more restrictive than EC regulations) and restriction against movement of trucks at night and on Sundays and holidays—irritates member states in the European Community. These regulations and restrictions interfere with highway commerce between the German Federal Republic and Italy.

As it is now, Switzerland suffers some economic disadvantage by not belonging to the European Community—the main disadvantage is that the community levies customs duty on all Swiss imports. The community, for instance, levies duty on Swiss cheeses imported by France, but France does not levy duty on Dutch cheeses because the Netherlands is a community member.

Some parts of Switzerland can be considered tax havens; other parts are not. Federal taxation comprises a small portion of the Swiss tax burden, the major portion consists of cantonal and communal taxes. Generally taxes are high in the urbanized cantons, such as Zurich and Geneva. The canton of Zug levies the lowest business taxes in the country; its government strives to attract foreign business enterprise. Its taxes are low enough that it succeeds.

Liechtenstein. In a way the Principality of Liechtenstein is a fairyland. Located in the Rhine valley between Switzerland and Austria, its 30,000 or so citizens live in one of the most beautiful spots on Planet Earth.

The Principality is bound to Switzerland by a customs union. Its currency is the Swiss franc, and Switzerland handles its foreign relations and military defense. The nation's only armed forces are a handful of police, and it does not cost much to finance a welfare state for so few citizens.

It levies a minimal income tax upon its residents (which might amount to as much as 18 percent of taxable income). Its banks are governed by a banking secrecy lawfully as strict as the Swiss law. Liechtenstein domiciliary and holding corporations pay no Liechtenstein income taxes. Their only tax burden is a nominal capital tax.

A domiciliary company transacts business anywhere on earth except in Liechtenstein. A holding company exists only to manage assets or investments. Though these companies are required to have a "seat" in the Principality, this need be no more than a mailing address.

Moreover, the Principality offers two types of organizations not found anywhere else in the world: the *Anstalt* and the *Stiftung*. The English translation of anstalt is "establishment." One or more persons may organize an anstalt for any lawful purpose, business or nonbusiness, with a minimal capital contribution. The anstalt may have one owner or several. The minimum capital for a one-owner anstalt is 30,000 Swiss francs (SFr 30,000). For a multiowner anstalt the minimal capital is SFr 50,000. For tax and secrecy reasons, there is usually just one owner. (If there are more than one, share certificates must be issued, stamp taxes must be paid, and several pieces of paper showing part ownership of the establishment are in circulation.)

The original founder(s) must appoint a Liechtenstein director. He represents the anstalt in dealings with the Liechtenstein government and, more importantly, manages its assets. In that respect he functions somewhat as the trustee of an American trust does.

When there is one founder he is issued a certificate of ownership. This is generally issued in blank, meaning that the bearer owns the anstalt. The founder may transfer ownership by transferring the certificate. Since it is a bearer certificate, the transfer will leave no paper trail. (Obviously, such valuable pieces of paper will spend most of their lives in bank vaults.)

Only the anstalt's director and the Liechtenstein government know the identity of its owner. Thus, ownership of a Liechtenstein anstalt provides about the most confidential, secret investment on Earth.

The stiftung (or foundation) is set up to benefit a family or charitable organization. It must not engage in any commercial activities except to help it carry out its purpose.

The founder (or settlor) establishes it by having a deed drawn up and signed, which describes the purpose of the stiftung and the assets that are being turned over to it. It will also appoint the trustees who will manage the assets and spell out how their successors will be appointed.

The deed need not mention the beneficiaries or describe their interests. These are generally described in a separate document. The deed is the one and only public document of a stiftung; a separate document naming beneficiaries is confidential. The advantage to secrecy here is that the public (and curious tax collectors) will have difficulty learning the identity of the beneficiaries and of the amount of income they receive.

Liechtenstein is the only country on the European continent where trusts of the sort that are so common in the United States and Great Britain may be established. Two types of trust are recognized: the business trust (*Treuunternehmen*) and the ordinary trust (*Treuhandschaft*). In both the founder (settlor) deeds assets to a trustee or trustees who manage them for the benefit of beneficiaries. These trustees operate the business of a treuunternehmen or manage the assets of a treuhandschaft.

The trust deed of the treuunternehmen must be recorded in the Registry of Commerce and is open to public inspection. The treuhandschaft trust deed is not a public document. Thus the treuhandschaft may be kept a secret from the world.

Many wealthy Europeans own or participate in Liechtenstein entities of the types just described. Americans are less likely to do so, because the Internal Revenue Service eyes American participation in such ventures with the greatest suspicion.

Money Laundering. The existence of tax havens, bank secrecy, and the mobility of people and money create great temptation to engage in criminal activity and conceal the origin of the proceeds thereof. Such conduct has the dual advantages of tax evasion and the creation of the appearance of lawful wealth lawfully acquired.

In order to increase the number and efficiency of weapons available to combat this, Congress in 1986 enacted the Money Laundering Control Act, Subtitle H of Title 1 of the Drug Abuse Control Act (Public Law 99-570, 100 Stat. 3207), 18 USC 1955, 1956. The act creates three new criminal offenses, which are: (1) money laundering — engaging in monetary transactions in criminally obtained property, or transportation of money or financial instruments for the purpose of money laundering; (2) monetary transactions in criminally derived property; and (3) evading monetary transaction reporting requirements.

The money-laundering offense is described in 18 USC 1956. To be guilty of the transaction portion of the money-laundering offense one must conduct financial transactions in property that represents the proceeds of specified unlawful activity. Financial transactions are those that involve: (1) moving money by wire or other means; (2) monetary instruments (checks, drafts, or the like); or (3) use of financial institutions. Specified unlawful activity consists of crimes associated with:

1. Bankruptcy fraud
2. Organized crime
3. Drug trafficking
4. Ordinary felonies such as counterfeiting, bribery, embezzlement, bank robbery, kidnapping, etc.
5. Hostage taking
6. Illegal arms sales
7. Making of illegal exports
8. Violation of Treasury Department Foreign Asset Control rules

The crime cannot be committed unintentionally. To be guilty of it the person committing the offense must: (1) have the intent to promote the carrying on of the specified unlawful activity; or (2) know that the transaction is designed to conceal or disguise the nature, source, ownership, location, or control of proceeds of specified unlawful activity; or to avoid a transaction reporting requirement under state or federal law.

To be guilty of the transportation portion of the money-laundering offense one must transport or attempt to transport a monetary instrument or funds into or out of the United States with the intent to either promote a crime or conceal a crime.

For the United States authorities to have jurisdiction to prosecute the crime it must either be committed within the United States or be committed by American nationals outside the United States. If the offense is committed outside the United States at least $10,000 must be involved.

For committing the transaction portion of the money-laundering crime one may be fined up to $500,000 or twice the value of the property involved, whichever is more, and or be imprisoned up to twenty years. For committing the transportation portion of the crime the minimum fine is $500,000. A civil penalty of $10,000 or the value of the property involved, whichever is greater, may also be imposed. This is payable to the United States.

He who knowingly engages in monetary transactions in criminally derived property is guilty of the monetary transaction crime, described in 18 USC 1957.

The property must come from one of the specified unlawful activities mentioned above, but the defendant need not know that. If he knows it derived from some type of criminal activity (like ordinary theft) that is sufficient.

The definition of "monetary transaction" is very broad. It consists of the deposit, withdrawal, transfer, or exchange, in or effecting interstate or foreign commerce, of funds or monetary instruments by, through, or to a financial institution.

The offense must be committed within United States territorial jurisdiction or the one committing it must be a "United States person."

The definition of "United States person" is much broader than that of "United States national." The following are considered to be United States persons under this legislation.

1. U.S. nationals

2. Aliens lawfully admitted to permanent residence in the United States

3. Any person within the United States

4. A business association composed primarily of United States nationals and or permanent resident aliens

5. A United States corporation

6. A foreign subsidiary of a United States corporation

Upon conviction the penalty is a fine of up to twice the value of the property involved and or imprisonment for up to ten years.

When either the money-laundering crime or the monetary-transaction crime is committed the gross receipts of the defendant from the crime are forfeit to the United States. If the owner of the property involved in the laundering or transaction knew the crime was being committed, his property is also subject to forfeiture.

The proceeds of certain criminal offenses against other nations are also subject to forfeiture. The offense must be a drug trafficking offense punishable by at least a year's imprisonment both in the United States and in the other nation.

It is unlawful to evade federal monetary transaction reporting requirements of the Currency and Foreign Transactions Reporting Act, 31 USC 5316 et seq. This act requires: (1) that all financial institutions must report to the Treasury Department all currency transactions exceeding $10,000; that (2) institutions or individuals moving more than $10,000 in currency or monetary instruments into or out of the United States must report these to the Treasury Department; and that (3) all individuals having financial interest in or signature authority over bank accounts, security accounts, or other accounts abroad must report this to the Treasury Department.

Formerly it was not unlawful to evade these requirements through evasion—such as dividing a $20,000 currency transaction into four $5000 transactions. Now to do such a thing with intent to evade the reporting requirement is a crime.

Racketeer Influenced and Corrupt Organizations Act. As a weapon in the struggle against organized crime Congress enacted the Racketeer Influenced and Corrupt Organizations Act (RICO), 18 USC 1961–1968, in 1970. It has not only become a potent weapon against the Mafia and other organized criminal gangs, but also a deterrent to certain types of marginally unlawful activity by normally honest businesses, including multinational businesses.

The act forbids:

1. The investment of income from a pattern of racketeering activity or collection of an unlawful debt in the establishment of or the purchase of an interest in any enterprise engaged in or whose activities affect interstate and foreign commerce (except for stock in such purchased on the open market amounting to less than 1 percent of its class, insufficient to elect a director or directors).

2. Acquiring or maintaining, through a pattern of racketeering activity or collection of unlawful debts, an interest in or control over such an enterprise.

3. Conducting or participating in the conducting of the business of such an enterprise through a pattern of racketeering activity or collecting of unlawful debts.

One might think that the ordinary business would never be guilty of racketeering activity. To be sure, the absolutely honest business never would be. However, 18 USC 1961 (1) provides a very broad definition of criminal activity. Aside from obviously criminal acts such as bribery, theft, counterfeiting, robbery, extortion, dealing in narcotic drugs, and the like, the following are defined as racketeering activity:

1. Mail and wire fraud

2. Fraud in the sale of securities (including violations of SEC Rule 10-b-5)

3. The money-laundering offense of 18 USC 1956 described above

4. The monetary transaction offense of 18 USC 1957 described above

5. Violations of the Currency and Foreign Transactions Reporting Act as described above

A pattern of racketeering activity consists of performing two or more acts of racketeering activity within a ten-year period.

Unlawful debts are defined as gambling debts or debts involving usury when the interest charged is over double the maximum lawful rate.

The purchase or sale of stock in an insider trading transaction is racketeering activity because it is fraud under SEC Rule 10-b-5. The mailing of a false financial statement in an effort to obtain credit is also racketeering activity because it is mail fraud. The sending of false advertising material through the mail may also be mail fraud and thus racketeering activity.

Violation of RICO is a crime. Conviction subjects the defendant to a fine of no more than $25,000 and or imprisonment of up to twenty years, plus forfeiture of any interest in an enterprise obtained in violation of the act.

Violation is also a tort. Anyone injured by elements of a pattern of racketeering activity may sue the party injuring him for triple damages.

The existence of RICO plus the new money-laundering crimes should make any international businessperson think many times before engaging in fraudulent activity or trying to launder the financial proceeds of unlawful activity.

Suits for triple damages under RICO are not exactly uncommon. Losing such a suit can be very expensive.

Chapter 15

Risks of Doing Business Abroad

Fraud. There are businesspeople everywhere on earth who will do anything for a dollar (or yen or pound or franc or whatever). In business dealings that cross national frontiers the tricksters have more opportunities than they do in transactions carried out within one country.

Mark S. W. Hoyle discusses several types of transnational fraud in his work, *The Law of International Trade.* One has already been discussed: the misuse of the letter of credit transaction. Through the mechanisms of forged documents or the shipment of nonconforming goods under conforming documents unscrupulous sellers have defrauded unsuspecting or careless buyers of huge sums. A related type of fraud is the counterfeiting of trade documents (such as bills of lading) and trademarks. Through the use of a counterfeit trademark nonconforming goods may be made to appear conforming, to the damage of unsuspecting buyers and their customers.

Charter party arrangements are open to fraud by both shipowner and charterer. The charterer may hire a ship and crew under a voyage charter. The crew take the ship and the charterer's cargo into an unscheduled port where the cargo is sold and the owner pockets the proceeds. The crew then take the ship out to sea and scuttle it, later claiming that the ship sank for legitimate reasons. The dishonest owner files a claim under the insurance policy he maintained on the ship; if the scheme works he absconds with the proceeds of the cargo and the insurance proceeds, leaving the charterer holding the big empty sack.

The dishonest charterer may take on a shipload of cargo belonging to third parties, having the shippers prepay the freight. The charterer then disappears with the freight proceeds, abandoning ship and cargo. As soon as the owners issue the bills of lading for the cargo, they are responsible for delivery of it even though the charterer collected the freight payments. Both the shipowner and the cargo owners lose.

There is no certain way to avoid being victimized by these kinds of fraud. The best course is to avoid doing business with people you do not know and trust, but often one must do business with total strangers; whenever this happens there really is no way to totally avoid the risk of fraud.

Foreign Exchange Rates. Probably the greatest economic risk of international operations in the First World is the risk posed by unstable currency exchange rates. In the old days of the gold standard, all developed country currencies were redeemable in gold at rates fixed by the issuing governments. The only way a currency could change in value in terms of another was through devaluation or revaluation by government action, which did not often happen. Under the later gold exchange standard, most currencies were no longer redeemable in gold (unless governments themselves were the would-be redeemers). However, they were still valued in terms of gold, and the exchange rates so fixed kept the value of one currency in terms of another relatively stable.

Under the Bretton Woods system, in effect from the end of World War II until 1973, currencies were valued both in gold and in U.S. dollars, the dollar serving as the world's reserve currency. Massive U.S. exports of dollars during the 1960s strained this system to the breaking point. In 1971 the United States devalued the dollar in terms of gold for the first time since 1934, and terminated the convertibility of dollars into gold.

The old system of fixed exchange rates was abolished in 1973, at the time of the second dollar devaluation. Under the present system each country determines how its currency will be valued in terms of others. The value of major currencies (the U.S. dollar, the Japanese yen, the Swiss franc, the English pound) in terms of each other is determined by market forces, modified by the actions of central banks. The currencies of most of the European Community nations (the German deutsche mark, the French franc, the Dutch guilder, the Belgian franc, the Italian lira, the Irish pound) are loosely pegged to each other and to the European Currency Unit (ECU). Generally each EC currency may float within a narrow band of 2.25 percent of the agreed parity of each in terms of the other (the Italian lira's band is 6 percent rather than 2.25 percent). This European "snake" also floats as a unit against other currencies.

Most third-world nations peg their currencies to one or more of the major world currencies; most use the U.S. dollar. Several former French colonies in Africa use the CFA franc as their currency, which is pegged to the French franc. A few nations peg their currencies to the English pound, a few others to the South African rand, and one to the Spanish peseta.

Thus, if Guatador pegs its peso to the U.S. dollar at a rate of GP 10 = US $1, the peso to dollar rate will remain constant. The peso's value in terms of other currencies will float along with the dollar's; as the dollar rises the peso rises, as the dollar falls the peso falls.

Other third-world nations, notably Brazil, use a "crawling float" to determine the exchange rate for their currency. Thus, if the Ruritanians peg their glotny to the U.S. dollar, but change the peg every month or so as inflation erodes the value of their currency, a "minidevaluation" of the glotny will take place once a month or so. In January the rate is 188 glotnies per dollar; in March Ruritania lowers the rate to 194 per dollar; in May the rate is lowered to two hundred per dollar. The value of the glotny in terms of U.S. dollars changes as the peg changes; its value in terms of Swiss francs will also be influenced by the fluctuation of the dollar in terms of Swiss francs.

A few nations peg their currency to the Special Drawing Right (SDR), the "paper gold" of the International Monetary Fund and an acceptable international currency of account. The value of the SDR is determined by the values of the U.S. dollar, Japanese yen, English pound, German deutsche mark, and French franc. In the early 1980s 42 percent of the value of the SDR was provided by the dollar, 19 percent by the deutsche mark and 13 percent by each of the other currencies. These percentages periodically change as the values of the five currencies in terms of each other change. Among the currencies so pegged are the Burmese kyat, the Jordanian dinar, and the Zambian kwacha.

Several other countries peg the value of their currency to that of a basket of foreign currencies, each defining its own basket.

Currencies of many Communist nations are officially inconvertible and are not traded on official world money markets. Examples are the Russian ruble, the Polish zloty, the Hungarian forint, and the Czech crown. The Russian government determines the exchange rate between its ruble and other currencies. It is unlawful to bring rubles into the Soviet Union, and unlawful to carry them out. An "unofficial" market for such currencies does exist outside the issuing countries, with the exchange rates determined by market forces.

No currency is allowed to float cleanly. National banks intervene in the world financial markets to stop undesired movements in their own and other currencies. Thus the Deutsche Bundesbank intervenes in the money markets to keep the deutsche mark from appreciating too much in terms of other EC currencies, or to keep it from depreciating too much in terms of the Swiss franc.

On occasion Europeans and Japanese have intervened in the marketplace to slow down the depreciation of the dollar — hence the statement that the United States finances its deficits through foreign national banks.

Currency fluctuations under floating exchange rates may be appreciable. In 1969 the U.S. dollar was worth 4.30 in Swiss francs. Then it went into a steady decline against the world's hardest currency, hitting a low of approximately U.S. $1 = SFr 1.50 in the late 1970s. Because of the extremely high U.S. interest rates circa 1980 the dollar rose, hitting a high against the Swiss franc of U.S. $1 = SFr 2.60. The rate was U.S. $1 = SFr 1.53 as of January 13, 1990.

Around 1985 the English pound sterling would buy only U.S. $1.30. As of January 13, 1990 it will buy U.S. $1.65.

The Italian lira stood at approximately 630 to the U.S. dollar in 1969. It now takes 1257 lira to buy a dollar.

The Japanese yen stood at 360 to the dollar in 1969. A Japanese may now buy a U.S. dollar for 145 yen.

Like stock prices, currency exchange rates are influenced by long-, middle-, and short-term trends. The high American inflation of the mid- and late-seventies created a long-term downward trend for the dollar. High interest rates and lowered inflation fueled the upward trend of the early eighties. Lower interest rates, the adverse American balance of trade, and fears of the consequences of the massive American budget deficits fuel the downward trend of the later eighties. However, shorter-term hopes and fears have added their peaks and valleys to the dollar's price charts, and will continue to do so.

No one can predict how exchange rates will fluctuate from day to day, let alone from year to year. They are influenced by political, economic, and psychological forces beyond the ken of individual human beings.

Floating exchange rates have added another element of uncertainty to international business. The decision to grant or withhold credit in international transactions may depend on informed guesses on future movements of these rates. Decisions as to the currency in which spare funds will be held may also depend on such speculation.

Any firm that possesses large cash balances may be tempted to engage in currency speculations. Large profits can be made by those who are able to forecast market trends. For those who possess defective crystal balls, however, this sport is an invitation to disaster.

Political Risk. Politically most first-world countries turned rightward during the late 1970s and early 1980s. Most noteworthy were the coming to power of Margaret Thatcher in Great Britain and Ronald Reagan in the United States, but the accession of Helmut Kohl in the German Federal Republic is also worthy of mention. In many nations the political climate is more favorable to the free market than it has been in the past.

However, the rightward trend has not been universal. In 1982 France elected its first Socialist government with the true power to govern; under President Mitterrand the French public sector grew considerably. To be sure Mitterrand lost his Socialist majority in the National Assembly in 1986 and appointed the rightist Jacques Chirac as premier. However, Mitterrand won reelection to the presidency against Chirac in May 1988, dismissed his opponent as premier, and appointed a Socialist in his place. He then dissolved the Assembly, enabling French voters to almost restore Socialist majority control there in June.

Spain and Greece have elected and reelected Socialist governments during the 1980s. The Greek Socialists, however, have lost their parliamentary majority and share power with others.

The British Labour Party continues under leftist domination, and remains the only viable governing alternative to Thatcher's Conservatives. The normal oscillation in power of parties in a two-party political system will almost inevitably put Labour in power again during the 1990s.

In the United States the same situation may not prevail. For the first time since 1928 Republicans have won three straight presidential elections. It is possible that a semipermanent Republican presidency is coming to pass.

In the German Federal Republic both Christian Democrats and Social Democrats lost votes at the last election to smaller parties. The Greens have apparently become a permanent force in German politics, while the left wing gains power within the Social Democratic Party. The coming to power of a Red-Green coalition is not at all unlikely; this could well change German hospitality toward the free market.

First-world economic and political risk in the coming years is not overwhelming, but the business climate in our part of the world will not remain the same. It may well become a bit more stormy than in the recent past. There is no indication that President Reagan, Prime Minister Thatcher, or any other conservative leader in our part of the world has brought off a true political or economic revolution.

Political risks of another order exist in the Marxist-Leninist world. A supremely rational Soviet government devoted to modernization of the national economy would probably throw open the door to Western trade and Western investment and indigenous private enterprise. Vladimir Ilyich Lenin did essentially that in 1921 when faced with an economy thrown into utter disorder by his revolution and the civil war that followed. He decreed a New Economic Policy that encouraged foreign aid and small-scale individual enterprise to get things moving again. NEP succeeded; by 1925 something resembling prosperity was returning to the Soviet Union. But Josef Stalin destroyed it all in the name of development of socialism and rapid industrialization; the present inefficient command economy of the USSR is one of Stalin's legacies.

Mikhail Gorbachev may be moving in the direction of a modified NEP in his effort to combat Soviet economic stagnation. Foreign investment is now to a degree welcomed, even though hedged about with strings to prevent foreign ownership of Soviet resources or enterprises. That foreign economic assistance will greatly benefit the Soviet economy is obvious. The big question is, would the Soviets leave foreign investments in place after they have served their purpose? Or might the ideologues one day eliminate them in the interest of restoring Marxist-Leninist purity?

In China, too, government seeks economic growth through the stimulation of local enterprise and the encouragement of foreign investment. The events of June 1959 have weakened proponents of this policy, however.

The year 1959 held unprecedented revolution in Eastern Europe, non–Communists rule Poland and Hungary, and free elections may take place in the German Democratic Republic, Czechoslovakia, Bulgaria and Romania. Free market economies may be established and foreign investment welcomed.

Governmental Instability. Governmental instability is a fact of life in many third-world nations. Though coups in Latin America and Africa do not often cause radical economic change, the altered political climate can be of concern to foreign investors. In many of these nations "connections" in the national capital are essential. A sudden change in government personnel can render old connections useless. Worse, those too closely associated with the old regime may be discriminated against by the new.

Political conditions are very unstable in this part of the world. Today's government may be swept away by a revolutionary tide tomorrow. Today's commitments conscientiously kept by today's government may be repudiated by tomorrow's. The political and economic policies of many third-world countries have changed in the twinkling of an eye over the past thirty years.

Iraq seemed to be a stable pro–Western nation during the 1950s, and thus a fairly safe place for long-term investments. The 1958 coup that destroyed the monarchy brought the Ba'ath Socialists to power and made Iraq one of the more radical anti–Western, anticapitalist Arab states. Libya, too, seemed to be stable and pro–Western until the 1969 coup that overthrew the monarch and brought Muammar Khadaffi to power. Iran's stance also changed when the Ayatollah Khomeini's government replaced that of the shah. Ethiopia, Cuba, and Nicaragua also turned rapidly from countries that welcomed Western capital to countries that spurned Western investment.

There are a few examples of countries that have changed policy in the other direction. Indonesia was anti–Western and anti–free market under President Sukarno. After the bloody suppression of Communist dissent in 1965, the country turned to the right. President Suharto has encouraged Western investment and Western-sponsored development. How long supporters of this policy will control the country, however, is an open question. Somalia was one of the more pro–Soviet countries of Africa at one time. She supported members of the Somali minority in Ethiopia who wanted to secede and join their ethnic brothers in an enlarged Somalia. The

Soviets supported this idea until the pro–Soviet Haile Mariam government came to power in Ethiopia; then they decided that Ethiopia offered more potential as an ally than Somalia. Soviet-armed Ethiopian troops smashed the Somali rebels in Ethiopia and threatened to invade Somalia herself. This induced the Somali government to radically change its policy; the country became pro–Western and remains so.

Several examples of other lands teetering near the brink of radical change are worthy of exploration. Consider the ABC nations of South America: Argentina, Brazil, and Chile. Here are nations that stand on the borderline between the Third World and the First World. These nations could, if they would, create industrial infrastructures that could give them first-world living standards within a generation.

Could Argentina make it? The Alfonsín civilian government has survived to the end of its term. Peronista presidential candidate Carlos Menen was elected as his successor and has taken office. Argentine inflation has often exceeded 100 percent per year recently. The Alfonsín government once had it under control, but it again threatens to ascend into triple digits. Argentina also has an immense foreign debt, upon which she is on the verge of default. Peronista economic nationalism is still alive and kicking; President Menen may some day introduce massive government regulation of business activity. The big pluses in the Argentine equation are that she can well feed herself, and that she has very few people living in abject poverty.

Brazil has recently combined high inflation with immense economic growth in a quasi-free market economy. Under the peculiar economic climate of that country the two seem to go together; when President Sarney tightened the economic screws to combat inflation economic growth declined. More recently he has released the screws and the inflation rate began to climb once more. A huge number of Brazilians live in poverty. The country has tried to alleviate this through economic growth, and opening the wilderness areas of the Amazon Basin in the north and the Matto Grosso in the west to settlement. This development runs the risk of causing great ecological damage to the colonized areas, the country, and the world, but success could put Brazil on the road to becoming a world power.

Brazil, too, has an immense foreign debt and is on the brink of default. During her last democratic experiment a government of the far left came to power, which is why the generals took control in 1964. Now the generals have stepped aside; democracy reigns once more. In December 1989 Brazil conducted her first presidential election by direct popular vote since 1960. Only literate Brazilians could vote in 1960; now virtually all citizens can vote. The winner, Fernando Collor de Mello, stands to the right of center. He was to take office in March of 1990.

Chile's democratic institutions of the 1960s elected the left-wing socialist Salvador Allende to the nation's presidency in 1970, with only 36 percent of the popular vote. He would have greatly strengthened the public sector of the country's economy and limited the scope of the free market in his country. General Pinochet's 1973 coup forestalled this change. The resulting 16-year military dictatorship ended on December 14, 1989. Thirty-five percent of those who voted chose Patricio Aylwin as their nation's new president. The new leader opposed both the Marxism of Allende and the dictatorship of Pinochet.

Unlike Brazil, Chile has relatively few citizens who live in abject poverty; unlike both Brazil and Argentina Chile is not burdened by massive international debt. The prognostication for the health of investments in Chile is at least somewhat favorable.

The Republic of South Africa will endure radical change sooner or later. The white-dominated government of that country faces ever-increasing pressure to dismantle its system of Apartheid and admit the country's black majority to the political process. Since most of the world will not be satisfied with any arrangement less than "one man, one vote," the black majority will almost inevitably assume political power in the near- or midterm future. If the precedent of Zimbabwe means anything, what may well follow black assumption of power is evolution toward a one-party political system.

Many argue that that is what the Republic of South Africa now has. This is true in the sense that the Nationalists always win national elections; but the elections are contested at least, and the votes are honestly counted. In the typical African one-party states, elections are not contested; only the names of official party candidates are on the ballot.

The fate of the nation's economic system under the new order will be open to question. Most African governments are hostile to significant foreign economic influence within their domains.

The Ivory Coast has one of the strongest economies of any country in sub–Saharan Africa. Its government encourages foreign investment and does not object to the investors repatriating some of their profits. This climate exists because President Félix Houphouët-Boigny wants it that way. He rules the country under a one-party political system, and has no substantial political opposition. The president is growing old, however; his tenure of office is growing short. The future of the Ivory Coast depends upon the will of Houphouët-Boigny's successor and the nature of his opposition.

Egypt for the moment is one of the most prowestern nations of the Middle East. It was not always so. While Egypt was under the rule of Gamal Abdel Nasser its government was hostile to the West, foreign investment, and the free market. Under President Anwar Sadat the country was to a degree opened to Western influence and investment; Sadat's assassins opposed this policy (as well as his policy of peace with Israel). President Hosni Mubarak is continuing Sadat's policy; but those who feel as Sadat's assassins did are still a political force in Egypt. They may well attain power some day through a coup or otherwise and then radically change the Egyptian political and economic environment.

Of all third-world states the three Asian nations of South Korea, Taiwan, and Singapore possess probably the fastest-growing economies on earth. None are American-style democracies, though South Korea has recently held a free presidential election and Singapore has regular parliamentary elections. Leftist sentiment is weak in all three, abject poverty is minimal, and oppressive inflation and massive foreign debt do not exist. Investment here is as safe as it could be in the Third World.

Nations with long-established regimes may still suffer coups. Liberia's first ever in over a century of history happened in 1980, when army Master Sergeant James Doe masterminded the overthrow and murder of President James Tolbert. Before that, Liberia was spoken of as one of the world's tax havens because of its favorable laws and political stability. Though the government established by Sergeant Doe has remained in place for over seven years, one cannot now claim that Liberia has political stability. A government that comes to power via the coup may well be ousted in the same way, especially when it is not Marxist-Leninist.

Inflation. Neither individuals nor governments ever seem to have enough money. Both groups strive hard to spend what they have not got. The individual accomplishes this trick by borrowing. In this age of easy credit borrowing is not too difficult in a wealthy country like the United States. With a little luck the debtor keeps his head above water, paying his bills as they come due or a bit later; without luck the debtor falls far behind in his financial obligations and escapes his bind via the bankruptcy court.

Private organizations and state and local governments behave in much the same manner. To be sure governments may raise taxes in order to—hopefully—meet increased expenditures. But heavy taxation excites political resistance, and higher tax rates do not necessarily bring in more revenue. When taxes grow so heavy that they stifle economic incentive, the taxers kill the goose that lays the golden eggs.

Central governments are as anxious to spend money they do not have as the rest of us; but they have an advantage denied to others. They may create their own money, either by selling bonds or treasury bills to the central banking system (which creates assets against which the banks can lend money to other borrowers, thus monetizing the government debt) or by printing new money.

Inflation has ravaged many a national economy during the twentieth century. After World War I France suffered moderately heavy inflation; the value of the franc dropped from approximately five to the U.S. dollar in 1914 to forty-nine per dollar in July 1926. Retail prices in Paris soared over 600 percent during this period. This rate of inflation would have been considered catastrophic in the United States, but was absolutely insignificant compared to what happened in other lands.

The economy of Austria was wrecked by World War I and the subsequent breakup of the Austro-Hungarian Empire. The value of the Austrian crown plummeted while prices skyrocketed. In 1924 the government abolished the crown as a monetary unit and replaced it with the schilling, with the Austrian citizen receiving one new schilling for 14,400 old crowns. The value of bank accounts, government bonds, and the like was much more than decimated, but much worse happened elsewhere.

After the Bolsheviks came to power in Russia in 1917 they were unable to create a stable monetary system for several years due to the civil war and the economic dislocation that followed. Horrendous inflation was rampant, but the new government was not really anxious to combat it, since it wiped out the savings of the formerly affluent classes and furthered the Communist goal of economic equality. By 1923 the civil war had ended and the continuance of Bolshevik power was assured. At that point the government issued the 1923 ruble to circulate alongside the old czarist ruble, decreeing that one 1923 ruble was worth one million czarist rubles. Inflation continued to erode the value of this new currency. Finally, in 1924 the government issued the gold ruble to replace the 1923 ruble. One gold ruble equaled 50,000 1923 rubles; thus, the gold ruble was worth 50,000,000,000 czarist rubles. The pre–World War I and wartime savings of the Russian people were totally wiped out, as the government had wished.

The story of interwar hyperinflation most familiar to most readers concerns Germany. The kaiser's government, like the others involved in World War I, financed its war effort by borrowing money, hoping to win the war and force its defeated enemies to repay the loans. Despite this borrowing, retail prices only doubled in Germany during the course of the war. But the dream of making the enemy pay went up in smoke when Germany lost the war. Instead of saddling her enemies with her war costs, Germany was forced to pay them reparations to compensate them for the harm done to their lands by German armies during the war.

The German economy, too, was dislocated by the outcome of the war. The government of the Weimar Republic (which had replaced that of the kaiser) resorted to the printing press for operating funds. Michael Jefferson described what now happened in his article "A Record of Inflation," appearing in the book *Inflation*. By the end of 1919 retail prices had gone up 800 percent since 1913 — a far greater rate of inflation than that suffered in

France between 1914 and 1926. By the end of 1921 they had gone up 3490 percent since 1913. By the end of 1922 the figure reached 147,500 percent. But it was during 1923 that the rocket of hyperinflation really took off. By the end of June of that year prices were up 2,461,000 percent over 1913. At the end of August the figure reached 169,510,900 percent. At the end of September it was 3,622,371,371,100 percent. In November the inflation peaked, with the percentage reaching 142,290,000,000,000 percent. In short, over a ten-year period, German prices rose one trillion four hundred twenty-two billion nine hundred million times.

At that point the government decreed a monetary reform. The old inflated worthless mark was demonetized and eventually replaced by the reichsmark. For 1,000,000,000,000 (one trillion) marks the German citizen obtained one reichsmark.

Unbelievable tales are told of events during this hyperinflation. One recounts the story of the German couple who frugally saved their money during the days before World War I, stashing away thousands of marks toward their retirement. The husband was drafted into the kaiser's army in 1914 and was killed in action during the war. The widow emigrated to Switzerland after the war but had to leave her money behind in Germany. She was still in Switzerland in early 1923. At that time she received a letter from her bank that contained a postage stamp. The letter said, essentially, "We're obligated to close your account, because our cost of maintaining it is now greater than your balance. The enclosed stamp represents your balance." With that stamp she could send one letter from one part of Germany to another. That was what remained of many years of saving.

Only three classes of Germans were not losers because of the hyperinflation. The working classes essentially broke even. They had little before the inflation, and had little after. Union power kept wages rising during these years. Since wages always rise slower than prices during times like these laborers lost purchasing power, but little else. Farmers were winners. Many of them refused to sell food for worthless paper money, demanding payment in more valuable commodities. Some of them acquired jewelry, art, fine furniture, and the like from city folks who needed to eat. The biggest winners were the clever speculators who knew how to profit from such catastrophic times. These were the men who borrowed every mark the banks would lend to buy hard assets, knowing that they could repay the loans when they matured with worthless paper. They bought all sorts of assets from those who played the economic game according to the conventional rules. Clever industrialists expanded their empires by buying out failed competitors. Real estate barons built empires by foreclosing on mortgages who could not keep up interest payments.

The German government rid itself of its massive (in normal terms) war debt, and German big business emerged from the horror debt-free. The

German experience proves well that in hyperinflation there are winners as well as losers, but the losers (people who believe in living debt-free, and in saving surplus earnings) get wiped out.

Depressions do not foster inflation, so there were no further examples of this sort of catastrophe during the 1930s. The dislocation caused by depression and deflation is of another order.

After World War II inflation again struck many lands, hitting hardest at the losers. The Japanese yen and the Italian lira plummeted in value, while the German reichsmark was demonetized and replaced by the deutsche mark in the currency reform of 1948.

In Hungary the most incredible inflation the world has ever seen took place. Jefferson summarized this tale, too, in the publication mentioned above. Hungary survived the war with almost no price change. On a price index counting the price level on August 26, 1939, as 100, prices stood at 105 on July 31, 1945. At the end of September of that year the index stood at 349. At the end of October it had reached 2431. By the end of 1945 it was 41,478. At the end of February 1946 it stood at 435,887. At the end of April it reached 35,790,361. By the end of May it was 11,267,000,000. By the end of June it was 954,000,000,000,000. At the end of July the inflation hit its peak, as the price index soared to 399,623,000,000,000,000,000,000,000. On August 1 the almost totally depreciated Hungarian pengo was replaced by the forint. To obtain one forint a Hungarian citizen needed 828,000,000,000,000,000,000,000,000,000 (828 octillion) 1938 pengo. So ended the world's record hyperinflation. Though the Communists had not yet come to power in the Hungary of 1946 the great inflation played perfectly into their hands by utterly ruining the country's urban middle class.

Since 1950 various nations have reformed their monetary systems due to persistent inflation. Shortly after Charles de Gaulle took power in France in 1958, he caused the creation of a new franc to replace the depreciated old franc, with one hundred old francs being required to obtain one new franc.

In the early 1960s Brazil replaced her old cruzeiro with a new cruzeiro, with one thousand of the old being equivalent to one new. More recently she replaced the new cruzeiro with the cruzado—one thousand new cruzeiros were worth one cruzado.

In 1980 Israel replaced the Israeli pound with the shekel at the rate of one thousand pounds per shekel. In 1986 she replaced the shekel with the new shekel at the rate of one thousand old for one new. Thus the new shekel is worth one million old pounds.

In 1983 Argentina replaced her peso with the peso argentino at the rate of ten thousand pesos per one peso argentino. In 1985 the peso argentino was replaced with the austral at the rate of one thousand to one. Thus one austral is worth 10,000,000 old pesos. Bolivia recently replaced her peso with the boliviano at the rate of 1,000,000 pesos per boliviano. Peru very recently replaced her sol with the inti, one thousand sols being required for one inti. Nicaragua replaced her old cordoba with the cordoba at the rate of one thousand to one in February 1988.

In terms of exchange rates against the U.S. dollar the following information is of interest. The Mexican peso was worth eight cents in 1961 — 12.5 pesos to the dollar. As of May 18, 1989, it stood at 2,425 per dollar. It took 215 Turkish lira to buy a dollar in 1983. As of April 15, 1988, it required 2,033.

In the developed countries of the world businesspeople show concern when the annual inflation rate of a nation reaches double-digit levels. One of the reasons why the Swiss franc is in such demand in world money markets is because Swiss inflation seldom climbs above 5 percent per year. Few other currencies have retained their domestic value so well.

The natives of nations where inflation is chronic have learned to live with it. The value of fixed assets will of course appreciate in monetary units as the currency depreciates. The value of accounts receivable will melt like the snowball in the sun if not collected, but delay in payment of accounts payable might be very profitable. Cash balances in local currency should be as small as possible. There is every incentive to borrow heavily, and to delay repayment. Though interest rates skyrocket, they usually remain below the rate of inflation.

Why do some of the world's nations tolerate high rates of inflation? When the value of money falls, the burden of old debts diminishes. It does not matter that your expenses exceed your income. You may have to scurry about to find the wherewithal to buy food, but at least the debt collector does not lie in wait to seize what you scrape together (unless you are a small businessman or the like who does not know how to play the borrowing and speculation game). Economic activity continues amid the storm; there are jobs to be had and maybe even profits to be made. If one survives the storm, he emerges from it debt-free.

When the value of money rises in times of deflation and recession the horror of economic dislocation is magnified. Debt becomes more and more onerous. Economic activity diminishes as the debt burden crushes more and more producers. Jobs become scarcer. Wages fall. Debt collectors become more diligent and more insistent.

In times of hyperinflation there is always money about; it just has very little value. In times of depression there is little or no money about, and it is very difficult to get more. In times of hyperinflation the frugal are crushed and the prodigal survive. In times of depression things happen in reverse. Since the prodigal outnumber the frugal depression is more painful to more people. That is why governments prefer inflation to depression many times over.

In nations such as Brazil the economy seems to boom during periods of near hyperinflation. There is plenty of money about, and more can always be found to invest. It does not matter that it loses its value rapidly; when properly invested it can earn profits far in excess of the inflation rate. Let the national government restrict the money supply in an effort to stop inflation and investment capital dries up. The economy slows down, unemployment grows, and people grow restless. Savers are happy that their stored capital does not melt away quite so rapidly, but such people are a small enough minority that their complaints carry little weight.

Summing up, inflation is bad, but recession and deflation are far worse in the minds of debtors. Debtors far outnumber creditors on Planet Earth, so inflation will always be with us.

Exchange Controls. Nations with balance of payments problems may enact legislation to control outflows of currency from their territory. If Ruritania has such a problem, it might do the following. First, it could either forbid anyone domiciled in Ruritania from purchasing large quantities of foreign currency for export outside Ruritania, or it could impose strict regulations regarding foreign currency purchases. Under these sorts of controls a Ruritanian wishing to import goods from the United States and to pay for them in U.S. dollars would have to have government consent, though he could pay in Ruritanian glotnies, the currency of the country. The Ruritanian subsidiary of an American multinational would not be permitted to convert its Ruritanian profits into dollars for remission to the U.S. without government consent. The importer would probably find it easier to get permission to buy dollars than the multinational.

Second, it could forbid or regulate the export of large quantities of glotnies outside Ruritania. If this sort of control is stringent enough, Ruritanian foreign trade would have to be done on a countertrade basis. The American multinational would be unable to repatriate Ruritanian profits in the form of cash; either it would have to do so in the form of Ruritanian products, or it would have to somehow invest its profits in the Ruritanian economy.

The more stringent exchange control becomes, the more power the host government may assert over the operations of foreign-owned businesses on its soil. The more difficult repatriation of profit becomes, the less point there is to having operations in the country. (Of course, such control could make it practically impossible for the foreign firm to profitably cease operations in the country; if the proceeds of liquidation of the enterprise could not be repatriated home what could be done with them?)

Bankruptcy of Customer, Supplier, or Bank. Virtually all nations with free market economies have bankruptcy legislation. The differences between bankruptcy under the common-law system and bankruptcy under the Romano-Germanic system have already been discussed.

There is little international cooperation or coordination in these matters. A bankruptcy proceeding is conducted in the courts of the country where filed under the law of that country, and the creditors and debtors of the bankrupt are all treated alike, whatever their nationality.

Perhaps the most aggravating problem in a bankruptcy with international ramifications is the question of whether a bankruptcy court will have jurisdiction over assets of the bankrupt located outside the country where the bankruptcy was filed. Some national laws assert such jurisdiction while others do not.

If the courts of the country where the assets are located try to assert jurisdiction over them sticky problems arise. Section 304 of the United States Bankruptcy Act allows American bankruptcy courts to assert control over the assets of foreign bankrupts within the United States and to preside over their liquidation in cooperation with the bankruptcy courts of the country where the bankruptcy was originally filed. It may turn out that the bankrupt's American assets are disposed of under American law while his foreign assets are disposed of under some other country's law.

Generally foreign bankruptcy legislation is nowhere as lenient toward the debtor as is American bankruptcy law. Remember that negligence by business managers leading to insolvency is a crime in some nations, and that in the majority of Romano-Germanic countries a debtor who goes through a bankruptcy proceeding is not discharged from his debts unless his creditors agree to discharge him.

Discriminatory Treatment. Host governments may discriminate against foreign enterprises operating on their soil in many ways besides the use of exchange controls. They may tighten regulations restricting the employment of foreigners within the country. The alien staff of such enterprises may be reduced simply by revoking the work permits of some of the staff members. This could force the enterprise to employ more natives, or it could force a contraction in operations.

All sorts of regulations of plant operations—from plant safety to product safety to environmental protection—could be enforced in a discriminatory fashion. All law enforcers everywhere have wide powers of discretion in determining enforcement policy; thus it is easy enough to watch foreigners more diligently than natives.

Governmental services may become lax. Customs inspectors may be slow about clearing shipments of imported raw materials. National bank personnel may dawdle over exchange control permits. Personnel of the nationalized railway system may be slow in arranging shipments to and from the plant.

Taxation may be discriminatorily enforced. Import duties may be raised on essential raw materials. Fixed assets may be appraised at high values for capital tax purposes. If the plant produces a unique product a high excise tax may be imposed upon it. The local equivalent of the IRS may harass the firm with continual tax return audits.

If the legislative branch of the host government involves itself in the pattern of discrimination the possibilities could be unlimited, depending on the sacredness of constitutional guarantees, the degree of independence of the local judiciary, and the like.

Expropriation. The ultimate host country act against an alien business is expropriation under which the alien owners are simply deprived of ownership of their property.

Expropriation as such was almost unknown before World War I. There were instances in which underdeveloped nations refused to pay interest and or principal on bonds issued to private parties in developed nations. But in that era of gunboat diplomacy, the result was likely to be military intervention. Thus, when Mexico defaulted on foreign debts in 1861, a joint French-British-Spanish military expedition landed at Vera Cruz to enforce collection. The liberal Mexican government of Benito Juarez was unable or unwilling to pay, so the French marched on Mexico City; the British and Spaniards meanwhile withdrew. In collaboration with conservative Mexicans the French sought to overthrow Mexico's republican government and establish Maximilian of Hapsburg as emperor. (The effort nearly succeeded, but Maximilian was ultimately deposed by Mexicans and executed by a Mexican firing squad in 1867.)

The first major expropriation of foreign investments was carried out by the Bolsheviks after their seizure of power. This act caused interesting legal controversies to erupt all over the non–Communist world. Among the properties expropriated by the Communists were the assets of Russian corporations operating internationally. The Soviet government claimed that their expropriation decrees reached the property of these Russian corporations everywhere in the world.

In many cases the preexpropriation managements of these corporations fled from their homeland and claimed the right to continue managing those corporate assets located outside Russia. In other cases the Russian managements of foreign branches residing outside Russia claimed a similar right. Almost without exception non–Communist courts held that, since expropriation without compensation is unlawful under international law, assets of expropriated Russian corporations located outside Russia still belonged to their former owners.

In the United States the New York state agency that regulated that state's insurance industry took control of the offices and assets of Russian insurance companies operating in that state and operated them for the benefit of American policyholders during the 1920s and early 1930s. The Soviet government claimed this action was unlawful, but since the Soviet Union and the United States had no diplomatic relations at that time, the

Soviets could do little to win redress. In 1933 the administration of Franklin D. Roosevelt decided to normalize relations with the Soviet Union. One of the sore points to be resolved was the proper disposition of these insurance company assets. Another involved the claims of American owners of expropriated assets in the Soviet Union for compensation.

In an executive agreement called the Litvinov Assignment, the two governments agreed that the United States government should take control of all Russian assets within the United States and use these as a fund to pay claims of the former American owners of expropriated property in the Soviet Union. The New York insurance regulators challenged the lawfulness of this agreement because it indirectly recognized the validity of the Soviet expropriation of Russian-owned assets located on American soil. However, the United States Supreme Court held that the Litvinov Assignment was a valid international agreement; therefore the United States government had the right to assume ownership of the assets in question.

In eastern Europe the governments of Poland, Czechoslovakia, and Romania expropriated land from large landowners and distributed it among farmers, generally paying no compensation. Though no foreign interests were involved, this was an indication that non–Communist governments were now willing to expropriate without consideration.

During the 1930s Turkish state banks began to buy up properties owned by foreigners in that country. Fair compensation was paid, but the Turkish government made it clear to the owners of these properties that expropriation would be invoked if they did not sell.

Bolivia expropriated some properties of Standard Oil Company in 1937, paying compensation after diplomatic pressure from Washington.

The major Western Hemisphere expropriation of the interwar period was the Mexican seizure of foreign oil properties in 1938. Though compensation was paid, oil company managements considered it to be utterly inadequate. However, the Franklin Roosevelt administration refused to exert diplomatic pressure on Mexico to help the oil industry, so the companies had to accept Mexico's compensation.

Expropriations occurred much more often after World War II. The new Communist regimes of eastern Europe expropriated most private property without compensation. The claims of foreign owners of such property were settled by mechanisms similar to the Litvinov Assignment; assets of expropriated Czech, Polish, Hungarian, and other such corporations located in the United States were taken over by the United States authorities, liquidated, and the proceeds used to pay American claimants.

Among the more noteworthy expropriations of the 1950s, 1960s and 1970s are the following:

1. Argentina's expropriation of British-owned railways and public utilities during Juan Perón's presidency

2. Expropriation of various foreign-owned public utilities by the Brazilian state of Rio Grande do Sul during the 1950s

3. Iran's expropriation of the Anglo-Iranian Oil Company in 1951

4. Egypt's expropriation of the Suez Canal shortly after the Nasser government assumed power in the early 1950s

5. Guatemala's expropriation of United Fruit Company property during the Arbenz Guzmán presidency in the early 1950s

6. Bolivia's nationalization of her tin mines in the 1950s

7. Cuba's expropriation of foreign investments in that country in 1960

8. Zaire's expropriation of Union Minière, the giant Belgian copper company operating in Katanga province, shortly after independence in the early 1960s

9. Chile's expropriation of copper mining properties in the 1960s

10. Peru's expropriation of various foreign investments during the 1960s

11. Saudi Arabia's expropriation of Arabian-American Oil Company properties

12. Libya's appropriation of various oil properties after Colonel Khaddafi's revolution

13. Venezuela's nationalization of her oil industry

14. Iran's expropriation of various foreign properties after the Khomeini revolution

15. Nicaragua's expropriation of various foreign properties after the Sandinista revolution

This list is by no means all-inclusive. Most of these expropriations occurred in the Third World, in widely separated countries. They are no longer uncommon, and are likely to become more common as political awareness grows in third-world lands.

As stated earlier, in theory the expropriating nation should pay compensation to the owners of the expropriated property. In practice this may not be done; or the compensation may be paid in a form that is not of much value to the property owners.

Within the United States the Fifth Amendment forbids the taking of private property for public use without payment of just compensation. Just compensation is generally considered to be fair market value. However, even within the United States or its territories government action may deprive a property owner of property rights without entitlement to any compensation.

Destruction of private property by American military forces to keep it out of the hands of the enemy is not compensable.

Zoning legislation may have the effect of reducing the value of the zoned real estate, but that is not compensable.

Impoundment of enemy assets in wartime is not compensable.

Reduction of property values because government chooses to locate an airport or military base or garbage dump nearby is not compensable.

Thus even pro–private-property regimes like American governments on occasion take private property without paying compensation. If the United States sometimes acts in this fashion, how much more likely are other national governments to do so, too?

If the expropriating government is Marxist-Leninist, it will not believe in private ownership of property. Its expropriation will be regarded as the triumph of the people over the capitalist-imperialist oppressors—the recovery by the people of their own. The profit the oppressors have earned from their wrongfully acquired assets was compensation enough for their capital investment; in fact it was too much. They deserve no more! The chances of the expropriators offering compensation are practically nil.

If the expropriating government is non–Marxist it may offer to pay compensation. However, the value of the compensation may well be less than the value of the expropriated assets, or the supposedly fair compensation may be reduced severely in value by the circumstances surrounding its payment. For instance, Ruritania may pay a fair price for Ace Company's expropriated plant in Ruritanian glotnies but then refuse permission to Ace to repatriate the glotnies outside the country. How will Ace spend the glotnies if it is not permitted to continue operations in Ruritania?

Guatador may pay for an expropriated Deuce Company plant with a quantity of government bonds denominated in Guatadoran pesos that amount to fair value, maturing on December 31, 2050. Deuce Company would be fairly happy if it could convert the bonds into cash and repatriate the cash. However, Guatador is so small and underdeveloped that it has no local exchange upon which bonds such as these are traded; the market that exists is a chaotic over-the-counter market. Besides, there is no market for Guatadoran government bonds outside Guatador. How will Deuce be able to turn these bonds into current assets? It will be difficult or impossible.

Gerolstein pays Trey Company for its expropriated plant a fair price in cash, Gerolsteiner thalers. However, the day after payment is made the Gerolsteiner government devalues the thaler by 25 percent. Suddenly Trey Company's compensation is worth only 75 percent of a fair price in U.S. dollars. Not only has Gerolstein expropriated the plant; it has also expropriated part of the compensation through the devaluation.

How can an alien investor contest an unfair expropriation? Such action varies from being difficult to being impossible.

A possible avenue is through the court system of the expropriating country. If the country has constitutional provisions like the Fifth Amendment to the United States Constitution and if it has an independent judiciary this approach will have potential. However, if the legal system is

Socialist or if the judiciary is under the thumb of the political rulers of the country this line of approach is useless.

Another possibility is taking action in United States courts. But if the investor's only argument is about the expropriation of assets within the expropriating country, this approach, too, will be useless. An American court would almost certainly hold that the expropriation was an *Act of State* and therefore cannot be challenged in a foreign court.

Courts in the United States have followed the custom of not questioning the lawfulness of acts of foreign government within its own country to avoid diplomatic complications. Before the era of expropriation of foreign assets with minimal or no compensation this approach worked very well. Recently, however, the American courts have come to recognize four situations in which the acts of foreign governments will be questioned:

1. The *Bernstein* exception. The Nazi government of Germany seized a ship belonging to Bernstein, a Jew, in the late 1930s and sold it to a Belgian corporation. The ship was later sunk during World War II, and the Belgians and Bernstein both claimed the insurance proceeds. The Belgians claimed good title to the ship because the Nazi seizure was an act of state. Bernstein sued for the money in an American court. The executive branch of the U.S. government informed the court that strict application of the doctrine would not advance the interests of American foreign policy, so the court heard the case. Bernstein lost after a trial; had the court applied the act-of-state doctrine he would not even have gotten a hearing.

2. The *Hickenlooper Amendment* exception. The Hickenlooper Amendment to the Foreign Aid Assistance Act of 1966 states that no American court may refuse to judge the lawfulness of a foreign expropriation of American property if done contrary to international law.

3. The *Commercial Activity* exception. Government actions in furtherance of state commercial activity are not considered to be true governmental actions.

4. The *Treaty* exception. Where a treaty unambiguously creates exceptions to the doctrine, American courts will abide by that treaty.

Austria and Switzerland tend to question foreign acts of state closely. France will also do this if there is some ground for questioning the basic fairness of the foreign act. West Germany, Italy, and Japan tend to apply the doctrine literally, not questioning the legitimacy of the governmental act. Great Britain recognized no immunity for acts of state—in the American sense—until the middle of the twentieth century. Now the British practice is somewhat similar to ours.

The significance of all this from the point of view of the American businessman is that one has little opportunity to question the lawfulness of acts of foreign governments in court. If the courts of the government's own country uphold its acts, so will the courts of other lands.

If the expropriating government owns assets within the United States things look a little brighter for the victim. If the assets are held by the expropriating government in its capacity as a government, an effort to attach these assets as compensation for the expropriation will fail. The expropriating government will claim that the assets are immune from claims of its creditors on grounds of *Sovereign Immunity.*

Under some circumstances it is possible to sue foreign governments in American courts under the Foreign Sovereign Immunity Act, which provides that foreign states may under some circumstances lose their immunity from suit.

Included in the definition of "foreign state" are "political subdivisions" of the state and "agencies and instrumentalities" of the state. Thus the commune of Maur in the canton of Zurich, Switzerland, would be entitled to sovereign immunity as a political subdivision of the country, and the Novosti press agency of the Soviet Union would be immune from suit as an agency or instrumentality of the state.

An entity normally entitled to sovereign immunity loses it when:

1. It expressly or impliedly waives its immunity. It would expressly waive immunity by so stating. It would waive by implication if it agrees to suit in an American court or it agreees to arbitrate disputes arising under a contract. A central government may waive the immunity of a political subdivision, agency, or instrumentality.

2. It is carrying on a commercial activity in the United States. Defining "commercial activity" is usually no problem, unless government or military procurement is involved.

3. It performs an act in the United States connected with a commercial act performed elsewhere. Perhaps making payment in the United States on a commercial contract performed abroad would be an example.

4. It performs an act outside the United States in connection with a commercial act performed outside the United States and that act has a direct effect in the United States. The meaning of this is somewhat uncertain. Air Ruritania, the government-owned airline of Ruritania, borrows money from the branch of Bank of America in Strelsau, Ruritania's capital. The airline does not repay the loan. Bank of America does not want to sue in Ruritanian courts to collect because it fears politically inspired bias against it, so it sues in an American court. The airline is clearly an instrumentality of the state of Ruritania, but the making of the loan is clearly a commercial act. Does the nonpayment in Ruritania have a direct effect in the United States? The answer is not clear.

It is one thing to sue a foreign sovereign and obtain judgment against it; it may be quite another to collect the judgment. If the judgment is against the foreign state or a political subdivision of the state assets of the judgment debtor may be seized if:

1. The immunity is waived. A waiver cannot apply to property used for governmental rather than commercial purposes, however. (Thus, an American with a judgment against the government of Ruritania could not seize a Ruritanian military aircraft in settlement of his claim even if the Ruritanians said that he could do it.)

2. The assets to be seized were or are used in the commercial activity upon which the claim was based.

3. The judgment establishes rights in property that was taken in violation of international law (perhaps property located in the United States that was expropriated by the foreign state without payment of compensation).

If the judgment debtor is an agency or instrumentality of the foreign government rather than the government itself or a political subdivision and the debtor is not immune, any of its commercial assets may be seized, whether used in the commercial activity involved in the claim or not.

Funds and other assets belonging to central banks are absolutely immune if "held for the bank's own account." Funds standing in the name of the central bank used to finance commercial activity by other instrumentalities of the state probably would not be exempt. The bank may expressly waive this immunity, but cannot do so by implication.

Military property is also absolutely immune. This immunity cannot be waived.

Prejudgment attachment of assets of a foreign sovereign will not be allowed unless the sovereign expressly waives the immunity. The foreign state must give official permission for the attachment.

A judgment against one agent or instrumentality of a foreign sovereign cannot be collected out of the assets of another. Thus an American with a judgment against Air Ruritania, the government airline, could not collect it out of the assets of Ruritanian Autoworks, the government auto manufacturer. The separate legal personalities of these organizations are respected, though both are instrumentalities of the Ruritanian state.

English law on sovereign immunity is very similar to American law. The laws of continental European countries diverge a little. Political subdivisions generally do not enjoy immunity in Romano-Germanic nations. Sweden and France are more likely to give immunity to nationalized industries and such then are Italy and Switzerland. Notions on exempt assets are about the same everywhere; commercial assets are fair game for the judgment creditor, while governmental assets are not. West Germany and Switzerland freely allow prejudgment attachment of a sovereign's commercial assets; other continental nations are not so generous.

The Soviet Union, China, and other countries of the Second World adhere to the old absolute theory of sovereign immunity. They become very upset when other nations permit them to be sued in their courts, and they do not generally entertain suits against foreign governments themselves.

Thus, when a foreign government breaches a contract with an American, the American may have trouble obtaining legal recourse — but recourse is not impossible.

Generally those who lose property through expropriation without compensation or with unfair compensation will get some sort of justice only if the United States and the expropriating nation agree to establish an arbitration tribunal to hear such cases. The expropriating nation will agree to do this only if the United States is able to exert control over its own valuable assets in this country.

What essentially happens is that the United States expropriates the expropriator's assets for the use of the American victims of the original expropriations. A procedure of this sort is now being utilized to settle the claims of American businessmen against Iran for the expropriation of American business properties after the 1979 revolution in that country.

Insuring Private Investment Through OPIC. An American wishing to insure the safety of a foreign investment may do so to an extent through the Overseas Private Investment Corporation, a corporation wholly owned by the United States government. OPIC will not insure an investment in a country unless it has entered into an agreement with the government of that country with respect to the status of U.S. investment in that country. Under these agreements OPIC will not commit to insure unless the host government approves the investment to be insured in advance.

To be eligible for OPIC insurance the investor must be: (1) an American national, or (2) an American corporation or partnership, if more than half of the partners are American or 50 percent or more of all classes of stock issued by a corporation are owned by Americans; or (3) an alien enterprise if all of the shareholders or owners are Americans, unless local law requires that up to 5 percent of the ownership be held by locals. Thus an alien corporation in which American shareholders own a 90 percent interest would not be eligible.

For the investment to be insurable it must be new. OPIC will not insure already existing investments. The new investment must take one of the following forms: (1) cash; (2) machinery, equipment, materials, or commodities; (3) services; or (4) intangibles, such as patents, processes, techniques, or licenses (trademarks, trade names, and goodwill are not insurable).

The following types of property interests are insurable: (1) equity; (2) loans, if made in U.S. dollars or currencies convertible to U.S. dollars; and (3) service or licensing agreements.

The following sorts of investments are ineligible:
1. In enterprises owned or controlled by the host government
2. Armament or munitions plants
3. Firms buying and selling real estate (but firms only developing real estate are acceptable)

4. Hotels containing gambling operations

5. Firms engaged in production of alcoholic beverages (though breweries might be eligible)

6. Investments for speculation purposes

7. Entertainment facilities (sports stadia, golf courses, etc.)

8. Establishment of an industry that is moving from the United States

OPIC insurance protects against the following risks: (1) currency inconvertibility; (2) expropriation; and (3) war, revolution, and insurrection.

Among the perils not protected against are the following:

1. Currency exchange rate fluctuations

2. Effects of exchange controls and the like in effect when the insurance was procured

3. Civil disturbances not caused by armed forces of the enemy in wartime or by organized revolutionaries or insurgents

4. Currency devaluations

5. Insolvency of customers, borrowers, and the like

The investment must be 100 percent insured. The maximum time for which it can be insured is twenty years.

Chapter 16

Multinational Dispute Resolution

Civil Jurisdiction

I have already discussed the criminal jurisdiction of national courts. Now I will consider the circumstances under which a plaintiff may sue a nonresident person or organization in the courts of his country.

In common-law systems the judges speak of *In Personam* jurisdiction and *In Rem* jurisdiction. In personam jurisdiction is jurisdiction over the defendant's being. Jurisdiction over this person is in theory jurisdiction over all of his assets. In rem jurisdiction is jurisdiction over assets. The court asserts in rem authority through *Attachment* of the asset. Any judgment obtained under such jurisdiction binds only the attached asset(s), not the person of the owner of the asset.

The usual method used to gain personal jurisdiction over the defendant is to serve him with a citation informing him that he is being sued. Under Texas state law this can be done only when the defendant is present in Texas under normal circumstances.

The citation may be served in one of two ways: by registered or certified mail deliverable to the addressee only, or by delivery of the documents to the defendant in person by a constable or deputy sheriff.

Most American states and other common-law jurisdictions have "long-arm" statutes under which defendants outside the jurisdiction may be properly served with citation. This may be done under Texas law when the litigation involves a tort committed against a Texan in Texas, or a contract made with a Texan in Texas. In such cases the defendant may be "served" by registered or certified mail even though he is not physically present in Texas.

Corporations doing business within common-law jurisdictions are required to have registered agents or business offices within the jurisdiction. Citations directed to the corporation may be validly served upon these agents.

243

Under English law personal jurisdiction may be obtained over a defendant if he is served a citation on English soil, though he does not reside there or have any assets there. Thus, an Englishman with a claim against a nonresident Frenchman who owned no assets in England learned that the Frenchman intended to attend the horseraces at Ascot. He saw to it that the Frenchman was served a citation at the racetrack; that provided the basis for him to obtain an in personam judgment against the defendant.

Some American states also permit this.

When the defendant has assets within a jurisdiction, he may be sued in that jurisdiction even if he is not physically present there. Through court process the plaintiff must attach the assets. This gives the court authority to hear the case. If the plaintiff wins he may have the attached assets sold to satisfy his judgment; but if the assets are of insufficient value to pay off the judgment he may not seize any other property of the defendant.

A judgment in personam theoretically binds the defendant and his assets wherever they might be found. However, no common-law jurisdiction will enforce another jurisdiction's judgment. It must convert the foreign judgment into its own.

Suppose that Smith sues Jones for damages for breach of contract in a Texas state court and obtains judgment for $100,000. Jones leaves Texas without paying off the judgment and leaves no valuable assets behind. Six months later Smith learns that Jones now lives in London, England. Smith may enforce his judgment against Jones in England, but first he must convert it into an English judgment. He must do this by filing another suit against Jones in England. Once the English court obtains personal jurisdiction over Jones Smith must merely prove that he has a valid unsatisfied Texas judgment against Jones. Jones will not be able to retry the case. Smith will obtain English judgment on the basis of the Texas judgment and will then be able to collect out of Jones's English assets. Had Jones lived in England at the time Smith filed suit against him — let us say that the Texas court had heard the case because Jones owned real estate in Texas and Smith had attached it — and Smith had gotten judgment for $100,000 and had the attached land sold for $50,000, the English court would not recognize the Texas judgment. Here the judgment is in rem, not in personam, and binds only Jones's Texas real estate.

When Smith sued Jones in England on his $100,000 Texas in personam judgment, would the English court give him judgment for U.S. $100,000 or for the equivalent sum in English pounds? The answer is that he would obtain the judgment in U.S. dollars. English courts will render judgments in foreign currency where appropriate. If Jones pays the judgment in pounds, the exchange rate as of the day of payment will apply; thus the value of Smith's judgment in pounds will fluctuate as the exchange rate between dollars and pounds fluctuates.

Suppose on the other hand that Brown sues Green in England and obtains valid judgment for 100,000 pounds against him. Green has no assets in England, but he has many in Texas. Brown therefore comes to Texas to convert his English judgment into a Texas judgment. Will Texas give him judgment for 100,000 pounds? The answer is almost certainly negative. American courts do not render judgments in foreign currency, though there is no legal reason why they cannot. Brown will be granted a judgment for the number of dollars 100,000 pounds will buy as of the day of rendition of the judgment. The value of the judgment in pounds will fluctuate as the exchange rate between dollars and pounds fluctuates until Brown collects; thus when he collects in dollars he may or may not realize 100,000 English pounds from the proceeds.

The Romano-Germanic system uses quite different standards for asserting jurisdiction. In France a French national may sue anyone anywhere in the world, the French court basing its jurisdiction upon the French nationality of the plaintiff. It does not matter whether the plaintiff actually lives in France or not. Thus a French citizen living in Belgium could sue a Swiss citizen living in Switzerland in a French court for breach of a contract that was to be performed in Denmark.

In the Netherlands anyone domiciled in the country may sue anyone else anywhere in the world, whether the plaintiff has Dutch nationality or not. Here the jurisdiction is based on the fact that the plaintiff has a permanent residence (domicile) in the Netherlands. Thus an American living in the Netherlands could sue a Canadian in a Dutch court for breach of a contract performed in France.

In Belgium a Belgian national may sue anyone anywhere in the world if the defendant's country lets its nationals sue anyone anywhere in the world. Thus, a Belgian could sue a nonresident Frenchman in a Belgian court because French law would let a French national sue a nonresident Belgian in a French court. However, a Belgian cannot sue a nonresident American in a Belgian court because American law will not permit an American to sue a nonresident Belgian in our courts.

Nations with legal systems based upon German law generally do not allow their nationals to sue anyone unless the defendant has some connection with the plaintiff's nation. However, the connection may be minimal. If the defendant has any asset whatsoever in West Germany the German court will assert the equivalent of in personam jurisdiction over him, and any judgment will theoretically bind all of the person's assets. Austrian law here is the same as German. An Austrian was able to obtain judgment on a claim against the French skier Jean-Claude Killy though Killy did not live in Austria because, when the skier checked out of a hotel, he left a pair of undershorts behind. This insignificant asset was enough to give the Austrian court jurisdiction over his person.

Belgian and Dutch law are similar — except that in these countries the plaintiff must get a court attachment of the defendant's asset(s) before the court will accept jurisdiction.

The same is true of Swiss law. A very common asset of an international businessperson is an account in a Swiss bank. It may be that an American has a claim against a Saudi citizen on a contract made and breached in Saudi Arabia. The Saudi has no assets in the United States, and the American does not want to get involved with Saudi courts. He discovers that the Saudi has a bank account in a Zurich bank. He may levy an attachment upon the account and file suit on his claim in a Zurich court. The Swiss will decide it, applying Saudi or American law as the case may be in order to do justice.

The connection with the plaintiff's country could be so simple a thing as the commission of a tort against the plaintiff there, or the breaching of a contract with the plaintiff there.

English law will allow a plaintiff to sue a defendant in England for breach of a contract made in England, whether it was to be performed in England or not.

In the Romano-Germanic system the serving of court papers on the defendant is of no significance at all. Personal jurisdiction must be obtained in other ways.

The average Romano-Germanic country enforces judgments of other nations in a somewhat simpler way than common law does; the plaintiff applies to a court of the enforcing nation for an *Exequatur* (a court order allowing enforcement of the judgment against the judgment debtor's assets in the country). If the enforcing nation recognizes the validity of the judgment the exequatur will issue with no problem, without any sort of trial.

However, in the absence of international agreements by which nations agree to enforce each other's judgments Romano-Germanic nations scrutinize carefully the judgment they are being asked to enforce.

A very few nations (such as Finland) will simply not enforce foreign judgments.

To the French the nationality of the judgment debtor is important. Suppose a Brazilian sues a Frenchman in a Brazilian court and obtains judgment. The debtor has no assets in Brazil, so the Brazilian wants to enforce his judgment in France. He will have difficulty. Any French person involved in litigation has the right to have his case tried in a French court. If he makes clear that he claims that right and has not given it up by accepting trial in Brazil France will not enforce the Brazilian judgment.

If the Brazilian sued an Egyptian in a Brazilian court, obtained judgment, and sought to enforce the judgment against the Egyptian's French assets it could be a different story. The French might well enforce the judgment.

German courts generally enforce foreign judgments if the country where the judgment was handed down enforces German judgments. With the Germans enforceability is a question of reciprocity.

Other matters taken into account in deciding whether to enforce the foreign judgment are the power of the court to hand down the judgment, whether or not the debtor got a fair trial, and the like.

Virtually all Romano-Germanic courts will render judgments in foreign currency when appropriate.

Because of the difference in jurisdiction requirements common-law courts may be reluctant to accept Romano-Germanic judgments at face value, and vice versa.

If an American vacationer commits a tort against a Frenchman in France and leaves that country without paying compensation the Frenchman may well sue him for damages in a French court. The court will assert jurisdiction even though the American is no longer in France and has no assets there. The American may be given notice of the suit, but may choose not to make an effort to defend himself. Or, the French effort to notify him may fail, so that he never learns of the suit.

The trial will probably proceed *In Absentia,* and the Frenchman may receive judgment. This judgment will be of no value in France, but the French plaintiff may well ask an American court in the state where the defendant lives to enforce it. No American court could hear a case against a Frenchman under such conditions, so the American judge may be reluctant to enforce the French judgment. It does not seem fair to us that the Frenchman could obtain judgment in such a manner without the American having a chance to defend himself.

If the Englishman who got his English judgment against the Frenchman because he had the defendant served with citation at the Ascot racetrack tried to have his judgment enforced in France he would have the same problem. The French would feel it was most unfair of the English to assert jurisdiction over their countryman through such underhanded trickery.

Brazil will enforce a foreign judgment only if it is approved for enforcement (homologized) by that nation's Supreme Court. At the other extreme English courts will enforce the judgments of certain Commonwealth countries if they are registered with the proper English authority. This registration requires no conversion into an English judgment.

The nations of the European Community have entered into a convention that provides that most civil judgments entered by courts of one member nation are directly enforceable by the courts of other member nations.

Two similar conventions, the Montevideo Agreement and the Bustamente Code, bind most Latin American nations to enforce each other's judgments.

Since the United States is a party to no such convention, she is under no obligation to enforce judgments from any nation; thus no other nation is absolutely obligated to enforce American judgments.

The following hypothetical cases illustrate some of the problems discussed above.

Ace Company, an American manufacturer with its main plant in Dallas, buys machinery from Kreuz AG, a Ruritanian manufacturer, for use in its plant. The machinery is defective and malfunctions, killing two of Ace's employees. Ace and the estates of the two deceased employees want to sue Kreuz for damages for selling the defective machinery. The contract contained no provision guaranteeing the quality of the machine.

The law of most nations holds a seller of a defective product liable for the harm it causes regardless of guarantee or lack thereof under at least some circumstances. Therefore the injured parties ought to be able to recover some sort of damages from Kreuz. Two important questions arise. Could the American plaintiffs sue in a Texas court, or must they sue in Ruritania? Which law, American or Ruritanian, will determine the outcome of the case?

The answer to the first question will depend on several factors: (1) where was the contract of sale made?; (2) does Kreuz AG do business in Texas or elsewhere in the United States?; and (3) does Kreuz AG have assets anywhere within the United States?

If the contract was made in Texas, the plaintiffs could sue in Texas because of the state's long arm statute. If Kreuz does business in Texas, the plaintiffs could sue there because citation could be served upon Kreuz's Texas agent, thus giving the Texas courts in personam jurisdiction over Kreuz.

If Kreuz does business elsewhere in the United States (say, in New York), the plaintiffs could sue in New York because service of citation upon Kreuz's agent would be possible there.

If Kreuz does no business in the United States but has assets here (for example, accounts in New York banks) the plaintiffs could obtain attachments on these assets, granting an American court in rem jurisdiction over them.

If the answer to all of these questions is negative, the plaintiffs have no way to sue in the United States. They must go to Ruritania.

What difference does it make whether the suit is in the United States or in Ruritania?

If the suit may be filed in the United States the plaintiffs need not cross the Atlantic to a foreign land to sue. They can hire American lawyers. The court proceedings will be in English, under the familiar common-law rules.

If the proceedings are in Ruritania, the plaintiffs will need to hire Ruritanian lawyers. The procedure will be Romano-Germanic rather than common law, and the court proceedings will be in the language of Ruritania.

Which law will govern the outcome?

The answer depends upon where the *Center of Gravity* of the contract was. This will depend upon the answers to the following questions, among others: (1) where was the contract made?; (2) where did title to the machinery pass from Kreuz to Ace?; and (3) where did Ace pay for the machinery?

The applicable law will make a great difference in the outcome of the case. The Texas law imposes no-fault liability upon the seller of a defective product. If Texas law governs, the plaintiffs win if they can prove the machine was defective when it left Kreuz's factory, whether negligence by Kreuz had anything to do with the defect or not. If they win, they recover actual damages. The estates of the deceased employees may also be able to recover damages for the pain and suffering of the deceased. In addition, it is possible for all of the plaintiffs to recover punitive damages.

Ruritania is not a member of the European Community, so EC product liability law does not apply there. Her law in this area is essentially what German law was before the mandated EC reforms. Therefore, Kreuz will not be liable under Ruritanian law unless the plaintiffs can prove negligence on its part; if there is no negligence, there is no liability. Even if there is negligence, Kreuz will be liable for only actual damages, because Romano-Germanic tort law does not allow recovery for pain and suffering. It also does not allow recovery of punitive damages in cases of this sort.

Depending upon the answers to the above questions, four possible sets of circumstances could govern the hearing of this case:

1. It could be heard in an American court that would apply American law

2. It could be heard in an American court that would apply Ruritanian law

3. It could be heard in a Ruritanian court that would apply American law

4. It could be heard in a Ruritanian court that would apply Ruritanian law

The set ultimately applied may well determine the outcome of the case.

Garcia AG, a Guatadoran corporation, contracts to sell a large quantity of Guatadoran alpaca wool to King Company, a Texas corporation. The contract is made in Texas; Garcia is to deliver the wool to King's branch in Santa Fe, Guatador. King is to pay the price in Guatadoran pesos there.

Garcia delivers at the last minute; King's agent rejects the delivery because the wool is not of the quality specified in the contract. Garcia protests because, it claims, the wool was exactly of the quality the contract called for. King claims Garcia breached by delivering inferior wool; Garcia claims King breached by refusing delivery of conforming goods. The argument cannot possibly be settled peaceably.

Garcia therefore files suit against King in Guatador to force it to accept the wool and pay for it. King's management knows that several people in Garcia's management are relatives of the president of Guatador; therefore they fear they will not get a fair trial in that country. They respond by filing suit against Garcia for damages for nondelivery in a Texas court under the Texas Long Arm Statute because the contract in question was made in Texas.

King asks the Guatadoran court to dismiss its case because King has filed suit in Texas; Garcia asks the Texas court to drop its case because Garcia has filed suit in Guatador. Would either case be dropped?

The answer is probably negative; rarely will courts dismiss cases in situations like the above. Both cases will wind down to their respective conclusions. If the same party wins in both, the argument is over. But what if Garcia wins in Guatador and King wins in Texas? Garcia could force King to accept the wool and pay for it in Guatador, while King would have a judgment for damages in Texas.

If Garcia had assets in Texas King could collect the judgment and recover some of what had to be paid to Garcia in Guatador. But what if Garcia had no assets in Texas and King had to try to enforce its Texas judgment in Guatador? It would probably be out of luck. When a foreign judgment conflicts with a domestic judgment, national courts will almost invariably assume that the domestic judgment is correct and the foreign erroneous; thus they will refuse to enforce the foreign judgment.

The parties to international contracts may remove some legal uncertainty from their bargains by including in them *Choice of Law* and *Choice of Forum* clauses. A choice of law clause simply says that the bargain shall be governed by and construed by the law of _____. Such a clause will make it probable that the governing law will be what is stated, but it does not make it certain. American and West European courts generally respect and enforce such clauses; courts of other nations may not.

When a party with superior bargaining power dictates a choice of law clause into the contract, the weaker party may seek to ignore it and may get away with it.

Deuce Company, an American firm, sells goods to Osuna SA, a Guatadoran corporation. The contract says that it will be construed by the law of New York. A dispute arises under the contract and each party accuses the other of breach. Osuna files suit against Deuce for damages in a Guatadoran court and asks the court to apply Guatadoran law to determine liability and damages. Deuce argues that this cannot be done: the Guatadoran court must apply New York law as the contract provides. The Guatadoran court holds that the choice of law clause was imposed upon

Osuna by the superior bargaining power of Deuce and is therefore invalid under Guatadoran law. It then decides the case according to the law of its country and imposes heavy damages upon Deuce.

Deuce has no effective recourse. Third-world courts in particular tend to look closely at clauses imposing first-world law upon their nationals. If a court system refuses to be bound by such a clause the clause is rendered ineffective.

The courts of Saudi Arabia refuse to apply foreign law. All cases heard in Saudi courts will be decided according to Saudi law, including all contract cases.

A choice of forum clause says simply that any claim or controversy arising out of the contract shall be heard in the courts of _____.

These clauses are generally respected by American courts. If the clause provides for an American forum, the court assumes jurisdiction over the parties based upon their consent. If the clause provides for a non–American forum, American courts will refuse to hear the case (unless the choice of forum clause is unconscionable or the result of a one-sided bargain or the like).

The court systems of some other countries may show less respect to these clauses. As with choice of law clauses, third-world courts might choose to ignore them and hear the case themselves.

A choice of law clause may specify that a contract will be governed by the law of a nation not involved with the contract; choice of forum clauses may provide that litigation will be heard in the courts of a nation not involved with the contract. It is not uncommon for transnational contracts to contain clauses that the contract will be construed according to English law and that litigation if necessary will take place in London, even though there is no English connection to the transaction.

Arbitration

Arbitration in General. The parties to an international contract may want to keep disputes arising under it out of national court systems. An agreement to arbitrate will accomplish this. Arbitration can be faster and less costly than litigation. In disputes involving business custom and procedure or specialized technical knowledge arbitrators may know more about the whys and wherefores of the argument than judges. If the issues in dispute are primarily legal, however, a court is a better forum for resolution.

Ad Hoc Arbitration. The parties may want to devise their own ground rules for arbitration. This has the advantage of allowing use of a procedure tailor-made for the type of contract involved.

There are two grave disadvantages to ad-hoc arbitration: (1) since arbitration awards are not enforceable without recognition by a national court system, care must be taken to make sure that the award will be in recognizable form; and (2) since it is so difficult to foresee all possible problems that can arise in contract interpretation and in arbitration proceedings, the ad hoc agreement probably will not cover all contingencies. When something totally unforeseen arises, what do the parties do? How are gaps in the arbitration agreement filled? Maybe they cannot be filled; maybe the arbitration effort will fail.

Institutional Arbitration. The parties may provide that the arbitration will be conducted under the supervision of an international arbitration authority. This may cost more and take more time, but the detailed rules used by these authorities touch all possible bases and ensure that the ultimate award will be recognizable by a court. The three most prestigious international arbitration authorities are: (1) The International Chamber of Commerce Court of Arbitration; (2) The London Court of International Arbitration; and (3) The American Arbitration Association.

The International Chamber of Commerce (ICC) and its Court of Arbitration have their headquarters in Paris, but ICC arbitration tribunals may sit anywhere in the world. ICC can provide experts in most conceivable areas of dispute to serve as arbitrators. Its arbitration panels have six months after the close of hearings to render a decision, which could be a disadvantage. Its fees are based upon the amount of money in dispute in the proceedings, assessed against the parties at the discretion of the arbitrators and paid out of a fund contributed by the parties at the beginning of the proceeding. Before handing down a decision, ICC arbitrators are required to permit a member of the Court of Arbitration in Paris to scrutinize it. This person has no power to reverse it or to alter it; the purpose of the procedure is to allow him to evaluate it and suggest revision that will make it more likely to be recognizable by a court.

The London Court of International Arbitration (LCIA) has its headquarters in London but will conduct arbitrations elsewhere. Its procedural rules are more precise and detailed than the ICC rules. Its arbitrators have especially wide discovery powers—powers to force parties to produce documentary evidence and the like. There is no time limit on how long LCIA arbitrators have to produce a decision after the close of hearings. Fees are assessed on an hourly basis rather than on a percentage of the money at stake. As with the ICC, these are divided between the parties at the discretion of the arbitrators.

The American Arbitration Association (AAA) may conduct arbitration proceedings anywhere in the world. It makes sure that its arbitrators are of nationalities other than those of the parties. Its rules are based upon common-law rules of court procedure. Its arbitrators must make a decision within thirty days of the close of the hearings. Its fees are a percentage of the amount at stake in the dispute, apportioned between the parties at the arbitrators' discretion.

The United Nations Commission on International Trade Law (UN-CITRAL) issued a set of rules for arbitration of international disputes in 1966. Though UNCITRAL is not an arbitration organization itself, its rules are often used in international arbitration—even in ICC, LCIA, and AAA arbitrations (parties may specify ICC arbitration under UNCITRAL rules, for instance). The arbitrator under these rules will be appointed by the secretary-general of the Permanent Court of Arbitration at The Hague, The Netherlands, unless the parties agree otherwise.

UNCITRAL rules give arbitrators much discretion in conducting the proceedings. There is no time limit within which the arbitrators must announce their decision. Cost is the main reason why parties choose to use these rules. Fees are based upon the cost of conducting the arbitration. The loser pays them all.

A specialized arbitration organization is the International Center for Settlement of Investment Disputes (ICSID). It hears only disputes between governments and their creditors. It will not hear private disputes. Located at World Bank headquarters in Washington, D.C., all of its proceedings take place there. It allows the parties to disputes to make their own rules, within reason. Its arbitrators must make a decision within thirty days of the close of hearings, subject to one thirty-day extension.

Other arbitration tribunals of importance are:

1. The Cairo Regional Center for Arbitration
2. Various tribunals in Switzerland
3. The Foreign Trade Arbitration Commission and the Maritime Trade Commissions of the Soviet Union
4. The Foreign Trade Arbitration Commission of the People's Republic of China
5. The Stockholm Chamber of Commerce

The Cairo Regional Center provides tribunals in locations convenient for west Asian and African nations. It is a relatively new institution, but it becomes more popular as time passes.

Switzerland has traditionally been a center for commercial arbitration. Arbitration tribunals exist in all major cities.

Soviet state enterprises generally include in their contracts with foreigners arbitration clauses calling for arbitration by the Foreign Trade Arbitration Commission or the Maritime Arbitration Commission, as the case may be. The Maritime Arbitration Commission heard disputes arising out of transport of goods by water; the Foreign Trade Arbitration Commission hears other cases. Foreigners find that these Soviet arbitration tribunals are thorough, fair, and unbiased.

Chinese foreign trade enterprises prefer to have disputes arbitrated by their Foreign Trade Arbitration Commission.

The Stockholm Chamber of Commerce Institute is gaining popularity as an arbitration tribunal. Arbitration is commonly used in Sweden as a medium for resolution of domestic commercial disputes; thus the Swedes have long experience to draw upon. Moreover, Sweden is perceived as neutral in both the East-West confrontation and in North-South disagreements. Communist-bloc and third-world parties will trust Swedish arbitrators when they might not be willing to trust Americans or Englishmen.

Elements of Arbitration Agreements. An arbitration agreement should contain several provisions. First, it should include the name of the arbitration institution, if any. Second, it should contain the rules to govern the arbitration. (Remember that all of the major arbitration institutions will use the UNCITRAL rules if the parties so specify.) Third, it should specify the place of arbitration. In what country and city will the arbitration tribunal sit? To insure judicial enforceability of an arbitration award the proceeding should be held in a country that has ratified the New York Convention on Recognition of Foreign Arbitral Awards. Sixty-two countries have ratified the agreement. An arbitration agreement handed down in one of these sixty-two will be enforceable in the other sixty-one. Fourth, it should specify the number, qualifications, and method of choice of arbitrators. Four common methods are used to choose arbitrators:

1. There is to be one arbitrator, to be appointed upon the agreement of the parties, or by a named person or organization if the parties fail to agree.

2. Each party appoints one arbitrator. These two hear the evidence and attempt to make a decision. If they cannot agree, they appoint an umpire, who makes the decision.

3. Each party appoints an arbitrator. These at once appoint the umpire who hears the evidence with them; but the umpire plays no role in deciding the case unless the two arbitrators disagree.

4. Each party appoints an arbitrator. These two at once appoint a chairman. These three persons hear the evidence and decide the case by majority vote.

Matters work more smoothly when each party is entitled to name an arbitrator. If there is to be only one chosen by agreement of the parties one of the parties may slow up the proceedings by refusing to agree to an arbitrator. If there are to be two arbitrators and Smith at once appoints his while Jones delays in appointing his, a court could threaten to appoint Smith's man sole arbitrator unless Jones makes his appointment. Thus under the two-arbitrator set-up more pressure could be brought to bear against a reluctant party.

The parties will probably want to specify the nationalities of the arbitrators; each may wish to appoint an arbitrator of his nationality with the umpire or chairman of a third; or they may specify that all three arbitrators shall be of a neutral nationality.

In technical cases the parties may want to specify that the arbitrators have the specialized professional training or knowledge to understand the background of the dispute.

Fifth, the arbitration agreement should specify a choice of language. In what language will the proceedings be held? What languages may witnesses use to testify? In what languages must written documents be prepared?

Sixth, it should specify the applicable law and basis of decision. The possibilities here are as follows:

    1. The arbitrators may be directed to decide in accordance with a recognized legal system (England, France, Switzerland, Texas)

    2. They may be directed to decide in accordance with the principles of the *Lex Mercatoria,* the custom of international trade

    3. They may be directed to decide *Ex Aequo Et Bono,* according to principles of equity and good will. Here the arbitrators are expected to be fair without adhering to the commands of any legal system.

    4. They may be directed to act as *Amiables Compositeurs,* literally, "friendly compromisers." Here they are not necessarily expected to choose a winner and a loser; they are to work out a solution in which both parties give a little and gain a little.

Appeal of Arbitration Awards. The decision of arbitrators is called an *Award.* Awards are not the equivalent of judgments; the winner will not immediately collect his award if the loser does not voluntarily pay.

If the loser will not voluntarily comply with the award compulsion will be necessary. The compelling agency will be a court. The winner, then, must have his award *Confirmed* and converted into a judgment to obtain judicial enforcement.

Confirmation will not occur until the award has become final. It has become final when there is no possibility of appeal.

The appeal of arbitration awards is usually made to the court system of the nation where the arbitration proceeding was held. In general, it is more difficult to appeal an award than it is to appeal a trial court decision.

Whenever a trial court makes an error in applying the law which injured a party to the case, the injured party has the possibility of appeal. The fact that an arbitrator made an error in applying the law does not give grounds for appeal. (Since arbitrators are usually not lawyers, they may be expected to make errors of law. Besides, if the parties wanted their dispute resolved strictly according to law they should have resolved it by litigation, not by arbitration.)

Generally, the only possible grounds for appeal of arbitration awards are the existence of circumstances under which one of the parties did not obtain a fair shake. Most countries consider the following as acceptable grounds for appeal:

1. The arbitrator(s) had no jurisdiction to hear the case — Perhaps the arbitration clause was invalid or the like

2. The appointment of one or more of the arbitrators was invalid (not done according to contract procedure or the like)

3. The arbitrator(s) were biased

4. The arbitrators did not properly apply the rules under which the arbitration was conducted

5. The award was obtained through fraud

Once the award becomes final, it is much more easily enforced internationally than a judgment if the arbitration was conducted in a New York Convention country. Rarely will a court of a New York Convention country deny the enforcement of an award handed down in another New York Convention country. It is paradoxical that this should be so, since arbitrators are so much less knowledgeable in law than judges.

There are a few disadvantages to arbitration as opposed to litigation. It is expensive, though cheaper than litigation if the matter is quickly disposed of. In lengthy arbitrations the supposed cost advantage may evaporate; some of the costs of litigation (the salary of judges and the like) are paid by states; the costs of arbitration are paid in full by the parties. Discovery procedures (forcing the other side to let you look at its documents and the like) are less efficient than common-law discovery procedures. It can be as time-consuming as litigation if matters do not run smoothly. A party may take his time about appointing his arbitrator; he may argue about the jurisdiction of the arbitration tribunal; the arbitrators may commit gross errors that tie the case up in court on appeal. Unforeseen circumstances may play so much havoc with an ad hoc arbitration that the proceeding must be cancelled after much expenditure of time and money.

Transnational Business and the Nation-State

These materials have hopefully given the reader an inkling of the complexities of the world of international business. The perils of dealing with unfamiliar legal systems, accounting systems, taxation systems, transportation systems, currencies and the like are obvious.

Yet, this world opens wide vistas of opportunity for those who know how to make use of them. Our ever faster, ever more efficient modes of transportation and communication shrink the globe. The hundreds of markets that existed in the world of seventy years ago are coalescing into one.

Indeed, we have one commercial world, governed by the laws of nearly two hundred political units.

When one plays the game of business in just one national ballpark, one has no choice but to play by the rules enforced there. It is the only game in town.

When one moves beyond the frontier of one's native land and begins playing the game of business in other ballparks, one is at first terrorized by the prospect of learning all of the new rules. Once the task is well in hand, tantalizing visions appear. New possibilities arise—what *may not* be done here *may* be done there. What would never pass muster there is standard operating procedure here.

The larger an international business organization grows, the less identification it may have with its original homeland. It acquires executives in all the lands where it operates; management becomes multinational.

The firm acquires a need for its own foreign policy; after all it must cultivate good relationships with the governments of all lands in which it does business. This foreign policy may not be in agreement with that of its homeland; what is good for the United States is not necessarily good for General Motors.

In a sense the successful multinational business entity acquires more power than any single government on earth. The firm operating in one country is in a sense at the mercy of the government of that country; it has no choice but to obey that government's will. The firm operating in many countries need not necessarily obey the will of one government; what Ruritania will not allow Gerolstein might find perfectly acceptable.

It is not lawful for nonbanks to control banks in the United States; thus a large corporation cannot incorporate its own bank as its subsidiary. In some tax haven countries there is no objection to this practice; the multinational may organize a captive bank in one of these lands.

The same principle holds good for insurance companies; American firms may generally not incorporate their own insurers in the United States. They may do so in several other lands, however.

The American minimum wage is relatively high, while many lands have very low or no minimum wages. Many firms locate manufacturing operations in areas of low wages to save payroll costs.

The United States allows more freedom for labor unions than many other countries do. An American management that wishes to avoid bargaining with union representatives could locate operations in lands where unions have less power.

American environmental protection legislation is stringent; compliance with it can be expensive. It is sometimes possible to locate polluting operations in lands with less tough environmental regulation.

American shipowners must meet very high safety standards and pay high wages to officers and crewmen to be able to operate their vessels under the American flag. By registering vessels in Liberia or Panama shipowners may escape some of these standards, hire cheaper crewmen, and reduce operating costs.

Yet, when the firm operates profitably abroad its success contributes to the economic well-being of the United States, through the profits it repatriates to this country and through the taxes it pays to our government.

Once a firm has broken through the barriers of uncertainty and fear and established itself internationally, the choices available to it multiply immensely. The more ballparks in which the firm plays, the more likely it is to find one in which it can accomplish today's objective.

How the international firm's management uses these opportunities is more a question of ethics than a question of law. The law, after all, is value-free.

May those who acquire the freedom and power that go with successful international business operations use it both wisely and well.

Glossary

ABUS DES DROITS (French, abuse of rights). The notion that a person who abuses rights given him by law in order to injure another should be liable to the injured party for damages.

ACT OF GOD. A natural catastrophe such as a storm, an earthquake, a volcanic eruption, or the like.

ACT OF STATE DOCTRINE. The principle that the act of a government is lawful within the boundaries of its territory.

AD HOC ARBITRATION. Arbitration in which the parties to the arbitration agreement draw up their own ground rules, not subject to the rules of any arbitration organization.

ADVISED LETTER OF CREDIT. A letter of credit under which a bank in the beneficiary's financial market (the *Advising Bank*) undertakes to advise the beneficiary of the issuance of the credit and to discount his drafts drawn under the credit without assuming any liability in the transaction.

AGREE. The French lawyer who represents clients in the commercial courts.

AKTIENGESELLSCHAFT (AG). The corporation in German-speaking lands.

ALLGEMEINE LANDRECHT. The Prussian law code put into effect in that country in 1794. It was repealed when the Burgerliches GESETZBUCH became law in Germany in 1900.

ALLGEMEINES BURGERLICHES GESETZBUCH. The civil code of Austria, enacted in 1811. Much of it is still in effect in the Austrian Federal Republic.

AMIABLE COMPOSITEUR (French, friendly compromiser). An arbitrator who is charged with working out a compromise of the dispute being settled rather than simply deciding who is most right and who is most wrong.

ANSTALT. The Liechtenstein "establishment," the owner of which can transfer funds to a secret entity known only to himself, its director, and the Liechtenstein government. It is the ultimate secret investment vehicle.

APPARENT AUTHORITY. The authority a stranger may reasonably assume that an agent possesses. In common-law countries agents may possess a considerable amount of apparent authority; in Romano-Germanic countries they possess very little.

AUFSICHTSRAT. The supervisory board of a German AKTIENGESELLSCHAFT, similar to our board of directors. In large corporations the employees are entitled to representation; in the coal and steel industries the public is also entitled to representation.

AUTHORITY TO PURCHASE LETTER OF CREDIT. A type of letter of credit issued by Far Eastern banks under which the advising bank is given authority to purchase the customer's drafts rather than discount them.

AVAL. A type of indorsement of commercial paper used in Romano-Germanic countries in which the indorser guarantees payment of the item even if the obligation of the party guaranteed is void.

AVOCAT. The French trial lawyer before the 1971 reforms.

AVOUE. The French office lawyer before the 1971 reforms.

BAB AL-IJTIHAD (Arabic, the gate of reasoning). The possibility of judges and scholars expanding the coverage of Islamic law through logical reasoning. This was declared to be closed during the tenth century of the Christian era. Since then, in theory, the body of Islamic law could not be changed; it was frozen in the form it had assumed by then.

BACK-TO-BACK LETTER OF CREDIT. An arrangement whereby a buyer obtains a letter of credit for the benefit of his seller. His seller then obtains another letter of credit for his supplier, pledging his interest in the original credit as collateral for his obligation under the second credit.

BAREBOAT CHARTER. The rental of a ship for a specified period under which the charterer agrees to furnish the crew. The charterer is responsible for all cargo carried during the duration of the charter party.

BARRISTER. The English trial lawyer.

BENEFICIARY. The person or organization for whose benefit a letter of credit or guarantee is obtained.

BILL OF EXCHANGE. A draft.

BOLSHEVIK (from Russian *Bolsheviki,* members of the majority). The Russian term for the faction led by Lenin that created the Communist government of Russia. The name makes clear the fact that Lenin's faction was the majority wing of the Russian Social Democratic party. The minority wing (the *Menshevik*) was destroyed by the Bolsheviks after they obtained power.

BOURGEOISIE. The middle class; in Marxist-Leninist theory it must be deprived of all political and economic power before the Communist revolution can come to pass.

BUNDESGERICHT. The highest court of Switzerland.

BUNDESGERICHTSHOF. The highest court of West Germany.

BURGERLICHES GESETZBUCH. The Civil Code of Germany which went into effect in 1900. It is still the law of West Germany; much has been repealed in East Germany.

CAUSA (Latin, reason). The concept found in Romano-Germanic law that a contract should be enforceable if both parties had logical reasons for making it, even if one party is not getting anything out of it.

CHARTER PARTY. A contract for the rental of a ship.

CIM (Convention on the International Movement of Goods by Rail). An international agreement adhered to by countries of Europe, Asia, and Africa defining the duties and liabilities of international rail carriers. It is not in effect anywhere in North or South America.

CLAUSED BILL OF LADING. A foul bill of lading, showing that the goods covered by the bill were damaged when the issuer of the bill took custody of them.

CLAUSULA REBUS SIC STANTIBUS. The Romano-Germanic legal concept that makes a contract remain valid only so long as the circumstances governing performance do not radically change.

CLEAN BILL OF LADING. A bill of lading showing that the issuing carrier received the shipment covered by the bill in undamaged condition.

CMR (Convention Concerning the International Movement of Goods by Road). An international agreement adhered to by most European countries defining the duties and liabilities of highway freight carriers. No non–European country has adhered to it.

CO-COM. The international committee of government representatives from the member nations of the North Atlantic Treaty Organizaton (NATO) plus Japan that coordinates policy on export of strategic goods to Communist nations.

CODE NAPOLEON. The French Civil Code which became law in that country in 1804, and is still in effect.

COMMERCIAL REGISTER. An official record in which all businesspeople and organizations must be registered. They exist in virtually all countries with Romano-Germanic law.

COMMISSIONAIRE. The French agent for an undisclosed principal. He may sue to enforce his contract made for the principal; the principal may not. His customers may not sue his principal for breach of contract; they may only sue the commissionaire.

CONFIRMED LETTER OF CREDIT. A letter of credit upon which a bank in the beneficiary's financial market assumes liability along with the issuing bank.

CONSEIL D'ETAT. The highest administrative court of France.

CONSEILLES DE PRUD'HOMMES. Special French courts that hear cases involving employment law.

CONSEILLES DES BAUX RURAUX. Special French courts that hear cases between rural landlords and tenants about rent claims and the like.

CONTRA BONOS MORES (Latin, against good morals). Under German law anyone guilty of conduct that is contra bonos mores in the negotiation or performance of a contract gives the other party grounds for rescission of the bargain. Conduct that is contra bonos mores is also a tort.

CORPUS JURIS CIVILIS. The most important of the volumes containing the codification of Roman law ordered by the Emperor Justinian in the sixth century A.D.

COUNTERGUARANTEE. An exporter obtains a guarantee for the performance of his contract from a bank in his area for the benefit of a bank in the importer's area. The guaranteed bank then issues the importer a guarantee. If exporter defaults importer may claim against the bank in his area under the counterguarantee.

COUR DE CASSATION. The highest court of France.

CROSSED CHECK. A type of check used in countries of Romano-Germanic law bearing two parallel lines across its face; such a check may not be honored by the drawee bank except for the account of its customers or for another bank.

CUSTOMER. The person or organization who obtains a letter of credit or guarantee for the benefit of the beneficiary.

DANSKE LOV. The Danish law code drafted by order of King Christian V and placed into effect in his realm in 1683. It has never been repealed in Denmark.

DEL CREDERE AGENT. An agent who agrees to pay his customer's delinquent accounts owed to his principal.

DEMISE CHARTER. A BAREBOAT CHARTER. The charterer rents a ship for a specified period, usually furnishing his own crew.

DIRECT AGENT. An agent for a disclosed principal.

DISCLOSED PRINCIPAL. The situation where an agent makes a contract on behalf of a principal whose identity is known to the third party.

DOSSIER. The file of documentary evidence accumulated by an investigating magistrate as he does his job.

DUAL NATIONALITY. The status of holding two or more national citizenships at once. The United States in general does not recognize this status; a few other nations (such as Switzerland) do.

EUROPEAN CURRENCY UNIT (ECU). The monetary unit of account of the European Community.

EX AEQUO ET BONO (Latin, according to equity and justice). Arbitrators may be instructed to decide a case on this basis. If so, they decide on general principles of fairness, not necessarily in accordance with the letter of the law.

EXPATRIATION. Loss of citizenship. It may be voluntary (renunciation of citizenship) or involuntary (deprivation of citizenship by one's government).

EXPRESS AUTHORITY. The authority directly and specifically delegated to an agent by his principal.

FORCE MAJEURE. Unforeseen circumstances making it difficult or impossible to perform a contract. Transnational business contracts should contain a Force Majeure clause spelling out what will happen to the contract in case such unforeseen circumstances arise.

FORFAIT TRANSACTION. An importer pays for very valuable goods with long-term promissory notes. He has the notes avalized by his bank or some other bank before turning them over to the exporter. The exporter sells them to a bank in his area at a small discount. The exporter runs very little risk of charge-back because of the bank AVAL; if the importer does not pay at maturity the avalizing bank will.

FOUL BILL OF LADING. A bill of lading showing that the carrier received the shipment in damaged condition.

GENERAL AVERAGE. The principle that, when it is necessary to sacrifice a part of the cargo of a ship (or of the ship itself) to prevent the loss of the ship and all the cargo, the cargo owners and the ship owners share the loss caused by the sacrifice ratably.

GESELLSCHAFT MIT BESCHRANKTER HAFTUNG (GmbH). The limited liability company in German-language countries.

GHARAR. In Islamic law, uncertainty. The entering into a contract, the outcome of which will be influenced by unforeseen factors, is almost always forbidden by Islamic tradition.

HABEAS CORPUS, writ of. A procedure by which the lawfulness of a deprivation of a person's liberty may be tested in common-law countries. If the petitioner for such a writ convinces a judge that such unlawful deprivation of liberty may exist, the judge will order the person in custody of the prisoner to produce him in court and explain why he holds the prisoner in custody.

HADD (plural Hudud). Criminal punishments mandated by the Qu'ran, such as amputation of the thief's right hand.

HADITH. The collected sayings and acts of the Prophet Mohammed.

HAGUE RULES. An international agreement defining the duties and liabilities of ocean carriers. It is the basis of the American Carriage of Goods by Sea Act.

HAGUE-VISBY RULES. An amended version of the Hague Rules. The United States has not adopted these.

HAMBURG RULES. A new convention defining the duties and liabilities of ocean carriers. They have not yet been adopted as law by any country.

HANAFI. A school of Sunni Islamic law dominant in most of the Middle East.

HANBALI. The most conservative school of Sunni Islamic law, dominant only in Saudi Arabia and Qatar.

HARAM. That which is forbidden by the Qu'ran. Contracts for the sale of haram goods (such as pigs and alcoholic beverages) are illegal and unenforceable in traditional Islamic law.

IBADI. The school of Islamic law that is dominant in Oman.

IJARA WA IQTINA. An Islamic contract under which a bank buys goods for a buyer and resells them to the buyer at a higher price, the buyer making his monthly payments into an account in his name. When the buyer has deposited the agreed price the bank takes the money and the contract is performed; if the buyer misses payments the bank takes the account balance and repossesses the goods.

IJMA. The opinions of Islamic scholars about the proper interpretation of the Qu'ran and the Sunna.

IMPLIED AUTHORITY. The authority of an agent to do what he must be able to do in order to carry out his express authority. This may be wide in common-law countries; it is narrow to nonexistent in Romano-Germanic countries.

IN PERSONAM JURISDICTION. In common-law countries, court jurisdiction over the person of the civil defendant and (in theory) all of his assets, wherever located.

IN REM JURISDICTION. In common-law countries, jurisdiction only over those assets of the defendant that are within the territorial jurisdiction of the court.

INDIRECT AGENT. An agent for an undisclosed principal.

INHERENT VICE. The tendency of perishable goods to spoil.

INSTITUTIONAL ARBITRATION. Arbitration under the rules of one of the organizations that conduct commercial arbitration, such as the International Chamber of Commerce or the American Arbitration Association.

INVESTIGATING MAGISTRATE. In Romano-Germanic lands, a person who has the training and power of a judge who investigates criminal matters in order to determine whether or not formal charges should be brought against the accused. He serves the same purpose as the American Grand Jury.

INVOLUNTARY NATURALIZATION. A change in citizenship brought about by a change in national frontiers; those who live in the territory that changes hands acquire the citizenship of the new occupant.

IRREVOCABLE LETTER OF CREDIT. A letter of credit that, once established, may not be revoked by the issuing bank without the consent of the customer and the beneficiary.

ISTISNA. An Islamic contract for the sale of goods to be manufactured in the future.

JURISDICTION. The authority of a court or arbitration tribunal to hear a case.

JUS CIVILE. The Roman law that was applied to Roman citizens.

JUS GENTIUM. The Roman law that was applied by Roman courts to non-Romans.

JUS SANGUINIS. The determination of the citizenship of a child by the citizenship of a parent or parents.

JUS SOLI. The determination of the citizenship of a child by the place where he was born; those nations using jus soli say that all persons born on the nation's soil are the nation's citizens.

LAND REGISTER. The Romano-Germanic public record where all transfers of land, mortgages on land, and the like must be recorded. Any unrecorded transfer or mortgage is void.

LAY ASSESSORS. Laymen who participate as decision-makers in Swedish trials.

LESION ENORME. The concept in French law that allows a party to rescind a contract if his performance is much more valuable than that of the other party.

LEX MERCATORIA. The merchant law developed by the traveling merchants of the Middle Ages.

LIMITED LIABILITY COMPANY. A type of business organization found in Romano-Germanic countries in which shareholders have the limited liability of corporate shareholders, but which issues no share certificates. Transfers of shares are made by recording them in the commercial register where the company articles are recorded.

LING. Ancient Chinese legislation that commanded that one do what was prescribed on pain of punishment set forth in the ling.

LORD CHANCELLOR. The English official who presides over the Judicial Committee of the House of Lords and acts as administrative head of the English court system. He also appoints the majority of English judges.

LU. Ancient Chinese legislation providing that if one did what was forbidden by it one would be punished as provided.

MAJLIS. The negotiating session at which Islamic contracts are sometimes negotiated. The contract is not finalized until the majlis ends; either party may back out before that time.

MALIKI. A school of Sunni Islamic law that is dominant in most of Islamic Africa and Kuwait.

MANDATE. The limited Romano-Germanic form of agency. The agent has the power to do what his principal specifically authorizes him to do and no more.

MINISTERE PUBLIQUE. The organization providing government attorneys to participate in the appeal of civil cases in Romano-Germanic countries. Public lawyers may take part under the theory that the public interest must be respected even if the government is not otherwise involved in the case.

MIRROR-IMAGE RULE. The rule that a response to an offer is not an acceptance unless it contains exactly the same terms as the offer. It has been abolished in American commercial law by the Uniform Commercial Code, but is still used in England and some other common-law countries.

MUDARABA. An Islamic partnership between an active partner and an inactive partner who does not participate in managing the business. In modern times, a contract between lender and borrower in which the lender becomes part owner of the borrower's enterprise until the loan is repaid.

MURABAHA. An Islamic contract of sale in which a bank obtains goods for its customer and resells to the customer for a higher price, the customer to pay at a later agreed-upon time. Either bank or customer may rescind before the payment is due.

NATIONALITY BY DERIVATION. Acquisition of nationality through an act other than voluntary naturalization (that is, by the naturalization of one's parents if one is a minor, by marraige to a national of another country, etc.).

NATURALIZATION. The acquisition of national citizenship by methods other than birth.

NEW YORK CONVENTION. An international agreement providing for the mutual recognition by its signatories of arbitration awards handed down in member nations.

NONTRANSFERABLE LETTER OF CREDIT. A letter of credit under which the beneficiary may not assign or transfer the right to draw drafts.

NORSKE LOV. The code of law drafted for Norway and put into effect there in 1687. It has never been totally repealed; small portions of it are still in effect.

NOTARY. A legally trained person who drafts and records legal documents (such as formal contracts, wills, and charters of business organizations) in Romano-Germanic and Socialist lands.

PACKING LETTER OF CREDIT. A letter of credit under which the issuing bank agrees to finance the beneficiary's production or acquisition of the goods he is to sell the customer. The issuer's obligation is usually triggered by beneficiary's presentation of proof that he has begun performance of his contract with the customer.

PAYS DE DROIT COUTUMIER (French, the land of customary law). The term applied to northern France before the French Revolution, signifying that local custom provided most of the law there.

PAYS DE DROIT ECRIT (French, the land of written law). The term applied to southern France before the French Revolution, signifying that Roman law played a large role in local legal systems.

PEOPLE'S ASSESSORS. The two laymen who participate in trying and deciding cases in Soviet PEOPLE'S COURTS.

PEOPLE'S COURTS. The trial courts of the Soviet legal system, consisting of one judge and two PEOPLE'S ASSESSORS. They decide the cases by majority vote.

PRAETOR. The official who exercised judicial power in the Roman Republic.

PRAETOR PEREGRINUS. The praetor who heard cases involving non–Romans and applied the JUS GENTIUM.

PRAETOR URBANUS. The praetor who heard cases involving Roman citizens and applied the JUS CIVILE.

PRESIDING JUDGE. The judge of a multimember Romano-Germanic court who directs the courtroom proceedings.

PROCURA. A form of agency that allows the agent to do almost anything his principal may do. It is found in Romano-Germanic countries influenced by German law only.

PROCURATOR. The most powerful lawyers of nations with Socialist legal systems. They act as prosecutors in cases involving serious crime; they assist civil litigants who are not getting proper legal representation; and they supervise the operations of government and state enterprises to see to it that Socialist legality prevails throughout the country.

PROCURIST. The agent appointed under a PROCURA.

PROLETARIAT. The working class; in Marxist theory a dictatorship of the proletariat must exercise all legal and economic authority until the power of the bourgeoisie is destroyed and men are willing to accept the coming of communism.

PROPISKA. The visa-type document each Soviet citizen must have attached to his internal passport. It is proof that the citizen has government authorization to live where he lives.

PROTOCOLIZED CONTRACTS. Contracts drafted by a notary and recorded in his files.

QADI. The judge in traditional Islamic courts.

QIYAS. In Islamic law, the process of deciding court cases by the use of analogy.

QU'RAN. The Holy Scripture of Islam.

RECHTSANWALT. The lawyer in German-speaking countries.

RECHTSMISBRAUCH (German, misuse of rights). See ABUS DES DROITS, above.

REVOCABLE LETTER OF CREDIT. A letter of credit that the issuing bank may revoke at any time without the consent of the customer and beneficiary.

RIBA (Arabic). Usury, or the charging of interest on loans; forbidden by traditional Islamic law.

SAKK (plural Sukuk). The certificate providing evidence of part ownership of an Islamic investment company.

SALAM. An Islamic contract for the sale of a future crop.

SPECIAL DRAWING RIGHT (SDR). The monetary unit of account of the International Monetary Fund.

SHARI'A. The body of traditional Islamic law.

SHIA. The largest non–Sunni body of Muslim believers. Also, the school of Islamic law followed by these believers, dominant in Iran.

SIEGE SOCIAL. The locality where a corporation has its headquarters and does most of its business.

SIETE PARTIDAS (Spanish, the Seven Parts). The medieval Castilian law code created by the order of King Alfonso X; the code has influenced the modern law of Spain.

SOCIEDAD ANONIMA (SA). The corporation in Spanish-speaking countries.

SOCIEDAD DE RESPONSIBILIDAD LIMITADA (SRL). The limited liability company in Spanish-speaking countries.

SOCIETE A RESPONSABILITE LIMITEE (SARL). The limited liability company in French-speaking countries.

SOCIETE ANONYME (SA). The corporation in French-speaking countries.

SOLICITOR. The English office lawyer.

SOVEREIGN IMMUNITY. The ancient principle that kings (or governments) can do no wrong and cannot be sued. The principle has been to an extent abrogated.

STANDBY LETTER OF CREDIT. A letter of credit under which the issuing bank acts as guarantor for the customer's obligation to the beneficiary. The issuer usually need not pay under the credit unless furnished proof of customer's nonfulfillment of his obligations.

STARE DECISIS (Latin). The principle under which common-law courts are required to follow precedent established by higher courts in deciding cases.

STIFTUNG. The Liechtenstein "foundation," which can be a secret organization known only to its director and the Liechtenstein government, established for the benefit of a family or charitable organization.

STRAIGHT LETTER OF CREDIT. A letter of credit under which the beneficiary need present no document to obtain payment and under which he must be both drawer and payee of his draft.

SUNNA. The body of Islamic writings that explains the way of life of the Prophet Mohammed.

SUNNI. The orthodox sect of believers in Islam.

SUPERGUARANTEE. An exporter obtains a guarantee of his obligation from his local bank. The local bank obtains a guarantee of its obligation from a large well-known bank for the benefit of the importer. The second guarantee is the superguarantee.

SVERIGES RIKS LAG. The Swedish law code enacted by the Riksdag in 1734. It has never been totally repealed; small parts of it are still good law in Sweden.

SVOD ZAKONOV. The Russian code of law promulgated by Czar Nicholas I in 1832. It was repealed after Lenin's revolution in 1917.

TAKAFUL MUDARABA. An Islamic insurance cooperative in which the members jointly assume all insured risks.

TAX HAVEN. A political unit (nation, colony, or dependency) that levies few or no taxes upon foreigners who do business there.

TENDER GUARANTEE. A guarantee obtained by a party bidding on a procurement or construction contract. The guarantor promises to pay damages if the bidder is awarded the contract but does not undertake performance.

TENDER OFFER. An offer made by a corporation to shareholders of another corporation it wishes to acquire offering to pay a named price per share for all shares tendered before the closing date, so long as a required percentage of outstanding shares are tendered.

TIME CHARTER. The rental of a vessel and its crew for a specified time. The charterer determines the use of the vessel, but the owner is responsible for cargo belonging to shippers other than the charterer.

TREUHANDSCHAFT. A Liechtenstein nonbusiness trust, the assets and beneficiaries of which may be kept secret from the world (except for the trustees and the Liechtenstein government).

TREUUNTERNEHMEN. A Liechtenstein business trust.

ULTRA VIRES (Latin, beyond the powers). An act performed by a corporation that is not authorized by its articles of incorporation.

VORSTAND. The managing board of a German AKTIENGESELLSCHAFT.

VOYAGE CHARTER. The rental of a vessel and its crew for one voyage or for a specified series of voyages. The owner is responsible for carried cargo belonging to parties other than the charterer.

Wᴀǫꜰ (plural Awqaf). The Islamic charitable trust in real estate, buildings, or the like, supposedly perpetual.

Wᴀʀsᴀw ᴄᴏɴᴠᴇɴᴛɪᴏɴ. An international agreement fixing the rules of liability of international air carriers.

Zᴀᴋᴀᴛ. The mandatory annual contribution by the believing Muslim of 2.5 percent of his net worth for the purpose of helping the needy. It is levied as a tax in Saudi Arabia.

Zɪᴠɪʟɢᴇsᴇᴛᴢʙᴜᴄʜ. The Civil Code of Switzerland, effective in that country in 1912 and still the basis of Swiss law.

Bibliography

General Works

Cheng, Chia Jui, ed. *Basic Documents on International Trade Law.* Dordrecht, the
   Netherlands: Martinus Nijhoff, Publishers, 1986.
Clasen, Thomas F. *Foreign Trade and Investment: A Legal Guide.* Wilmette, Ill.:
   Callaghan & Company, 1987.
Day, D.M. *The Law of International Trade.* London: Butterworth's, 1985.
Fox, William J. *International Commercial Agreements: A Functional Primer on
   Drafting, Negotiating, and Resolving Disputes.* Deventer, the Netherlands:
   Kluwer Law and Taxation Publishers, 1988.
Herrmann, A.H. *Judges, Law, and Businessmen.* Deventer, the Netherlands:
   Kluwer Law and Taxation Publishers, 1983.
Hoyle, Mark S.W. *The Law of International Trade.* 2d ed. Bicester, England: CCH
   Editions, 1985.
Kelso, Robert Charles. *International Law of Commerce.* 2d ed. Buffalo, N.Y.:
   Dennis & Co., 1961.
Kohona, P.T.B. *The Regulation of International Economic Relations through
   Law.* Dordrecht, the Netherlands: Martinus Nijhoff Publishers, 1985.
Kolde, Endel-Jakob. *Environment of International Business.* 2d ed. Boston: Kent
   Publishing Company, 1985.
Nanda, Ved P., ed. *The Law of International Business Transactions.* New York:
   Clark Boardman Company, 1983.
Schmitthoff, Clive M. *Schmitthoff's Export Trade: The Law and Practice of Inter-
   national Trade.* 8th ed. London: Stevens and Sons, 1986.
Schnitzer, Martin C., Marilyn L. Liebrenz, and Konrad W. Kubin. *International
   Business.* Cincinnati: Southwestern Publishing Company, 1985.
Streng, William P. *International Business Transactions: Tax and Legal Handbook.*
   Englewood Cliffs, N.J.: Prentice-Hall, 1978.
_____, and Jeswald W. Salacuse. *International Business Planning, Law, and
   Taxation.* 3 vols. New York: Matthew Bender, 1982.
Vernon, Raymond, and Louis T. Wells, Jr. *Economic Environment of Interna-
   tional Business.* 3d ed. Englewood Cliffs, N.J.: Prentice-Hall, 1981.

Export Regulation

Liebman, John R., Rauer H. Meyer, and Robert L. Johnson. *Export Controls in
   the United States.* Englewood Cliffs, N.J.: Prentice-Hall Law and Business,
   1988.

Import Regulation

Rossides, Eugene T. *U.S. Import Regulation.* Washington, D.C.: Bureau of National Affairs, 1986.

Simmonds, Kenneth R. and Brian H.W. Hill. *Law and Practice under the GATT.* Dobbs Ferry, N.Y.: Oceana Publications, 1988.

Comparative Law

Butler, W.E., and V.N. Kudriavtsev, eds. *Comparative Law and Legal System: Historical and Socio-Legal Perspectives.* Dobbs Ferry, N.Y.: Oceana Publications, 1985.

David, Rene, and John E.C. Brierly. *Major Legal Systems in the World Today.* 3d ed. London: Stevens and Sons, 1985.

Delaume, Georges R. *Law and Practice of Transnational Contracts.* Dobbs Ferry, N.Y.: Oceana Publications, 1988.

Derrett, J. Duncan M., ed. *An Introduction to Legal Systems.* London: Sweet and Maxwell, 1968.

Ingraham, B.L. *The Structure of Criminal Procedure.* New York: Greenwood Press, 1987.

Katz, Alan M., ed. *Legal Traditions and Systems: An International Handbook.* New York: Greenwood Press, 1986.

Mueller, Gerhard O.W., and Fre Le Poole-Griffiths. *Comparative Criminal Procedure.* New York: New York University Press, 1969.

Schlesinger, Rudolf B. *Comparative Law.* 4th ed. Mineola, N.Y.: Foundation Press, 1980.

Zweigert, Konrad, and Hein Kotz. *An Introduction to Comparative Law.* 2d ed., rev. Oxford: Clarendon Press, 1987.

English Law

Ingman, Terence. *The English Legal Process.* 2d ed. London: Financial Training Publications, 1987.

European Community Law

Agnew, John. *Competition Law.* London: Allen & Unwin, 1985.

Goyder, D.G. *EEC Competition Law.* Oxford: Clarendon Press, 1988.

Lasok, D., and J.W.B. Bridges. *Law and Institutions of the European Communities.* 4th ed. London: Butterworths, 1987.

Mathijsen, P.S.R.F. *A Guide to European Community Law.* 4th ed. London: Sweet and Maxwell, 1985.

Rudden, Bernard, and Derrick Wyatt. *Basic Community Laws.* 2d ed. Oxford: Clarendon Press, 1986.

Van Bael, Ivo, and Jean-François Beills. *Competition Laws of the EEC.* Bicester, England: CCH Editions, 1988.

Woodroffe, Geoffrey. *Consumer Law in the EEC.* London: Sweet and Maxwell, 1984.

Islamic Law

Ahmad, Khurshid, ed. *Studies in Islamic Economics*. Leicester, England: The Islamic Foundation, 1980.

Amin, S.H. *Islamic Law in the Contemporary World*. Glasgow, Scotland: Royston, 1985.

Anderson, Norman. *Law Reform in the Muslim World*. London: University of London Press, Athlone Press, 1976.

Coulson, Noel J. *Commercial Law in the Gulf States: The Islamic Legal Tradition*. London: Graham & Trotman, 1984.

Iqbal, Zubair, and Abbas Mirakhor. *Islamic Banking*. Occasional Paper, no. 49. Washington, D.C.: International Monetary Fund, 1987.

Liebesny, Herbert J. *The Law of the Near and Middle East: Readings, Cases and Materials*. Albany, N.Y.: State University of New York Press, 1975.

Mallat, Chibli, ed. *Islamic Law and Finance*. London: Graham and Trotman, 1988.

Saleh, Nabil A. *Unlawful Gain and Legitimate Profit in Islamic Law*. Cambridge: Cambridge University Press, 1986.

Schacht, Joseph. *An Introduction to Islamic Law*. Oxford: Clarendon Press, 1964.

Romano-Germanic Law

Lawson, F.H. *A Common Lawyer Looks at the Civil Law*. Ann Arbor: University of Michigan Press, 1955.

Merryman, John H., and David S. Clark. *Comparative Law: Western Europe and Latin America*. Charlottesville, Va.: Michie & Company, 1978.

Von Mehren, Arthur Taylor, and James Russell Gordley. *The Civil Law System*. 2d ed. Boston: Little, Brown & Co., 1977.

Socialist (Soviet) Law

Butler, W.E. *Soviet Law*. 2d ed. London: Butterworth's, 1988.

Farnsworth, E. Allen, and Viktor P. Mozolin. *Contract Law in the USSR and in the United States: History and General Concepts*. Washington, D.C.: International Law Institute, 1987.

Hazard, John N., William E. Butler, and Peter B. Maggs. *The Soviet Legal System*. 3d ed. Dobbs Ferry, N.Y.: Oceana Publications, 1977.

_____. *The Soviet Legal System: The Law in the 1980s*. Dobbs Ferry, N.Y.: Oceana Publications, 1984.

Johnson, E.L. *An Introduction to the Soviet Legal System*. London: Methuen & Company, 1969.

Kudryavtsev, V.N., et al., eds. *The Soviet Constitution: A Dictionary*. Moscow, USSR: Progress Publishers, 1986.

International Law

Boyle, Francis Anthony. *World Politics and International Law*. Durham, N.C.: Duke University Press, 1985.

Brownley, Ian. *Principles of Public International Law*. 3d ed. Oxford: Oxford University Press, 1978.

D'Amato, Anthony. *International Law: Process and Prospect*. Ardsley on Hudson, N.Y.: Transnational Publishers, 1986.
De Lupis, Ingrid Detter. *International Law and the Independent State*. Brookfield, Vt.: Gower Publishing Company, 1987.
Janis, Mark W. *An Introduction to International Law*. Boston: Little, Brown and Co., 1988.
Kennedy, David. *International Legal Structures*. Baden-Baden, German Federal Republic: Nomos Verlagsgesellschaft, 1987.
Shaw, Malcolm N. *International Law*. 2d ed. Cambridge: Grotius Publications, 1986.
Wallace, Rebecca M.M. *International Law*. London: Sweet and Maxwell, 1986.

Legal History

Berman, Harold J. *Law and Revolution: The Formation of the Western Legal Tradition*. Cambridge: Harvard University Press, 1983.
Robinson, O.F., T.D. Fergus, and W.M. Gordon. *An Introduction to European Legal History*. Abingdon, England: Professional Books, 1987.
Tigar, Michael E., and Madeleine R. Levy. *Law and the Rise of Capitalism*. New York: Monthly Review Press, 1977.
Trakman, Leon E. *The Law Merchant: Evolution of Commercial Law*. Littleton, Colo.: Fred B. Rothman & Co., 1983.
Watson, A. *The Evolution of Law*. Baltimore: Johns Hopkins University Press, 1985.

Transnational Law Casebooks

Folsom, Ralph H., Michael Wallace Gordon, and John A. Spanogle, Jr. *International Business Transactions—A Problem-Oriented Casebook*. St. Paul, Minn.: West Publishing Company, 1985.
Katz, Milton, and Kingman Brewster. *International Transactions and Relations*. Mineola, N.Y.: Foundation Press, 1970.
Steiner, Henry J., and Detlev F. Vagts. *Transnational Legal Problems*. 3d ed. Mineola, N.Y.: Foundation Press, 1986.
Vagts, Detlev F. *Transnational Business Problems*. Mineola, N.Y.: Foundation Press, 1986.

Carriage of Goods

Gilmore, Grant, and Charles L. Black. *Admiralty Law*. Mineola, N.Y.: Foundation Press, 1958.
Hill, D.J. *CMR: Contracts for the International Carriage of Goods by Road*. London: Lloyd's of London Press, 1984.
Longley, Henry N. *Common Carriage of Cargo*. New York: Matthew Bender, 1967.
Poor, Wharton. *Poor on Charter Parties and Ocean Bills of Lading*. 5th ed. New York: Matthew Bender & Company, 1968.
Sorkin, Saul. *How to Recover for Loss or Damage to Goods in Transit*. New York: Matthew Bender, 1978.

Countertrade

Ehrenhaft, P. *Countertrade: International Trade without Cash.* New York: Law & Business, Inc.; Harcourt Brace Jovanovich, 1983.

Verzariu, P. *Countertrade, Barter, and Offsets: New Strategies for Profit in International Trade.* New York: McGraw-Hill, 1985.

Welt, L.G.B. *Trade without Money: Barter and Countertrade.* New York: Law & Business, Inc.; Harcourt Brace Jovanovich, 1984.

Documentary Credits

De Rooy, F.P. *Documentary Credits.* Deventer, the Netherlands: Kluwer Law and Taxation Publishers, 1984.

Kurkela, M. *Letters of Credit under International Law: UCC, UCP, and Law Merchant.* Dobbs Ferry, N.Y.: Oceana Publications, 1985.

Wheble, B.S. *Documentary Credits, UCP 1974/1983 Revisions Compared and Explained.* Paris: International Chamber of Commerce, 1984.

Expropriation

Jain, S.C. *Nationalization of Foreign Property: A Study in North-South Dialogue.* New Delhi, India: Deep and Deep Publishers, 1983.

Transnational Aspects of Antitrust Law

Atwood, James, and Kingman Brewster. *Antitrust and American Business Abroad.* New York: McGraw-Hill, 1981.

Frazer, Jim. *Monopoly, Competition, and the Law and Regulation of Business Activity in Britain, Europe, and America.* New York: St. Martin's, 1988.

Fugate, Wilbur. *Foreign Commerce and the Anti-Trust Laws.* 2 vols. 3d ed. Boston: Little, Brown & Co., 1981.

Hawk, B.E. *United States, Common Market, and International Antitrust: A Comparative Guide.* 2d ed. New York: Law & Business, Inc.; Harcourt Brace Jovanovich, 1986.

Kronstein, Heinrich. *The Law of International Cartels.* Ithaca, N.Y.: Cornell University Press, 1972.

Neale, A.D., and M.C. Stephens. *International Business and National Jurisdiction.* Oxford: Clarendon Press, 1988.

International Accounting

Arpan, Jeffrey S., and Dhia D. AlHashim. *International Dimensions of Accounting.* Boston: Kent Publishing Company, 1984.

International Finance

Chambost, E. *Bank Accounts: A World Guide to Confidentiality*. New York: John Wiley & Sons, 1983.

Deak, N.L. *International Banking*. New York: New York Institute of Finance; Prentice-Hall, 1984.

Gold, Sir Joseph. *Exchange Rates in International Law and Organization*. Washington, D.C.: American Bar Association, Section of International Law and Practice, 1989.

Rendell, Robert S., ed. *International Financial Law*. 2d ed. London: Euromoney Publications, 1984.

Robinson, J. Michael, ed. *International Securities: Law and Practice*. London: Euromoney Publications, 1985.

Wood, Philip. *Law and Practice of International Finance*. New York: Clark Boardman Co., 1984.

Labor Law

Blanpain, R., ed. *Comparative Labour Law and Industrial Relations*. 3d ed. Deventer, the Netherlands: Kluwer Law and Taxation Publishers, 1987.

Taxation

Bischel, J.E. *Fundamentals of International Taxation*. 2d ed. New York: Practicing Law Institute, 1985.

Glautier, W.E., and Frederick W. Basinger. *A Reference Guide to International Taxation: Profiting from Your International Operations*. Lexington, Mass.: D.C. Heath & Company, 1987.

Grundy, M. *World of International Tax Planning*. Cambridge: Cambridge University Press, 1984.

Pechman, Joseph A., ed. *Comparative Tax Systems: Europe, Canada and Japan*. Arlington, Va.: Tax Analysts, 1987.

Tait, Alan A. *Value Added Tax: International Practice and Problems*. Washington, D.C.: International Monetary Fund, 1988.

Tax Havens

Faith, Nicholas. *Safety in Numbers: The Mysterious World of Swiss Banking*. London: Hamish Hamilton, 1982.

Langer, Marshall J. *How to Use Foreign Tax Havens*. New York: Practicing Law Institute, 1975.

Walters, John. *Grundy's Tax Havens: A World Survey*. 4th ed. London: Sweet and Maxwell, 1983.

Transnational Arbitration

Carbonneau, T., ed. *Resolving Transnational Disputes through International Arbitration*. Sixth Sokol Symposium. Charlottesville, Va.: The University Press of Virginia, 1984.

Lew, Julian D.M. *Contemporary Problems in International Arbitration*. Dordrecht, the Netherlands: Martinus Nijhoff Publishers, 1987.

Redfern, A., and M. Hunter. *Law and Practice of International Commercial Arbitration*. London: Sweet and Maxwell, 1986.

Schwebel, Stephen M. *International Arbitration: Three Salient Problems*. Cambridge: Grotius Publications, 1987.

Transnational Litigation

Badr, G.M. *State Immunity: An Analytic and Prognostic View*. Dordrecht, the Netherlands: Martinus Nijhoff Publishers, 1984.

Born, Gary B., and David Westin. *International Litigation in United States Courts*. Deventer, the Netherlands: Kluwer Law and Taxation Publishers, 1988.

Dellapena, Joseph W. *Suing Foreign Governments and Their Corporations*. Washington, D.C.: Bureau of National Affairs, 1988.

Greiter, Ivo. *How to Get Your Money in Foreign Countries*. Deventer, the Netherlands: Kluwer Law and Taxation Publishers, 1988.

Index